Endless Intervals

Endless Intervals

Cinema, Psychology, and Semiotechnics around 1900

Jeffrey West Kirkwood

University of Minnesota Press
Minneapolis
London

The University of Minnesota Press gratefully acknowledges the financial assistance provided for the publication of this book through the generosity of donors to the Harpur College Advocacy Council Faculty Development Endowment, an endowed fund that invests deeply in the research, creative activities, and professional development of Harpur College of Arts and Sciences faculty at Binghamton University.

Chapter 5 was originally published as "The Cinema of Afflictions," *October,* no. 159 (Winter 2017): 37–54, copyright 2017 by October Magazine, Ltd., and the Massachusetts Institute of Technology.

Published by the University of Minnesota Press
111 Third Avenue South, Suite 290
Minneapolis, MN 55401-2520
http://www.upress.umn.edu

ISBN 978-1-5179-1253-6 (hc)
ISBN 978-1-5179-1254-3 (pb)

Library of Congress record available at https://lccn.loc.gov/2022015144

Printed in the United States of America on acid-free paper

UMP BmB 2022

Contents

Introduction

Signifying Nothings

This book is about nothing. It is about the many nothings that form the stops, breaks, pauses, gaps, and fleeting moments of quietude underlying the work of machines that have governed human life since the nineteenth century. The machines propelling the "werewolf-like hunger for surplus-labour" amid the hellish drone of factories in Manchester, England, detailed by Friedrich Engels in the 1840s, and the digital machines of computational capitalism used to datafy and monetize work, sleep, and meditation alike share a feature often denied to their human counterparts: they rest.[1] For all the justified concern with the ceaseless nature of the devices that now harry screen-tired subjects to the edge of madness, the dominance of digital computation emerged from an ability to define and to control the moments when machines—if even for the briefest periods—stop.

To stop is to discretize, to measure, to temporalize, to quantify, and to digitize. This book will argue that these operations are all theoretically bound to one another in an unlikely history of early cinematic mechanisms. As is well known, what is often vaguely referred to as "digital" is not essentially defined by graphic user interfaces, platforms, screens, front-end design, or data but rather is rooted in the simple binarization into two possible states, expressed most commonly as 1 or 0. The long digital trajectory from Gottfried Wilhelm Leibniz's early descriptions of binary notation and plans for a binary calculator in his unfinished, three-page 1679 text "De Progressione Dyadica" to neuromorphic processors, whose architecture seeks to mirror the spiking functions of neurons, departs from this common foundation.[2] Leibniz's aspiration for a *characteristica universalis*, or a universal mathematics that would (arguably) first be implemented in Konrad Zuse's Turing complete machine in the 1940s, reckoned with a simple notion with profound consequences. Namely, it made it possible to encode all mathematical problems as a series of steps based on one of two states. Following the work of Alonzo Church and Alan Turing writing separately in 1936, as well as Claude Shannon's remarkable master's thesis on the expression of Boolean algebra using switching relays, such steps and the digital revolution they would enable became inseparable from the operations of the machines that executed these binary instructions through a series of starts and stops.[3]

Typically, the first half of the twentieth century is historicized as a period of fragmentation marked by mechanization. The second half of the twentieth century has been primarily marked by discretization in the form of digitization. The paradigmatic machine of the former is the cinema; of the latter, the computer. In the digital age, the big questions have stemmed from parallelisms between organic human processes and computer processes: autopoiesis, artificial intelligence, and deep learning. By contrast, modernist histories concerned with the late nineteenth and early twentieth centuries have generally fixated on the explosive, interruptive, and traumatic effects of technologies like early cinema on the human psyche. By returning to early, sedimented, and largely obscured cinematic and psychological discourses, this book uncovers foundations of digital-age thinking that were already at work around 1900.

That most digital computers we encounter are electronic devices, or that they rely on microchips with the silicon transistors for which that famous area south of San Francisco is named, or that most computers rely on screen-based interfaces is all incidental to the machine logic that organizes them. Alan Turing commented on this in a 1947 lecture to the London Mathematical Society about his recent work on the Automatic Computing Engine (ACE) for the National Physical Laboratory.

> From the point of view of the mathematician the property of being digital should be of greater interest than that of being electronic. That it is electronic is certainly important because these machines owe their high speed to this, and without the speed it is doubtful if financial support for their construction would be forthcoming. But this is virtually all that there is to be said on that subject. That the machine is digital however has much more subtle significance.[4]

On the one hand, digital operations are independent of the highly contingent history of machines through which they are articulated. Turing is clear that the principles he has in mind could be implemented just as easily by the fleshy hardware of a "human computer."[5] This fact would become a vital fixture of powerful theories that found ontological distinctions between things like humans and machines irrelevant to their operational participation in structuring and transmitting information. Albeit with divergent objectives, such an informational thesis has guided work such as a panoply of cybernetic and informational theories from Norbert Wiener in the 1940s through Donna Haraway's watershed text, "The Cyborg Manifesto," which identified the codability and recodability of all matter as a potentially liberatory political path.[6]

On the other hand, the systems of discretization that form the backbone of our digital universe are fully wedded to the idiosyncratic developments of technical apparatuses. As part of an often misinterpreted theoretical program, known for its supposed "technological determinism," Friedrich Kittler wrote that "Claude Shannon, in 1937, proved" that "simple telegraph switching relays can implement, by means of their different interconnections, the whole of Boolean algebra," and therefore that the entire world of human-meaning production could be operated by the open/closed switching mechanisms that had been pioneered in the nineteenth century and comprised the root of digital computation.[7] If the possible functions of every "and," "or," and "not" can be materially operated as "true" or "false" using a series of open or closed circuit gates, then every hermeneutic question can become a question of electrical engineering. This is especially true of digital technologies, which are able to encode perceptually distinct content (moving images, images, audio, text) according to a megalithic binary regime that does not mimic the shape or character of their inputs in the mode of storage and transmission. It governs everything—Covid-19 pandemic heat maps, meme stocks, and algorithmically optimized streaming playlists are all made possible by the same reasoning.

An artificially synchronic view of the sequential path through on/off switching mechanisms is not enough, however, to fully account for what is meant by "the digital." It is not merely that the whole of Boolean algebra can be mapped and executed through the arrangement of sequential circuit gates. The momentary position of those gates (whether open or closed) must also be remembered once the electrical impulse that determined their positions passes and vanishes into a larger cosmic-level heat death. One might say that this is the moment that machines begin to *signify,* indicating an absent state of the machine as a part of its operations. It is the moment that they are transformed from purely technical mechanisms into the *semiotechnical* mechanisms that are the subject of this book. For this reason, Joseph Henry's development of the electromagnetic relay in 1835, important for the telegraphic switching that informed later digital computation, was not itself a digital mechanism, despite instituting alternations between two positions. Absence only makes the heart grow fonder when we have a system for remembering the departed. This requires cultural technical systems for managing the intervals of absence such that they come to signify. Or as the cybernetician and anthropologist Gregory Bateson frequently defined the concept of information, it requires "difference that makes a difference."[8]

How did the question of machine signification come to be asked in the first place? Its theoretical origins can be found in the cinematic management of discrete machine operations. The term *digital* is less important than the fully operationalized conception of identity, unity, autonomy, and ontological distinction that the history of digital systems made possible. This is the point at which this book seeks to intervene. The theorist and filmmaker Jean Epstein explicated the central position of cinematic apparatuses within the technical reconception of human experience by pointing to exactly this mechanical hinge between discontinuity and continuity. The cinematic mechanism, according to Epstein, "proves to be endowed with its own subjectivity."[9] In "the discontinuity of still images (still at least during the time of projection, in the intervals between their abrupt substitution), a discontinuity acting as a real foundation to the imaginary human content of the projected film as a whole, ends up, in turn, being but a ghost, conceived and thought-out by an apparatus."[10] This ghost is much older than Epstein acknowledges, and the operations he presciently describes place cinema in contact with a burgeoning technical domain of digital computation that would shape the coming century. The discretized "intelligence" he locates is not unique to cinema but would develop in tandem along a path that has traditionally been framed, paradoxically, as almost entirely divergent from analog technologies like cinema. Where Epstein's observations are essential, however, is in their insistence that the focus on cinema be shifted from the deceptive indexicality of images to the underlying operations of discontinuity that were systematized to signify as continuities.

In 1918, roughly the year that the historical cases considered in this book end and several years before Epstein's text, the British physicists William Henry Eccles and Frank Wilfred Jordan introduced what would become known as the Eccles-Jordan trigger relay, commonly referred to as the "flip-flop" circuit that was later integral to the Colossus computer and the Electronic Numerical Integrator and Computer (ENIAC).[11] Eccles was a close longtime friend of Ludwig Wittgenstein, which is more than a charming historical factoid, as the effects the flip-flop would eventually have on the shape of philosophical questions about meaning and language rival those of Wittgenstein, albeit quietly and without named attribution.[12] As a figure of media theoretical interest, the flip-flop has become both a "paradigm and apparative [*apparativer*] myth of digital memory in the technical history of digital computers," despite the many years between the introduction of the highly particular vacuum tube–based invention and the rise of digital computers.[13] No doubt the reason for its dispositive significance within the history of digital theory is that it was the mechanism central to signaling the difference of difference that was the wellspring of digitality.

Despite what the term *flip-flop* might suggest, its purpose was not only to switch between two positions, as this had indeed been possible since the mid-nineteenth century. Instead, it recorded—in its own simple function—the fact of having switched in the first place. As a result, it turned the seemingly deterministic process of electric switching into a matter of signification that would allow one to build sequences of circuits that could account for their own previous positions. The transformative significance of the flip-flop's modest arrival in the world of telecommunications has not been lost on theorists, and, as Bernhard Siegert notes, it constituted "the historical originating element [*Urelement*] of all digital processor and memory circuits."[14] It turned on/off, stop/start into a metatechnical operation that would evolve into the complex computational architectures that would summon the specter of machine "intelligence." Computers would not, however, be the first machines to raise such questions. The cinema too, in its transition from a site of pure fascination with the marvels of a machine, or what Tom Gunning calls the "cinema of attractions"—to an elaborate setting for subjective identification with alternating images, would raise questions about signification as a matter of technics.[15]

The Eccles-Jordan flip-flop also reveals a theoretical path along which cinematic mechanisms can (and perhaps should) be dislodged from their traditional position within the pantheon of analog technologies. It shows how the cultural-technical linkage between discontinuous and continuous states—stops and starts—instituted by a technical mechanism can create contact between the supposedly deterministic workings of machines and the signifying operations that have long characterized human meaning making. If meaning is woven into a seamless fabric of experience through operative chains that substitute the presence of signs for that which is absent, there is a natural tendency to view the halting increments essential to machines in diametric opposition to the gliding, unified contours of human experience.[16] At some level, even in the absence of concepts like "artificial intelligence," which suggests a replication or imitation of an ill-defined but nevertheless uniquely human capacity, what it means to be digital is to bridge between these two states: continuous and discontinuous.

The flip-flop did just this. It was a bistable multivibrator with "a pair of vacuum tubes" that, as the term *bistable* implies, switched between two possible stable logic states.[17] The "stability" of the states is the result of "back-coupling," whereby the state (either on or off) triggered by the initial input is maintained such that the output becomes an input that partially determines whether the device is switched to another state.[18] Through a purely operational feat, flip-flops are thus able to signify for the absence of their initial inputs as an element of their future operations.[19] This represents the first bit of digital memory, storing the fact of a binary difference operated by a simple mechanism and opening a vast horizon of meaning. What the device implemented can be understood in systems of theoretical terms, which arose in no small part because of the same work in mathematics and technical design that accompanied digital computing. When Niklas Luhmann argued more generally that if "a distinction is supposed to become operational as a unity, it always already presupposes a distinction within the distinction," he could have just as easily been writing about the birth of the digital with the flip-flop.[20] The ability to signify for the fact of difference that gives rise to the apparent unities of systems like consciousness is thus analyzable as having been built and maintained by sequenced discontinuities.

The long-contested opposition between machines and humans that has become the hallmark of popular debates about artificial intelligence and deep learning has brought into focus larger questions about machines' basic abilities to signify. N. Katherine Hayles, whose work has vigorously resisted both the ontological immurement of humans as separate from machines and the inclination to fully etherealize information as if it were not always inseparable from the materials it defines, has more recently turned to consider the crossing paths of emerging ideas in bio- and cybersemiotics.[21] Hayles recognizes the question of "computer cognition" as a semiotic one, which, following Charles Sanders Peirce, is a matter of a recursive process of "interpretation" enabled by "logic gates" whose sequenced intervals of switching between binary positions move beyond their "deterministic base."[22] The capacity for meaning, and that which seems to serve as a bright-line between deterministic machines and "artificial cognition," depends on the capacity to signify for something that is no longer present.[23] For informational machines, this is an operational activity, since storage and transmission do not actually retain or convey analog inscriptions or signs. As Hayles describes it, the sign is a "relational operator" that "creates possibilities for meaning making because it brings a behavior (the interpretant) into relation with the object, the absential phenomenon for which the sign stands."[24]

In essence, the *meaning* associated with neurobiological experiences of cognition resides in making continuous what was discontinuous. This is how machines—and I will argue, *cinematic machines*—began to allow the question of mechanical meaning making to be posed as well. They systematically assembled intervals in such a way that the absences and breaks they introduced signified as continuities. If one considers that the experimentation with machine intervals that was the premise for both scientific psychology and cinema in the nineteenth century confronted familiar questions of mechanical meaning making, the philosophical questions of artificiality surrounding binary computation defining the twenty-first century look to have a long theoretical legacy.

Discretization is the hallmark of artificiality, but it was also the primary gateway to consciousness as a scientific object of study. No doubt, the architecture of neuromorphic, manycore microprocessors like Intel's recent Loihi chip, built to serve neural networks intended to simulate the dynamic systems of one-bit impulses that constitute "spikes" between neurons, offers a compelling morphological and operational parallel with the human mind.[25] Yet the shape of the distinctly digital-age questions it poses with respect to the difficult relationships between discrete and continuous states, meaning and determinism, and machine and mind were theoretically at play in the smoky movie houses of the early twentieth century.

At the level of their technical mechanisms, the history of digital computers is in many ways braided into the history of cinema. Konrad Zuse's partner in designing and constructing the first programmable relay computer, Helmut Schreyer, was a friend who had worked as a film projectionist.[26] In addition to suggesting that Zuse implement vacuum tubes instead of a series of metal plates he had been using to operate as logic gates, Schreyer engineered a system that ran on discarded 35mm film.[27] With this method, Zuse's Z3 and Z4 ran on celluloid using a series of holes—its discrete steps sequenced into the frames of exposed films, annihilating the analog photographic storage of the medium in the simple act of programming. Similarly, engineers of the Ferranti Mark I, one of the first commercial, general-purpose stored-program computers, and an updated version of the famous Manchester Mark I, solved the problem of the thin, fragile high-speed tape that was the machine's store by replacing it with "standard 35mm stock with a magnetic coating."[28] The revised version was purchased by the Royal Dutch Shell Company following the 1956 Suez Canal crisis to optimize crude oil transport around the Cape of Good Hope, representing one of the unlikelier genealogies following in the wake of filmic technologies' first introduction.[29] However, the technical crossover between cinematic machines and computers traditionally viewed as a part of distinct medial lineages obscures a deeper theoretical entanglement that unifies the two.

The theoretical watershed of digital machines resides in their capacity to sequence discrete steps to produce conceptual, perceptual, and mathematical unities. Binary instructions could eventually be used to deal with real numbers, model continuous surfaces, perform natural language processing, conduct unsupervised machine learning, and display films. As the Eccles-Jordan flip-flop makes evident, however, the groundwork for these wide-ranging possibilities was not its function of switching between two binary states but of being able to signify for the difference of difference—what would be called, anthropomorphically, memory, though it would also entail feedback and recursion. The mechanism signals the fact of there having been a difference, which then integrates the absent input in the reception of future inputs. How unities emerge from these systems of self-reference and "observation" as symbols, objects, and ontologies would be a primary matter for cyberneticians and particularly later questions of the second and third order in cybernetics advanced by figures like Heinz von Foerster. This is ultimately what Alexander Galloway takes up in his book motivated by the nonphilosophy of François Laruelle when he describes the "transcendental" nature of digitality.

> The digital says that the one divides into two. So, within the modal condition of the two (or the three, or the four, or the multiple), a

> universe populated by a purely homogenous substrate of standardized atoms, there must be some way in which these atomic entities—so absolutely separate, so absolutely standard—can overcome their stifling congruity and relate to each other.[30]

What is important, then, is not just that which divides into two but that which reinscribes the fact of that division. This is a transcendental function that is operationally built into the flip-flop and what, in a feat of functional circularity, brings the continuous world of objects, signs, symbols, and minds into contact with the discontinuous workings of machines. It is also, as we shall see, a function of early narrative cinema, whose robust semiotic capacity had less to do with analog images than it did with technical patterns of alternation. The philosopher Nelson Goodman contended that a "digital scheme," as opposed to an analog one, "is discontinuous throughout," though "to be digital a system must be not merely discontinuous but *differentiated* throughout, syntactically and semantically."[31] It is not enough to be discrete. It requires that discrete steps be systematized in such a way that they can signify for their own distinctions.

Hiding in theories of digitality—whether it is rigorously eschewed or actively embraced—is a theory of meaning. Within semiotic theory, Umberto Eco framed it as a matter of signification versus communication. Machines can communicate, according to Eco, in traditional Shannonian terms through "the passage of a signal" from "a source (through a transmitter, along a channel) to a destination," but in a "machine-to-machine process the signal has no power to signify," as it lacks the "interpretive" process that "couples present entities with absent units."[32] The challenges of contemporary artificial intelligence and neural nets to the protected domain of humanness, then, are not, as papers on spiking neural networks or even the frequent references to the McCulloch-Pitts neuron might indicate, based purely on morphological or structural likeness between processors and brains.

Instead, these challenges should be analyzed according to what can be called a *semiotechnics*—a theory of technical systems focusing on their management of absences, breaks, and gaps for the production of meaning.[33] Ernst Kapp, the eighteenth-century German philosopher, Texas abolitionist, and geographer who formulated the first explicit philosophy of technology, laid the foundations for such analysis.[34] In his estimation, *Technik* or technic (imagined as an operational unity predating the idea of technical objects captured in the term *technology*) created a dialectical relationship between the human body and our tools.[35] The workings of bodily organs, including the brain, were "projected" into technologies, whose exteriorized operations allowed the organs themselves to be understood as differentiated parts of a whole.[36] Kapp drew heavily on Franz Reuleaux, a revolutionary theorist of engineering, for such observations (discussed in chapter 1). Where Reuleaux moved the analysis of machines from a focus on the piecemeal workings of individual mechanisms to the "universal grammar of machine movement" that defined what he called the "*Gestell*," for Kapp that grammar would also determine the emergence and shape of human cultural forms.[37] This was the bridge between the discontinuities of technical operations and continuities of meaning making that is the backbone of a semiotechnical analysis. Focusing on the technics of semiotics opens the door to thinking about how it was that the problems of meaning and machines were theorized well prior to and differently from the explicit imitations of human capabilities like sentence construction, object identification, and prediction that have propelled anxieties about the artificiality of artificial intelligence.[38]

Within the realm of more contemporary theories of media that find their roots in the nineteenth-century work of theorists like Kapp as well as cybernetic theories, such a union of technics and meaning production have been taken up under the aegis of cultural techniques or "*Kulturtechnik.*" As the uniquely German nominalizaton of "culture" and "technics" in a single term suggests, neither the machinations of technologies nor the immense world of cultural meanings they convey, store, and shape can be considered separately. The term *Kulturtechnik* first entered the vocabulary to describe "large-scale" agricultural processes like "irrigating and draining arable tracts of land, straightening river beds, or constructing water reservoirs" that morphed the natural landscape for human exploitation.[39] This early usage already makes clear the deep interdependence between technical operations and the ability of physical distinctions to signify (parceling arable land into procedurally defined spaces for human consumption). The power of the observation, however, really achieves significance once—following the insights of twentieth-century information theory—one sees their potential for second-order operations. As Thomas Macho notes, the hallmark of cultural techniques is thus a "potential self-referentiality" and "a pragmatics of recursion" essential to "self-reflection, identity formation and identification."[40] Yet the symbolic, technical, and real are not preestablished, neatly separated ontological categories set into motion or regulated by various technics. They are mutually constitutive, emergent properties of one another that require specific histories of the operative chains through which they become visible. On this point, Siegert notes:

> It is problematic to base an understanding of cultural techniques on static concepts of technologies and symbolic work, that is, on an ontologically operating differentiation between first- and second-order techniques. Separating the two must be replaced by chains of operations and techniques. In order to situate cultural techniques *before* the grand epistemic distinction between culture and technology, sense and nonsense, code and thing, it is necessary to elaborate a *processual* (rather than ontological) definition of first- and second-order techniques. We need to focus on how recursive operative chains bring about a switch from first- to second-order techniques (and back), on how nonsense generates sense, how the symbolic is filtered out of the real or how, conversely, the symbolic is incorporated into the real, and how the material signifier is present in the signified and manages to create a physical presence effect.[41]

It is not just that technical systems of distinction get made in the real, nor that they come to operate symbolic distinctions. Rather, it is a matter of revealing the shifting registers that allow operative chains to be viewed as chains at all, and therefore symbolically unified at a level of secondary observation, which then makes its way into the definition of those operations themselves. This is where the history of cinematic mechanisms becomes so instructive for media theoretical engagements with the technical and philosophical underpinnings of the digital age.

Cinematic technologies emerged from a long period of mechanical discretization in the nineteenth century that also gave rise to scientific psychology. The aspiration to scientifically quantify the world, and with it the mind, was enabled by the development of technologies that instituted a regime of measurement according to mechanical discontinuities. The virtue of machines like the chronoscope, tachistoscope, and galvanometer was precisely that they could be made to stop rapidly and regularly. Such instruments' role in early psychological experimentation and its impact on the science, philosophy, and aesthetics of the period has been widely and brilliantly examined, though their implications for subsequent theoretical shifts have remained by and large historically circumscribed. The purpose of these machines was to introduce rapid, regular breaks, below the threshold of perception, that could scientifically quantify human phenomena related to attention, sensation, perception, cognition, and memory.

As but one instance considered in chapter 3 demonstrates, early scientific psychologists of the late 1800s like Wilhelm Wundt, his student James McKeen Cattell, and Hubert von Grashey used various chronometric tachistoscopes to understand the essential meaning-making task of reading according to mechanically defined intervals. They took words—the bedrock of human meaning making—and mechanically discretized them by measuring the intervals according to which recognition tasks were performed. How many fractions of a second did it take an experimental subject to recognize a word, a letter, or a series of nonsense letters, and how long did it take that subject to substitute these elements with the things for which they signified? It would be difficult to argue that this splitting of the one (in perception and cognition) into many constituted a digital event on its own, as the discontinuities it introduced worked against the linguistic exercises they quantified. Where the question of a proto-digitality, and with it meaning, appears is in the cinematic reassembly of the moments when the machines stop into sequences that signify.

The same technical mechanisms that had been used to render the human psyche a discrete, scientific object were deployed later to create the cinematic illusion of continuous movement. Filmic continuities of movement—and later of narrative—were predicated on devices like the Geneva Drive or Maltese Cross, patented by the early film pioneer Oskar Messter, that, much like the Eccles-Jordan flip-flop, unified discontinuous and continuous operations. In the case of the Geneva Drive mechanism, the continuous rotation of a disc intermittently engaged a driven disc to advance the filmstrip at regular intervals—eventually projecting twenty-four frames per second. Laura Mulvey designates this "co-presence of movement and stillness, continuity and discontinuity" as cinema's "central paradox," which is what suits the medium to the Lacanian analyses that find endless chains of absences and deferrals at the heart of every signifying act—not least of all in the formation of the ego itself.[42] Jacques Lacan, however, was interested in digital computers, and there is a good reason for that. The flatness of binary operations, which lack the fantasy of photographic indexicality, lay bare the purity of alternation and absence structuring the universe of human meaning. In *Seminar II,* he argues:

> The more or less confused, accidental traversal of the world of symbols is organized around the correlation of absence and presence. And the search for the laws of presence and absence will tend toward the establishing of the binary order which leads to what we call cybernetics.[43]

The tenuous union between presence and absence guiding interest in the rudiments of digitality was, as this book explores, likewise the theoretical center of early cinematic semiotechnics. This was especially true as cinema emerged from a deterministic machine logic of producing only the illusion of movement to create semiotically rich, psychological narratives based on the alternations and absences of editing. Writing in the wake of the high-cybernetic upheaval in linguistic theory, Christian Metz sketched a cursory blueprint of this bridge from semiotics to cinema to computation as a matter of psychology.

> The machine has ground up human language and dispenses it into clean slices, to which no flesh clings. Those "binary digits," perfect segments, have only to be assembled (programed) in requisite order. The code triumphs and attains perfection in the transmission of the *message.* It is a great feast for the syntagmatic mentality. There are other examples. An artificial limb is to the leg as the cybernetic message is to the human sentence. And why not mention—for amusement and a change from erector sets—powdered milk and instant coffee? And robots of all kinds? The linguistic machine, at the forefront of so many modern preoccupations, remains nevertheless the privileged example. The attitude that conceives and produces all these *products* is broadly the same: The natural object (whether human language or cow's milk) is considered as a simple point of departure. It is analyzed, literally and figuratively, and its constituent parts are isolated; this is the moment of *breakdown analysis,* as in the cinema. . . . The grand moment, which one has been waiting for and thinking about since the beginning, is the syntagmatic moment. One reassembles a duplicate of the original object, a duplicate which is perfectly grasped by the mind, since it is a pure product of the mind.[44]

The mechanical discretization that drove nineteenth-century industrialization of the human psyche—itself viewed as a machine—toward ever-greater rationalization, fragmentation, disaggregation, quantifiability, and fungibility has remained the primary touchstone for critical theories of film. Cinema's challenge to an already long-shattered fiction of a shattered unitary subject, who was thought overwhelmed, shocked, or broken down by the advent of electrical modernity, was in its ability to reinstitute, by entirely mechanical means, semiotic fullness. This was perhaps a greater danger to the notion of sui generis human thought than any posed by the monstrous and deafening machines of the industrial age, whose challenge to humanity was external, identifiable, and dialectical. Once the absences of cinema were not just mechanical but also the raison d'être of a narrative, visual syntax achieved through filmic editing beginning in the early twentieth century (chapter 1), the truly frightening semiotechnics of film became more evident (chapter 2). This is something traced in part by Mary Ann Doane in her magnificent analysis of the scientific and philosophical ramifications of cinematic discretization.

> A gap or interval is required and is found in the form of editing. On the other hand, the solution to the threat of the overpresence of the image—editing—generates its own anxieties about discontinuity and absence. As a reinscription of the gap between film frames, editing potentially constitutes a persistent reminder of the abyss of darkness that subtends cinema.[45]

One could argue that such an abyss was not only a purely existential matter but the absence at the heart of systems of signification. Once the intervals of cinematic editing recursively incorporated themselves, making the breaks that were the foundation of moving-image technologies a tool of narrative, symbolic, experiential continuity, the challenge of machines to the sovereign domain of human psychology was not simply external and oppositional but artificial and substitutive. No doubt this is a familiar concern, as much of what is unsettling about the contemporary applications of artificial intelligence stems from the uncanny nearness to the products of human thought achieved through alien reasoning. It was also a part of a transformation that Gilbert Simondon described as a move from a purely thermodynamic model of technics to an informational one.[46] Both were built on the organization of mechanical absences from which forms arose, but in the latter case, absences were understood to signify. And this difference, according to Simondon, partially accounted for the difference between humans and machines. That cinema summoned the possibility of a machine that could also potentially make meaning represented a far greater challenge to human primacy than the bombardment of modern psyches with electrical stimuli that has long characterized the period of early film's maturation.

What this book presents is a theory of an epochal shift in the understanding of the mechanical intervals that undergird technical conceptions of thought—both human and machine. It explores how evolving technologies for manufacturing cinematic narrative revolutionized the relationship between continuity and discontinuity and, therefore, between psychology and machines. The mechanical intervals of devices such as the chronoscopic tachistoscope were seen as a means for both functionally and theoretically breaking down the seamless flow of experience into measurable units, allowing the mind to become a legitimate object of scientific study. At the same time, the ubiquitous staccato of machines around 1900 was the source of broader cultural anxieties about the interruptive and damaging effects of technologies on the psyche. Scientifically, disaggregation of the human subject into reaction times made the mind into an empirically verifiable machine. Culturally, the onslaught of rapid, discontinuous machine stimuli was viewed as the end of the unitary subject. However, both scientists and social critics of the early 1900s began to take the newly robust narrative technics of cinema seriously for their ability to produce psychologically continuous states from series of discrete stimuli. The outcome, described in chapter 2, was multiple. Cinema was seen as an even more formidable psychological menace by its opponents, and in the process the epistemological structures underlying theories of mind were entirely revised.

One of this book's objectives is to unravel dominant "nervousness discourses" about the early twentieth century and to locate an inchoate logic of the digital age within cinematic modernity.[47] By the 1910s, cinema had become the explicit object of inquiry for psychologists. Their interest in cinematic mechanisms, however, was radically different than that of the previous generation of pioneers in experimental psychology, such as Wilhelm Wundt, who had relied so heavily on proto-cinematic instruments. The standardization of cinematic mechanisms that allowed film to become a relatively sophisticated narrative medium transformed the breaks and pauses between stimuli from a mode of measurement into a form of mechanical ego formation. This was a conceptual upheaval that migrated from the laboratory to the movie theater, rapidly altering the nature of technophobic outcry about the medium's psychological impacts. When it was just a machine acting on another physiological machine, cinema merely exerted a strain on the nervous system. As a narrative machine, it jeopardized the media-technical reasoning of reading, education, and subject formation.

The intervals through which discretized units become cinematic unities are not theoretically or historically uniform. Chapter 1 encounters cinema at a decisive point in its analogy with the human psyche—in its transition from a mode of pure stimulus to a narrative medium. Psychophysicists of the nineteenth century like Gustav Fechner, who viewed the nervous system as an elaborate machine, had already sought to determine the minimal thresholds of perceptibility, focusing particularly on illusions of movement. Proto-cinematic devices were ideal for this purpose because they established a quantifiable relationship between continuities of experience and the discontinuities of stimuli. The earliest cinema, which grew out of such optical devices, was thus understood as a kind of psychological heuristic. It modeled the synthesis that allowed discrete mechanical processes to be experienced as continuous perceptual states. Hence, the earliest psychological engagements with cinema were concerned with reducing what were called "flicker" effects: the technical infelicities that caused one to experience the breaks between frames as a punishing stroboscopic blinking. What scientific psychologists like Paul Linke and Karl Marbe soon realized, however, was that the pauses between images were as crucial to the experience of continuity as the speed of their succession. Chapter 1 thus explores how pauses, absences, and intervals were no longer seen as something to avoid but instead became the conceptual bedrock for the possibility of a thinking machine. This would turn out to be a dangerous proposition for humanists, and one that would change the basic character of thinking about machines and how they affected human subjects.

In the 1910s, the semiotechnical possibilities of cinema were articulated in fears about the mechanical *replacement* of essential human faculties rather than their destruction. Chapter 2 argues that cinema of this period was transformed from a physiological medium into a psychological medium. As a result, its techno-dystopian detractors moved from criticizing its taxing overstimulation of the nervous system to the much grander claim that it mechanized the very logic of human subjectivity in a way that parallels contemporary worries about artificial intelligence. The effect was that cinema was not—as the modernist thesis goes—simply feared for its shocks to the nervous system, with one machine acting on another. Its regulation of intervals through new projection mechanisms and editing techniques supplanted human semiotic systems. The chapter explores a colorful history of critiques by members of what has come to be known as the cinema reform movement (*Kinoreformbewegung*), a group of doctors, jurists, educators, and social critics who mobilized psychological studies to oppose or mitigate the potentially deleterious effects of cinema. Much of the most important work by these critics, including Robert Gaupp, Richard Guttmann, and Adolf Sellmann, has never been translated into English, and what has been lost in its obscurity is the crucial opposition it entails for modernist theses about the fragmentation of the subject in the age of machines. As the chapter argues, the mutation of these critics' anxieties signaled a ground shift in cultural technical ideas about signification, subjectivity, and mechanization with profound effects that spanned pop psychological theory to psychoanalysis.

The conceptual shift from the deterministic mechanics of experimental psychology to the semiotechnics of narrative cinema described in the first two chapters had far-reaching consequences for what it meant to be a subject. Because the power of the filmic operations of discontinuity, sequence, and semiosis the book describes had little to do with the actual images that appeared on screen, the mode of reasoning they imposed could—like universal digitization later—cross between perceptual media. Indeed, as chapter 3 considers, beginning in the nineteenth century, proto-cinematic experimentation came to govern the scientific study of the cultural practices of reading, which had existed for centuries as the primary media-technical vehicle for training subjects.

Prior to what film theorist André Bazin designated as "the evolution of film language," written text was submitted to the rules of discretization—before cinema was readable, reading became cinematographic.[48] In the nineteenth century, the readerly psyche was technologically dismembered using variations of proto-cinematic apparatuses like the chronoscopic fall tachistoscope, which tested word and letter recognition times. Experimental psychologists such as James McKeen Cattell, Wilhelm Wundt, Friedrich

Schumann, Hubert von Grashey, Carl Wernicke, Ludwig Lichtheim, Benno Erdmann, and Raymond Dodge used such instruments to define the textured field of association and signification according to machine protocols and quantifiable intervals. As such, hermeneutics was turned into a matter of latent intervals. At the same time, many of these same figures would also be central to understanding illusions of movement and the cognitive processes by which those same discrete intervals could be reassembled into continuous, symbolic inner experiences. With this in mind, chapter 3 argues not only that cinematic technologies mechanized the reading subject but also that they subjectivized human reading machines.

There was also a larger question posed by reading machines: namely, how the most historically obdurate of signifying functions—subjective identification—could be achieved mechanically. Educational objectives have always been based on modes of media training and their attendant psychological ideals. The Bildungsroman of the nineteenth century, for instance, was essential to determining the character of the silent, highly interior, and autonomous reader. By contrast, the subjects produced by the discretized proto-cinematic practices described in chapter 3 upset expectations about *Bildung* and ideas of completion as they had been defined by textual practices of signification. In their place, chapter 4 argues that early cinematic subjects, whose logic of assembly was industrial in nature, were products of montage. Specifically, it considers psychotechnical experiments conducted by Hugo Münsterberg, the high priest of experimental psychology turned film theorist (who also coined the term *psychotechnics*). In his explicit union of cinematic technologies and psychophysical methodologies, he investigated film as the ideal medium for training the psyches of modern workers. Rather than a symptom of pure industrial rationalization, however, he grants insight into the possibility that machine intervals could be built into a signifying system. Pursuing the material outcomes of this possibility, the chapter thus turns to the systems of assembly inherent in the earliest industrial Edison films. The narratives of these films were regulated by the syntax of industry and were explicitly linked to educational ideals of modernization. In each case, the qualitative properties of the older educated subject were replaced by quantitative, interval-based protocols. Yet the reduction of the psychic apparatus to a discretized machine was not the final step in the process. Like the sequences of logic gates following on the heels of the flip-flop relay, the cinematic subject was shown to be programmable and reprogrammable.

Of course, machines are also prone to malfunction, produce unexpected results, or function differently than anticipated. In his *Philosophical Investigations,* Wittgenstein contended with the supposedly deterministic, hyper-rationalized notion of machines that bore little relation to the internal complexities and contingencies of their actual functions. The projection of a unified image of a "machine as a symbol" onto real machines elides the fact that they could always "move quite differently" than we initially expect and treats their operations as if they were not just predetermined but "already *present.*"[49] What is in fact already present in such a case is the cultural consolidation of a dynamic system of technics into a static signifier for something that is not at all mechanical. A typewriter, for instance, has a multitude of structured technical operations that determine the range of possibilities for what and how one may write. But at the same time, few would claim that the many books written by hunting and pecking across the keys of a Remington were preordained by the device itself, or that its many ways of jamming are normally considered as a part of its signifying potential. Such divergent and errant operations are, however, structured elements of its cultural technical makeup. This has been taken up by Simondon, whose work has been revived as a part of a recent turn to technics. The "necessity of a culture of technics," as he argues, is demanded by a false antagonism between human culture and the technical relationality of machines.[50] The perceived "opposition between culture and technics comes from the fact that the technical object is considered identical with the machine" and will survive until "culture discovers that each machine is not an absolute unit, but only an individualized technical reality that is open."[51] The antidote to this symbolic simplification, which substitutes a stable cultural signifier for the dynamism of mechanical systems, is to interrogate the ways that the modalities of technical arrangement open semiotic spaces. And this is most effectively demonstrated where machines—including psychic machines—seem to function improperly.

Chapter 5 examines instances where cinematic technics exerted a force on categories of pathology, capturing even aberrant states as a part of a monolithic logic of intervals. It is composed of two case histories. The first looks at Viktor Tausk's now famous 1919 essay "On the Origin of the 'Influencing Machine' in Schizophrenia."[52] In it, Tausk, a brilliant early disciple of psychoanalysis, discussed a rare variant of schizophrenia in which patients hallucinated persecution by a mysterious cinematographic machine. As the section argues, Tausk's paper surreptitiously offers the first psychoanalytic theory of film by explaining how a discretized image machine could produce conditions of subjective identification, even if only in cases of extreme mental illness. In other words, it retheorizes pathology as a matter of cinematic semiotechnics capable of creating subjective closure despite what was deemed a malfunction. Needless to say, this was extremely heterodox for cultural-linguistic Freudians whose model of the psyche had long sought to abandon its technicity. The chapter then locates the consequences of this new period in which cinema acted as both a technical and normative influence on the designation, representation, and resolution of pathologies in Léonce Perret's 1913 film, *The Mystery of the Rocks of Kador.* This is a film that Tausk likely saw, and one that reconfigured psychoanalytic treatment as a "watching" rather than "talking" cure, revealing along the way a pernicious gendering of technical pathologies.

The second and final case history the chapter addresses is about Ernst August Wagner, who in 1913 was one of the earliest recorded mass shooters and one of the first people in Germany to be found not guilty on grounds of insanity. Not only has the case itself remained largely unknown, but the fact that his psychiatric evaluation was conducted by the psychologist and eminent Cinema Reform Movement critic Robert Gaupp has received almost no attention. The incident showcases a dramatic contest between the logic of readership and the new semiotechnics of cinematographic machines. Wagner was a literature teacher and writer who suffered from megalomaniacal delusions but was nevertheless a hypertraditional literary subject. The method of diagnoses, however, relied on tachistoscopic testing informed by Gaupp's work with the experimental psychologists Carl Wernicke and Emil Kraepelin. The result was a clash between medial regimes that proposed radically different logics of psychological health and pathology—one discretized, proto-digital, and filmic, and the other atavistic and readerly.

The psychological revolution brought about by cinema is often viewed as the endpiece of a long nineteenth century of mechanical industrialism. Yet the questions of autonomy, ontology, and semiotics that have troubled cyberneticians, systems theorists, and philosophers of the digital age were already present in psychocinematic discourses of the 1910s. Where early cinema has remained a paradigmatic technology of modernism, this book asks whether its forms of discretization could not just as well be theorized as a part of the informational epoch that followed. What this requires, however, is that we look back rather than forward, to examine machines heralded for their magnificent speed precisely when they stop. That is where this book begins.

1

Engineering the Interval

> The physiological utopia of seeing things "together" is replaced by an approximation: seeing them quickly.
>
> —Jean Epstein, "Cinema and Modern Literature"

Gilbert Simondon argued in 1958 that we had entered "a new phase of the philosophy of technics" that followed a long period concerned with "thermodynamics and energetics."[1] The new phase was one of information, which, as he claimed, still failed to make "a clear distinction between *form* and *information*."[2] Broad application of the nineteenth-century scientific materialism born of research on the laws of thermodynamics to matters of industrial, philosophical, and social significance found a vanishing boundary between the human and the machine. After Hermann von Helmholtz, "energy was a transcendental principle" that allowed little regard for the metaphysical constructs that uniquely enthroned humanity.[3] Everything was interpretable in terms of energetic quantities. And those quantities were determined through the regularities of mechanical intervals. This was a flat principle of uniformity that would be carried over into the computational era, which acknowledged the shared thermodynamic limitations of machines and humans while shifting to a framework that analyzed events in terms of information. It is with this in mind that Norbert Wiener wrote in 1950 that "the theory of control of engineering, whether human or animal or mechanical, is a chapter in the theory of messages."[4]

Where Simondon found fault with the first wave of theories of computational technics among cyberneticians was in their refusal to recognize "the important gap between the living thing and the machine," which was that "the living transforms the information into forms."[5] For Simondon it was human beings that "discover significations," which are "the meaning [*sens*] that an event takes on with respect to already existing forms; signification is what makes an event have value as information."[6]

To signify was to recognize absence—not merely as absence but as a governing feature by which information was reconstituted according to recognizable forms. What was at stake in this transition from thermodynamics to information was not the particular mechanisms involved but the ability for technics to become semiosis. As this chapter contends, the first steps to finding this hinge between purely technical operations and semiotics became apparent in the cinematic definition of the scientific psyche beginning around 1900. Proto-cinematic instruments in the nineteenth century were used to quantify matters of mind according to the discretized measure of machines. It was in recognizing that the intervals between movements were the key to what Simondon called "form" that allowed the idea of signifying machines to become thinkable.

Hard Stops

In 1910 the psychologist Karl Marbe ventured to explicitly connect the field of experimental psychology with cinematic technologies. Together with Oswald Külpe, one of Wilhelm Wundt's most influential students, Marbe had cofounded the experimental psychology lab at the University of Würzburg in 1896. While there, he became an exponent of systematic experimental introspection as well as investigations into higher-order volitional processes. His most significant contribution to the history of psychology was arguably his monograph on the experimental psychological study of judgment, *Experimental Psychological Investigations of Judgement,* which was likely the "first unified study of complex thought processes."[7] As it would turn out, these were complex processes that found a native analogy in the cinema.

The groundwork for Marbe's revelation can be found in early psychophysical experiments. Psychophysics, which analyzed mental phenomena in terms of underlying physiological events, and which took universities by storm at the end of the nineteenth century, sought to quantify and discretize the relationship between stimulus and perception. Erica Fretwell describes the novel nineteenth-century discipline as an "experimental science" first developed between 1840 and 1880 that tested "people's subjective responses to auditory, gustatory, olfactory, tactile, and visual stimulation," and that has been received in contemporary discourses as either "a footnote in the history of ideas or a hegemonic science in the service of liberal biopower."[8] It was marked by a disaggregation of the senses into measurable inputs and outputs that could be mechanically quantified, albeit not according to any simple linear correspondence, as has often been assumed. Gustav

Fechner, the founder of psychophysics, described the quantitative link between stimulus and response not as a flat one-to-one relationship but instead in terms of perceptual thresholds.[9] What one experienced was not determined by a perceptual input but by a series of differences. Although Fechner complicated the law of proportional correspondence between stimulus and perception by demonstrating a threshold value (*Schwellenwert*) determined by a logarithmic relationship, it was still a model based on mechanical causality. The "conditions of excitation of the organism" stood in relation to the world of inputs that was "not inalterable" but was nonetheless deterministic.[10] Perceptual states were still a function of the intensity of stimuli. Increases and decreases in sequential stimuli signified to the perceiver only if they crossed a certain threshold of difference built into the perceptual mechanism, which Fechner thought could be scientifically pinned down and mapped. Such a mechanical, psychophysical view ensured a proportionality between input and output that guaranteed the predictable function of the psyche as a machine.

The presence of images, however, complicated the ostensibly direct relationship between inputs and outputs, and especially where it involved apparent motion. For the cinema, the issue would not be merely one of minimal thresholds for the detection of difference as it was for Fechner but the minimum threshold for *concealing* difference in order to experience movement. The gaps between frames had to be rendered invisible. Moreover, a cinema capable of symbolic, narrative operations beginning in the 1910s would require that films also elide representational discontinuities of place and time. Elaboration of narrative editing techniques like parallel editing, which really took shape in the 1910s in films such as D. W. Griffith's *The Lonedale Operator* (1911), presupposed a certain level of technical precision with respect to the regulation of mechanical intervals. The filmic alternation that allowed viewers to move effortlessly back and forth between a train station and a fast-approaching locomotive (as was the case in *The Lonedale Operator*) were based on the fundamental breaks between images becoming less conspicuous. In this way, narrative, semiotic, and psychological functions of film were wedded to a psychophysiological mirroring of the psyche and the cinema from their very beginning.

Returning in 1898 to earlier histories of psychophysical research on apparent motion, Marbe noted that the property of perceptual continuity linked to the illusion of movement was primarily marked by the interval.[11] It was the absence, break, or cut, not the indexical image, that was of utmost significance for cinematic realism. This early work seems to suggest that the notion of psychological continuity itself could only be of a signifying order, meaning that it functioned as a process of systematic exclusion, structured primarily by periods in which no image was presented. From these intervals, a secondary state emerged that was not reducible to the stimuli. Instead, the character of the experience relied on an alternation between discrete states. The optical nature of these phenomena had been initially investigated in the 1830s by Simon von Stampfer, who first engineered the scientifically indispensable visual toys of "stroboscopic discs," which created a very simple illusion of movement by presenting a series of drawn images through a slatted wheel.[12] The standards of verisimilitude for such toys was already a matter of managing intervals rather than standards of pictorial realism, even if the illusions would not receive proper scientific theorization until later in the century. It was the breaks between images, not the pictures themselves, that were responsible for the visual delight.

Reference to optical devices as models of psycho-phenomenological interaction would become standard, particularly following Sigmund Freud's *The Interpretation of Dreams* (1899).[13] This has been much commented upon with respect to Freud's move from an "echo of Fechnerism" in his early mechanistic model of the psyche to a psychoanalytic model that signaled a shift from a straightforward mechano-materialist attitude of psychic causality to a semiotic ordering.[14] Freud's departure around 1900 from a thermodynamic or mechanical model of the psyche to one ordered by the sedimentations of language, substitution, and interpretation drew on the heuristic power of "optics," which had already found expression in Fechner's reckoning with how images became present to consciousness.

The plausibility of a bridge between discrete mechanical operations and the autonomy of psychological experience was grounded in cinematographic research long before cinema ever existed. Experiments on the perception of apparent motion using precinematic instruments, such as the pedemascope and tachistoscope, which presented rapid series of stimuli for testing reaction time responses, functioned as much to show how the psyche worked like the instruments that measured it as they did to show how subjects physiologically responded to them. The climate for arguments at the end of the nineteenth century and the beginning of the twentieth century, especially with respect to the all-important matter of apparent motion, was one in which "the brain, and with it consciousness, became an apparatus among others."[15] In many ways, this experimental setting bore greater likeness to early cinema than early cinema would to later narrative films.

For Marbe, the shift was expressed through a critical focus on the interval that, in the context of later film criticism, became a theoretical linchpin in the understanding of film as diegetic, and therefore psychological rather than merely physiological. The interval, as would likewise be evident in Freud, indicates the move from *positivism* to *hermeneutics*—or from technics to semiotechnics—recognizing the breaks and pauses essential to the process of signification.[16] In Marbe's matter-of-fact estimation, alternation and absence, not continuous succession, were the source of the experience of movement.

> The ones, however, with which the impression of moving objects is generated (and these are truly the most interesting and important), are based on a second moment. That is to say, we also find ourselves in the circumstances to believe we see continuous movement if the individual, sequential periods of image exposure do not fall side-by-side on the retina. If a real object swings up and down before our eyes, then it illuminates corresponding points on the retina, side-by-side. If we want to produce the impression of a point swinging up and down by means of the stroboscope, then there must be a certain *interval* between the illumination of adjacent retinal points. Without this, the stroboscopic effect would be dispersed. We can also express this fact as such: *To stroboscopically depict* [*darstellen*] *movement,* several phases of the movement must be *absent,* without us noticing.[17]

Marbe realized that the appearance of movement was based as much on the frequency of breaks between stimuli as it was on the speed of their succession. Albeit a seemingly minor observation, it was of inestimable importance for the later interpretations of how film produced both perceptual and narrative continuity by psychoanalytic film theorists of the 1960s, 1970s, and 1980s. The interval was essential to a sense of continuity for both producing scientific conceptions of the psyche from empirical data and for producing perceptual experiences of movement and later diegesis. By introducing the idea of the calculable absence to the experience of a continuous state, Marbe prefaced a change that would take place fifteen years later with respect to cinema, whereby criticism and interpretation of films would relocate their point of engagement with the medium from *physiological* effects to *psychological* effects—from a mechanical-causal mode of continuity to a model of continuity as a space of signification. This was a change, however, based largely on concepts of moving images that were already present in purely mechanical understandings of psychic operation.

Early forerunners in experimental psychology maintained interest in proto-cinematic apparatuses and toys like the zoetrope and phenakistoscope as well as psychophysical instruments like the pedemascope (a modified thaumatrope) used in the experiments of Paul Linke (an opponent of Marbe on the issue of intervals in illusions of movement).[18] However, the discursive direction of writings about the nature and effects of imagistic "blending" (*Verschmelzung*), "after-image effects," and general "after-image phenomena" changed in the 1910s. This was particularly true as films cultivated an increasingly standardized set of technical practices for creating diegetic closure. Although Wolfgang Jacobsen attributes this to the fact that early films in the *varieté* format "merely reproduced the spectacle of the stage," maintaining the "spatial and temporal" continuity of theater, it is nonetheless true that "the technical effect" of films from this period are "more interesting than the content of the film."[19]

Cinematographic machines offered a nexus between a technologized conception of the psyche that had arisen over the course of the late nineteenth century and the more continuous experience of consciousness. In his 1910 book *Theory of Cinematographic Projections,* Marbe writes:

> After a long time having promoted scientific theory and praxis in the areas of mathematics, medicine, and the natural sciences, the text attempts—in the golden age of technology [*Blütezeit der Technik*]—to establish a connection between psychology and technology within the theory of cinematographic projection.[20]

In the "golden age" of *Technik* (meaning both "technology" and "technique"), the cinematographic projector became a proxy for thinking about the relationship between physiological mechanisms and the qualitative properties of subjective experience. This was the case precisely because the physical operations of the cinematograph had been calibrated to conjure visual and cognitive effects that concealed those very operations. In a sense, it became a model for exploring the mind/body dilemma during a period when the psyche came to be treated as a machine. The more the machine was hidden, the more convincing was its play of images—for both the cinematograph and the psyche.

Scientific treatises on cinema worked like projects of reverse engineering, suggesting adjustments for the mechanisms of the camera and projector to produce desired cognitive states. On this basis, Marbe could make the normative claim about cinematographic presentations that "they should produce in us the subjective impression of a continuous, running scene without disruptive interruptions."[21] His contention about the necessity of a connection between technical, scientific, and psychological investigation into the cinematograph demonstrates a tendency during the period to see a parallel between physiological processes and mental states on the one hand, and cinematographic mechanisms and diegetic functions on the other. From its inception, studies of proper cinematographic function centered on a chiasmic interaction between the operations of technical presentation and the sensorial and psychological conditions produced in the viewer. Both practical interest on the part of the film industry in "improving" the experience as well as social, moral, and psychological conversations about the impacts of film took as their starting point an assumption about the ideal union of machines and the corresponding cognitive continuities they produced.

Films from the late nineteenth century through the 1910s were a punishing affair for the eyes. In 1913 Naldo Felke went as far as to call the experience a form of "optical torture."[22] The "flicker" of early films was the result of a number of infelicitously combined technical elements. Several revised mechanisms were introduced in the 1900s to deal with the problem. The three-bladed shutter became a standard feature of Oskar Messter's projector in Germany and those made by the Biograph Company in the United States starting in 1903, and the Maltese Cross mechanism for smoothly regulating the intervals of the filmstrip's movement became standard in the early 1910s. But prior to such inventions, much of the movement was simply hard to watch—precisely because the audience was watching movement. They were confronted with the perceptible fact of the visual intervals responsible for the experience.

Experimental psychologists of the nineteenth century, while far from marching in theoretical lockstep, initially contended that the appearance of movement using stroboscopic and proto-cinematographic apparatuses was "determined by the fatigue of the visual organs, and in all probability, by the retina itself."[23] Cinema's success, according to this view, was definitionally a failure of the perceptual apparatus and therefore necessarily harmful. Illusions of movement were evidence of a limitation and breakdown of the physiological apparatus. Such risks, however, were predicated on a specific mechanical model of psychic and cinematic movement. That cinema would later be recognized, as well as feared, for reproducing the proper (which is to say, symbolic and narrative) functions of the psyche in the 1910s indicates a radical reconception of the mediating operations of both cinema and the psyche. The moving images of the earliest films were not thought to wreak their havoc through the replication of interior, subjective space because their effects were the mere malfunction of the perceptual apparatus. The understanding of a mechanical—meaning scientifically valid—psyche at the end of the nineteenth century mirrored the cinematograph. Paradoxically, however, one only experienced the illusion of movement when something went unnoticed, when the experience one was having could not be reduced to the individual mechanisms and one could no longer see things as they actually were.

With special attention to these visual effects, Carl Forch provided an overview of the history and function of cinematographic apparatuses in which the operations of the various projective mechanisms were treated as inseparable from their perceptual effects. In a section on the persistence of punishing flicker phenomena in early cinema, Forch writes:

> A good film camera must have a shutter that is able to modify the ratio of the exposure time to the duration of full cycle, independent of the rotating speed of the mechanism. It is different for cinematic presentation [*Vorführungskino*]. There, the duration of the film's full stop [*Filmstillstandes*] should be fully exploited. Subsequently it is desirable for achieving the physiological phenomenon at issue that either the dark periods are brightened somewhat, or conversely, that the lighting, in the time available, is interrupted by one or several short dark periods.[24]

The very terms for the discussion of cinematic mechanisms were—especially in 1913, with the explosion of long-format narrative films—guided by the conditions for perceptual continuity that would allow for an uninterrupted space of signification and narrative. Overcoming the jarring discontinuities of cinematographic presentation related to phenomena like flicker effects, which bound cinema to purely physiological consideration (its effects on the eyes, nerves, and body), also allowed it to become an art form. That is, it was transformed into a mode of visual presentation whose mechanical prowess could be ignored in favor of its content—an evolution that gave way to what could be called "style." The maturation of "projection operations toward projection art" entailed the "development of an autonomous form" capable of using "the possibilities of pictorial form [*Bildgestaltung*], the movement of the images or its components, and above all else the sequence of images as dramatic elements."[25] This is an observation that Siegfried Kracauer made central to the historiography of film, noting that the "days when films were allowed to run one after another" disappeared in favor of "a self-contained show, which integrates the film into a larger whole" representing a "*total artwork* [*Gesamtkunstwerk*] *of effects.*"[26] At the same time, meditations on how to mechanically manufacture a purely semiotic space of narrative always wound their way back to the question of how to control the periods of pause, darkness, and discontinuity. For all of cinema's putative realism, its powers as a psychological medium were tied to a history of discretization and the regulation of moments in which nothing at all was shown.

Forch appears to be among an early group of researchers and psychologists who identified the technical objectives for the further development of the cinematic apparatus with the production of a continuous, uninterrupted perceptual state based not on the speed of succession but on intervals. Siegfried Zielinski has summarized these technical improvements as part of a larger constellation of related developments connected to both narrative cinema and the psychologically motivated observations of figures like Marbe.

> Without changes to the material basis of this medium, the expansion of the single film event into a full evening's entertainment would have been impossible. Only with the doubling and tripling of the brightness enabled by the introduction of the three-bladed projection shutter at the beginning of this century—systematically described in Karl Marbe's history of cinema projection—were the relatively flicker-free pictures on the screen guaranteed. The physical fatigue resulting from eye-strain, characteristic of the first years of film, was thus ameliorated. . . . Such modifications to the apparatus were not motivated by the production of filmic entertainment alone.[27]

Instances of apparent motion and the devices for manufacturing them came to occupy a central position in understanding how the psyche worked because they were thought to provide a controlled setting for investigating the transition from discontinuous mechanical operations to states of continuous consciousness. They presented the problems of empiricism in miniature, namely, how one can get from discrete images to conceptual continuities. For experimental psychology—which had only really matured into a discipline in the late nineteenth century—there was an imperative to understand the continuity of mental states in terms of the intervals of measure, with scientific measure itself being a process of discretization. Conversely, for cinema the objective was to arrive at states of perceptual continuity by calibrating the functions of discontinuous filming, editing, and projection. The outcome of work on the conditions for perceiving motion, both cinematically and psychologically, was an increased attention to the operational character of the devices that produced them. Indeed, the connection between how the physiological apparatus could be understood as a network of discrete physical operations represented the very beginning of scientific psychology. And these were precisely the same sorts of machinations that ensured the seamless experience of cinema.

In 1911 Hans Lehmann analyzed the new cinema-technical mechanisms, filmmaking techniques, and psychology of film, notably recovering the apparatus-driven feel of earlier psychophysical experimentation. At various moments of media-sensitive, anthropological reflection, Lehmann gives a surprisingly agile theoretical account of the dialectical evolution of the psyche and technological devices. In the first instance, he argues that beyond the categories of tools and implements identified by the arch–social Darwinist Herbert Spencer as imitating and expanding native human capacities for perception, a new group of apparatuses, which included the cinematograph, "are capable of not only perceiving external stimuli, but also of retaining them—that is to say, registering them—and reproducing them on demand."[28] In other words, cinematic mechanisms functioned much like the Eccles-Jordan flip-flop described in the introduction to this book. They used purely discrete operations to produce a memory of previous operations that were no longer present. Lehmann goes on to add that they "not only form an external replica of the natural organs, but also exercise certain brain centers of the relevant organs."[29] Unlike older tools that simply extended human faculties, new technologies changed the organization of perceptual capacities. Both participated in social and cultural evolutions, but the new category of cinematographic machines restructured the organs they originally imitated.[30]

There is no doubt a sense of profound familiarity for the contemporary reader in Lehmann's argument about the education of the senses through technology, particularly in the case of film. Walter Benjamin's much later (1939) and exhaustively cited observation has become the touchstone for such a vision of modernism.

> Thus, technology has subjected the human sensorium to a complex kind of training. There came a day when a new and urgent need for stimuli was met by film. In a film, perception conditioned by shock [*chockförmige Wahrnehmung*] was established as a formal principle. What determines the rhythm of production on a conveyor belt is the same thing that underlies the rhythm of reception in film.[31]

Albeit with a Marxist attachment to the modes of industrial production that inform the sequential logic of film, Benjamin recognized that principles of sensorial training had *already* become formalized as principles of film by the time he was writing. Indeed, the emphasis on the mechanistic nature of the training involved in the perception of film highlights an important additional step that Lehmann makes, which is related to a diegetic organizing principle derived from the operations of the camera and the projector.

As a second aspect of his analysis, Lehmann was also attentive to the difference between the physiological and psychological responses to film. Drawing on the work of Linke and Marbe, who were at odds about the reasons for the perceived stability of objects in moving images, Lehmann was clear to note that the continuities of stroboscopic effects must be considered as psychological and not only physiological problems.

> Initially a precise test shows that the foundation of cinema is not only *physiological*, but also of a *psychological* nature—and truly above all else of a psychological nature. Because we really do not see real movement, rather only pseudo-movement. That is to say, our consciousness gets deceived and all problems pertaining to consciousness are primarily psychological in nature. The credit for having first pointed this out is due to Paul Linke, a student of the famous Wilhelm Wundt. Previously the cause of stroboscopic illusions had been assumed to be so-called after-image effects and blending [*Verschmelzung*].[32]

Physiological processes were mechanical, positive, and measurable. Psychological processes emphasized pauses and intervals, whose structures of absence allowed for an impression of continuous movement. In the passage, the cinematograph offers a parallel to psychic processes through which the symbolic space of mind can be explained in terms of the machine of the body. In earlier theories explaining illusions of movement as deriving from the positive, continued "duration of retinal stimuli" (a position Linke perhaps falsely attributed to Marbe), bridging from one image to the next without break, the explanatory model remained purely mechanical.[33] It could not be psychological because the model was one of direct input/output, stimuli/response. In this way, Lehmann was not only claiming that psychology was predicated on the signifying power of absences as a core psychological process but also that such processes could best be explained by new cinematic apparatuses. He writes, "If the stroboscopic effect is to be brought about, a definite, relatively small interval must be present."[34] Psychological continuity was no longer believed to be a simple internal reproduction of structurally coherent objects in the world but the result of breaks. There is a detectable movement from an emphasis on content, which would entail a replication of the world in the mind, to an emphasis on the logic and technics of assembly as the determining force in the continuity of inner life.

Wilhelm Wundt, perhaps the most important figure of experimental psychology during the nineteenth century, articulated the conceptual problem faced when thinking of the mind as a discrete state machine almost as soon as psychology emerged as a legitimate field of study. Although he would become known as a defender of introspection as a legitimate tenet of scientific observation, he also scoffed at the idea that psychological processes could not be measured and thus discretized. This was made particularly clear in a dispute with Eduard Zeller about the nature and meaning of perceptual thresholds. Zeller arrived in Heidelberg as a professor of philosophy in 1862, where Wundt was the assistant to Hermann von Helmholtz and would later become a professor. Defending a religious metaphysical unity of the soul, Zeller used Weber's law of perceptual thresholds as a "principle of relativity for all psychical conditions" and therefore evidence that "psychical processes are not measurable"—essentially disputing the basic precepts of the field of psychophysics.[35] Zeller had made a two-part claim that "sense impression" was "a conscious phenomenon and as such, absolutely different than mechanical movement."[36] Wundt replied lovelessly that both formulations of Zeller's objection "embark from the fiction that there is a world outside of us and a world in us, which admittedly share a boundary, but share no internal connection," and that this "fiction is untenable."[37] According to Wundt, the character of the movements in the machine and the impression of movement in the subject were not qualitatively but only quantitatively different. In this way, the world he was describing—and with it the psyche—was informational. The ability of the psyche to be treated as an autonomous, symbolic unity was not at odds with its mechanical character as a series of discrete operations. Rather, both the symbolic and the psychological were tied to such machinations.

Continuous by Design

The psychophysical architects of cinematic experience drew from nineteenth-century theories of engineering that found in machines a powerful union between the discontinuities of their many parts and the continuities of what those parts meant when they worked together. In his watershed 1875 work on kinematics, the theorist of mechanical engineering at the Berlin Royal Technical Academy, Franz Reuleaux, explained mechanical operations in terms of limitations (*Beschränkungen*), through which a specific set of modalities of machine articulation became possible.[38] By establishing and combining the limitations of individual movements within a machine and then sequencing them, something like a machine syntax could be elaborated with deep implications for the interpretation of how the mind worked for experimental psychologists, and therefore the connection between technics and semiosis. Reuleaux helped shift the analysis of machines from a static concern with individual forces within a machine to the shape of its entire range of possible movements. What a machine did (or was capable of doing), and thus what it meant, was evaluable in terms of a continuous geometric shape that emerged as a gestalt from the sequence of discontinuous operations.

For Reuleaux, limitations—those rules governing the organization of intervals among mechanical components—acted as a logic in the sense that they made certain movements possible and excluded others, making way for the assembly of "chains" (*Ketten*) that eventuated themselves in a single, perpetual movement unifying the device as a whole. This was true for both the machine's function and its appearance to an observer, and it is an insight that would be a guiding premise for the understanding of filmic apparatuses. It would also inform the reception of earlier histories of stroboscopic effects conducted by Michael Faraday, Simon von Stampfer, and Charles Wheatstone. Oftentimes, as was true of the cogwheel (*Zahnrad*) and the Geneva drive (*Maltesekreuzantrieb*), in the case of the cinematograph, it was precisely in the discontinuous workings of the individual mechanism that a continuity, whether kinematic or perceptual, became possible.

Following the generation of French engineers influenced by Leonhard Euler, Reuleaux claimed, "We take all questions belonging to what we have called the special study of machinery and the study of machine-design as solved, so that only geometrical properties remain for us to consider."[39] Kinematic analysis for engineers of the nineteenth century, which would be so influential for anthropotechnical theories by figures like Ernst Kapp, was geometrical in nature, which had a number of ramifications, the first of which was that it privileged possible states over existing ones (modality over actuality).[40] It also constituted those relationships as a kind of image that signified for a spectrum of possible states.

The unity of function, and the appearance of a single movement, was made possible by a technological Gestell, for both Reuleaux and for his later readers, such as Kapp and Martin Heidegger. What was present in Reuleaux, and either accidentally or intentionally lifted by Heidegger in his reflections on the origins of art, was a relationship between a Gestell that defined the limitations and possibilities structuring an image of movement but that emerged only through the synchronized intervals and operative chains of linked mechanical movements.[41] In the case of Reuleaux and his advances in mechanical engineering, machine design benefited from a theoretical distance from the empirical movements of actual apparatuses. In the place of a static empiricism, "kinematic chains" established a range of possible articulations that could be best viewed as continuous images.

After Reuleaux, natural, mechanical, perceptual, and mental operations could be seen to participate in a kind of mechanical syntax, producing continuities that were the effect of limitations, breaks, and the assembly of shapes that signified for a spectrum of potential movements. On the rotating mechanisms that were all-important for the cinematograph, Reuleaux wrote:

> Just as the ancient philosopher compared the constant, gradual transformation of a thing to a flow, and condensed it into the adage "everything flows," so too can we summarize in a word the innumerable phenomena of movement in the wonderful products of the

> human mind that we call machines: "everything rolls!" . . . By itself the rolling geometric forms, which can be deciphered in the cosmos, are not the continuity of nature. They have a part in the general "flowing"; they endlessly transform themselves in the fluctuation of appearances, and in so doing, either dissolve into nothing, or they reshape themselves in perpetually mutable formations, precisely locatable in each moment within only the rolling itself. . . . In the machine, by contrast, the artificial limitation of movement means that the rolling figures have a continued existence. At the very least it is these that we seek to fundamentally bring about and to ascertain in every manner; it is here, observed in itself, therefore, that it is available to us. Here these figures pass through their reciprocal changes in position, periodically and innumerable times. They rest when the machine stands still, yet begin again in the unvarying form of their game, as soon as the animating force reinfuses life in the whole. Continually only parts stop, which, as connectors, link the idle area to the rest. For practical mechanics, which has made itself familiar with recent phoronomics, and more still theoretically, it is for this reason that the machine of a particular type is animated by the rolling, geometrical forms throughout it. Individual parts physically emerge. . . . They all carry out their strange tireless game, in part physically, in part in the mind's eye of the machinist. Amid the often perceptually bewildering roar of their physical representatives, they perform their noiseless life function [*Lebensfunktion*] to roll. *They are, so to speak, the soul of the machine* [Seele der Maschine], *which dictates the physical expression of movement* [Bewegungsäusserungen] *and reflects them in a pure light. They are the geometrical abstractions of the machine.*[42]

In the passage, Reuleaux identifies a relationship between the circumscribed individual movements that produces the overall operations of the machine and the *idea* of the machine. As an idea, it omits the specific arrangements of multiple, sometimes discontinuous movements, in favor of a conceptual, geometrical image of the whole.

Nature was thought to be marked by movement since the pre-Socratics, even where (or even especially where) it was seen as a merely an illusion, as Parmenides had claimed.[43] Yet the impression of its continuity was an analytical construct and a tendency of the mind to abstract and unify discontinuities. The transmission or production of such a continuity in consciousness, or *of* consciousness, however, bore traces of the specific character of the technological medium that produced it. Peter Berz wrote of the "universal grammar of machine movement" elaborated by Reuleaux that "the machine of the nineteenth century rolls, runs, cranks, and be plotted in continuous arcs. However, that which blocks, halts, hinders, clicks shut, clicks open, suddenly starts and stops again, does not belong to the machine."[44] Reuleaux's observations indicate a preliminary step toward not only a notion of how the disjunction between the real operations of a machine and the continuities of signification could occur but also of the technical nature of such an occurrence. As Wolfgang Schäffner notes, "The rolling, rotating machine always already looks to Reuleaux the engineer to be an image machine [*Bildmaschine*]," and therefore machines "generate an entirely new kind of image [*Bildtyp*] that is as new as the wheel of the nineteenth century: 'everything rolls' and produces images."[45]

It was not simply that the machine became an image machine but that Reuleaux noticed the way that discrete technics could come to signify as a single moving object. The very fact of the early connection between the logic of discontinuous mechanisms and the impression of continuity serves to demonstrate an approach to the problem of how semiotechnical continuities could arise from purely mechanical processes. The "soul of the machine" and its "life function" were already significantly involved in the theorization of the psyche with respect to continuous and discontinuous mechanisms. From the calculated elisions of individual, mechanical functions, a shape emerged that expressed the essence of a machine. The soul was a moving image and one not reducible to any single element.

These observations about machines were almost directly transmitted to scientific psychology, in which the psyche had already long been treated as a machine. In his 1891 dissertation "On the Perceptions of Movement," for instance, Edmund Burke Delabarre, a student of the psychophysicist and film theory pioneer Hugo Münsterberg, contended:

> All of our complicated psychological [*geistigen*] ideas and functions—space, time, selfhood, feelings, psychological activities, etc.—are nothing other than combinations of sensory perceptions with the perception of movements or muscle contractions, and the association of these combinations with their reproductions of one another.[46]

He went on to make an even more machine-oriented declaration about the premises and limitations for any scientific view of the psyche.

> The presuppositions from which we would now like to proceed are a total dependence of psychological life on bodily conditions and the necessity for all events of consciousness to be understood as sensations and reproductions of sensations as the contents of consciousness [*Bewusstseinsinhalt*]. This perspective forecloses on the possibility of an immaterial will as the source of any part of our voluntary movements. To admit the existence of such an influence would absolutely negate the validity of the mechanical laws in the physical world.[47]

Theorizations of the psyche that sought to reduce the complexities of experience to observable inputs assumed a likeness between all mechanisms, of which the psyche was just one. The problem of apparent motion had been essentialized as *the* problem of consciousness in experimental psychology, as it captured the simultaneous interdependence and internal conflict between mechanical causality and consciousness. The relatively young field of experimental psychology had taken up the contentious issue of where perceptions of movement were located, as it remained a question of mechanical causality until after the introduction of the cinema. Psychophysicists and experimental psychologists such as Johannes Müller, Wilhelm Wundt, William James, Hugo Münsterberg, and Friedrich Schumann—many of whom would later be involved in accounting for the *psychological* implications of images in cinematographic apparatuses—were forced in their earlier work to confront the problem of where the source of perceptual impressions of continuous movement resided. Münsterberg, for instance, would maintain that all "contents of consciousness were reducible to sensations," involving a "model of the mind as essentially a registering mechanism."[48]

Although written much later, Wolfgang Köhler's gestalt psychological opposition to "psychical causality" was given voice in his argument against what had pejoratively been named "machine theory."[49] In a section addressing the history of psychology in the first two decades of the twentieth century, Köhler argues that "we are surely not exaggerating if we say that the machine theory of the nervous system is quite unable to do justice to the nature of sensory experience."[50] Not coincidentally, it is in this section that Köhler supports his claim by making reference to "motion pictures" and recalling Max Wertheimer's 1912 experiments on apparent motion, which have been the darling of film theoretical scholarship since Rudolf Arnheim, who was a student of Wertheimer's and who quoted him at length in his classic work *Film as Art* in 1932.[51] If one is to simplify the results of Wertheimer's experiment, the argument is that measuring only the physical conditions and intensities of stimuli involved in the rapid succession of images is insufficient for explaining the impression of continuous movement experienced in front of a moving image machine.[52] Arnheim cites his teacher to establish the correspondence between the principles of film and those of mental, perceptual coherence:

> In his investigation of "apparent motion" [*Sehen von Bewegung*] Max Wertheimer has described experiments in which he let two illuminated slots, at a small distance from each other, bob in rapid succession before the eyes of a person in a darkened room. If the distance and the exposure time were correctly chosen, the person had the overwhelming impression that there were not two separate slots lighting up one after the other and beside each other, but that one slot appeared on the left, ran over to the right and was there extinguished. This stroboscopic fusion of objectively separate stimuli into one unified impression also occurs in film by montage. In fact, fundamentally, the whole existence of the motion picture is dependent on this principle. For actually, objectively, there is nothing but a succession of single motionless images, phases of motion, on the celluloid strip. It is only because the images succeed one another so rapidly and because they fit one another so exactly that the impression of continuous movement is given. Fundamentally, therefore, film is the montage of single frames—imperceptible montage [*Unmerkbare Montage*].[53]

Arnheim's comparison of perceptual continuity on the part of the experimental subject to the effects of film montage set the "objective" conditions of perception in opposition to the "impression of continuous movement." Not only did montage offer a technological model for reinterpreting perceptual operations, suggesting that film became a template for understanding how the mind worked, but it also found no fundamental difference between the objective and the perceived. Neither the single stimulus nor the individual image was the primary determining factor in the perception and comprehension of stimuli.

It was the intervals between, and the speed and order of the presentation of successive "light slots," that produced the impression of a perceptual unity. Rather than the psyche acting as an organizational apparatus, sorting and internally transmitting stimuli, film in Arnheim's description mechanically prefigured these mental operations, such that the psyche received—instead of created—a "total impression." If thought was conceived of as the apparent coherence emerging from the sorting and arrangement of external stimuli by the psychic apparatus, then the diegetic space created by films had to also be seen as a parallel mechanism going from individual frames to psychological uniformity. This point is made all the more explicit when Arnheim writes in a section titled "Artistic Uses of the Absence of Spatiotemporal Continuity" about the relation of the potential failure to achieve continuity:

> Since montage separates things that are spatially continuous and merges together things that have no inherent space-time continuity, the danger arises that the process may not be successful and that the whole may disintegrate into pieces, which the spectator cannot combine according to the wishes of the artist.[54]

The continuity he describes here is not that of mere movement instituted by the rapid pace of successive images, nor the intervals of shutter closure that separate them. The threat of incoherence he describes is a failure of the film to produce a closed diegetic space. When a film properly instituted a narrative logic in the presentation of images, its spatiotemporal discontinuities disappeared and were replaced in the viewer with a continuous space of signification. A diegetic space came at the cost of the viewer's own spatiotemporal faculties for detecting discontinuities.

While the illusion of movement was an essential element of the experience of film, its real power, and the threat that would be intuited by its early opponents discussed in the next chapter, was not just a failure as described by Arnheim but its *success* in replacing the viewer's mechanisms of apperception. Where early physiological theories saw apparent motion as a failure of the viewer to notice discontinuities, this failure was reconfigured as an essential precondition of thought, and therefore not a failure at all. The real threat to the integrity of the human subject would be that the logic according to which psychological continuities emerged was the result of an apparatus engineered in much the same way that Reuleaux had described; it just would not be a human apparatus.

The Soul of the Machine

If science seeks explanations that structurally correspond with or bridge the chasm between the perceived and the real, film seeks visual formulations that structurally correspond with or express the "reality" experienced in the obfuscation of the real. Scientific deployments of proto-cinematic instruments in the late nineteenth and early twentieth centuries first introduced the breaks that made the psyche measurable. But they also sought to explain how those mechanical breaks could be operationalized to resemble consciousness. This was—by no means accidentally—also the heart of the cinematic experience. In a certain way, it proleptically addressed the issues that would motivate the apparatus theory of the 1970s. It did so not by disenchanting the well-developed machines that produced the ideological, disembodied subjects of cinema after the classical Hollywood period but by attempting to reenchant the machines that had mechanically dismantled such subjects in the first place. Apparatus theorists located filmic subject effects in the "displacement of the codes of cinematic verisimilitude from the plane of the impression of reality along to the more complex planes of fictional logic (narrative codes), of psychological verisimilitude, of the impression of homogeneity and continuity."[55] The "real" appeared as only a specific set of psychological operations that established a coherence among perceptual impressions that were themselves disparate and did not reside in the content but in the order provided by the apparatus. The origins of this interval-based subject building were engineered into the machines themselves from their very beginning.

Photographically excerpting moments from a continuous movement had the advantage of allowing scientists to reconstruct the event using the analytical precepts of scientific method rather than the undifferentiated and likely deceiving flow of perception. The logical relationship between images was to be interpreted and imposed by the neutral apparatus of scientific observation, not by the photographic or cinematographic apparatus. In the history of the development of cinematographic technologies, this dispute was already visible in the acrimonious end of the relationship between Étienne-Jules Marey and his assistant Georges Demenÿ. Marey was dedicated to the scientific value of his chronophotographic devices, and therefore their ability to stop and sequence movement, and Demenÿ to the possible commercial applications: namely, the reproduction of the impression of movement.[56] As Tom Gunning has written, Marey's "deep and abiding suspicion of human vision" and his "lack of interest in the illusion of motion strongly expresses the scientific disdain of motion pictures as a betrayal of the possibilities of scientific photography."[57] However, the initial aspiration to create a scientifically valid, fully standardized reproduction of the movement of objects by initially breaking them down into discrete moments, then reassembling them according to a standardized incremental measure, did not come to fruition, and the cinematograph fell into the near-exclusive domain of entertainment.[58] Movement, as Marey discovered, could be decomposed into scientifically useful chronophotographic images, but the impression of movement produced when they were then sequenced and projected came to be seen as exclusively the result of the apparatus's logic, which was subjective rather than objective. Jimena Canales has similarly claimed that "the connection between analysis (shooting) and synthesis (projecting) largely lost its *raison d'etre* rapidly after it was achieved."[59] As such, the mechanistic order that was the foundation of cinematographic projection, even in scientific discourses, doubled as a reference to the idiosyncratic construction of human subjects. Machine logic was not human, to be sure, but it was treated as subjective nonetheless.

Henri Bergson captures the dilemma when he draws a parallel between the concepts governing scientific measurement and the mechanical intervals that initiate a continuous mental space.

> *Instead of attaching ourselves to the inner becoming of things, we place ourselves outside them in order to recompose their becoming artificially.* . . . Perception, intellection, language so proceed in general. Whether we would think becoming, or express it, or even perceive it, we hardly do anything else than set going a kind of cinematograph inside of us. We may therefore sum up what we have been saying in the conclusion that the *mechanism of our ordinary knowledge is of a cinematographical kind.*
>
> . . . Our knowledge of the operation of nature must be exactly symmetrical, therefore, with the interest we take in our own operation. In this sense we may say, if we are not abusing this kind of illustration, that *the cinematographical character of our knowledge of things is due to the kaleidoscopic character of our adaptation of them.*
>
> The cinematographical method is therefore the only practical method, since it consists in making the general character of knowledge form itself on that of action, while expecting that the detail of each act should depend in its turn on that of knowledge.[60]

Canales has claimed that by 1907, when Bergson was writing (and even before that), the cinematograph was no longer seen as a useful scientific instrument because the irregularities involved in "synthesizing" movement were at odds with the expectations about precision and "analysis." Yet Bergson seems to support the idea that scientific thinking, and thinking in general, was *already* modeled on the operations of the cinematograph. Unlike Marey, Bergson "criticized this techno-mathematical discretization of time as the misapprehension of the phenomenological being of time: duration."[61] Yet at the same time, duration for the cinema was precisely a matter of managing absences.

Whether the cinematograph was still deployed as an instrument in the service of scientific objectives was not what was at issue. Instead, cinematographic operations provided a model for thinking about how technics produced semiotic unities from mechanical discontinuities. Scientific psychology did not need to use cinematographs to be cinematographic. This was because its models of psychological coherence had already internalized the relationship between discrete empirical measure and abstract concepts, and between measurable perceptual inputs and consciousness. Or as Bergson had claimed: we place ourselves outside events "in order to recompose their becoming artificially."

Around the turn of the twentieth century, when flicker in films still made apparent the mechanisms by which continuity arose, the science of the psyche proceeded cinematographically. Films offered a vision for how perceptual continuities were related to the sequence of discrete operations. The fear about cinema being more than a physiological threat only occurred once the conspicuous mechanisms were erased from view, flicker disappeared, narrative appeared through editing, and the continuities were not only perceptual but also cognitive. At this point, the fact that the "mechanism of our ordinary knowledge is of a cinematographical kind" meant something entirely different. It meant that it was no longer just the basic mechanisms for physiological perception that imitated or could be reproduced with the cinematograph; rather, the very logic of psychological continuity could perhaps be dictated by a machine.

One of the better-known examples of such an anxiety about cinema's operationalization of human psychology was made by Georg Lukács in 1911. He argued that cinema had granted the "how" of events "a power that dominates everything else."[62] His pronouncement about filmic techniques, which would resonate so profoundly with later Freudian contentions about images' primitive, unconscious derivation and inability to structure the ego, diagnosed this problem.[63] Lukács writes:

> Silent: the spoken word, the sonorous concept are vehicles of fate; only in and through them does binding continuity arise in the psyche of dramatic people. The *revocation of the word* and, with it, of memory, of duty, and of the faithfulness to oneself and to the idea of one's own selfhood makes everything—if the nonverbal develops into a totality—light, sprightly, and quickened, frivolous, and terpsichorean.[64]

This leads him to the elegiac insight about the introduction of cinema that "man has lost his soul and gained a body in return," a comment that could have easily—and, in fact, had—been made about the tendency toward mechanical measure in experimental psychology.[65] Lukács already ascribes any notion of continuity to technical operations, arguing that the cinematograph, in spite of its ability to produce perceptual continuities, destroyed an irreducible psychic unity. The timing of the essay is important because it was written on the cusp of the eruption of long-format narrative feature films such as Walter Friedemann's *Der Müller und sein Kind* (1911) and Urban Gad's *Die Verräterin* (1912), starring Asta Nielsen, where the techniques of continuity editing, like parallel editing in chase scenes, were just being fully elaborated.[66] These would be the same machine-based subjectivizing narrative techniques that would be critiqued by apparatus theory sixty years later.

The result is that we are presented with a limit case, where the transition from pure perceptual continuity to diegetic continuity had not fully arrived. Lukács recognizes that the core concept of subjective autonomy is continuity and therefore that film, up to the point that he was writing, influenced the construction or destruction of the psyche but could not itself produce the coherence associated with thought. As the evolution of thinking about flicker demonstrated, perceptual continuity was the effect of bridging the gaps between stimuli. Conversely, the psychological, semiotic continuity that formed something like a human subject relied on a technics that bridged the gaps that formed the basis for signification. That film would also come to master these gaps and with them the techniques of subject formation would serve as grounds for a general outcry about its dangers to not just the sensorium but the entire species as well.

2

The Semiotechnical Subject

Piglets cannot be both Piglets and words at the same time.

—Jacques Rancière, *The Intervals of Cinema*

Between 1907 and 1917, film was transformed from an itinerant attraction in varieté theaters and traveling cinemas into an increasingly permanent fixture of urban entertainment in storefront cinemas and cinema palaces.[1] As the cinematic *dispositif* underwent accelerating standardization—regulating projection speeds, shutter mechanisms, film formats, and theater architecture—editing techniques governing the organization of multiscene narrative films followed suit.[2] During this time, cinema's institutionalization was met with institutional criticism. This took the form of state censorship and a proliferation of conservative religious, medical, juridical, and *bildungsbürgerliche* associations, initiatives, and publications aimed at controlling for the potentially deleterious effects of films. Although they advanced no one unified thesis about the virtues and dangers of the medium, critics associated with this milieu are collectively referred to as a part of the cinema reform movement (Kinoreformbewegung) and have come to occupy an established area of inquiry for contemporary scholarship on early cinema.[3]

What is evident in texts about the reception and theorization of early cinema on the part of its social critics is that its development as a narrative medium, and as a locus for a public, collective, visual experience, was accompanied by a preoccupation with its mass-psychological ramifications. In large part, these concerns were limited to versions of the banal objection that the native subjects for film were sex, suicide, and the unredeemed criminal life (*Verbrecherleben*), capitalizing on the basest desires of viewers and inuring an international audience to a hyperbolic vision of eroticism in darkened rooms filled with smoke, alcohol, and women.[4] Writers and critics affiliated with the cinema reform movement lamented the salacious content of the many films popular with female audiences about topics such as the white sexual slave trade in films like *The White Slave Trade* (1910) and *Traffic in Souls* (1913), alongside detective and adventure films like the Stuart Webbs series produced in the 1910s, which was thought to celebrate acts of criminality. From such films, they extrapolated to a crisis of civilizations, which, as in the case of films like *Traffic in Souls,* even partially guided sinister anti-Black legislation.[5] Where early critics—from the United States to Germany—often ignored damaging racist fantasies about imagined threats to the purity of young white women and corruptible young men, they remained extremely attentive to the semiotechnical dangers of the medium itself. Reformers frequently drew upon earlier movements aimed at eliminating pulp literature (*Schundliteratur*) in their attempts to contextualize their own objectives and were propelled by the opposition of morality movements (*Sittlichkeitsbewegungen*) to many forms of popular entertainment, which included films as well as novels and magazines.[6]

Following the second "reading revolution after 1850," Europe was awash in trivial printed materials, from postcards to colportage novels, religious literature, and ten-pfennig fantasy magazines for young readers, all of which were subject to scrutiny by conservative educational critics.[7] Otto von Leixner, the vigilant anti–pulp literature campaigner, coiner of the literary designation "smut" (*Schmutz*), and founder of the Volksbund zur Bekämpfung des Schmutzes in Wort und Bild (People's Federation for the Prevention of Smut in Word and Image), drew analogies between physical, national, and moral health to decry the contamination of German moral character through lurid novels and comic papers.[8] Others, such as Karl Brunner, went as far as to make the claim that trashy literature inspired a pervasive milieu of criminality. Brunner's moralistic publication *Die Hochwacht* (The Watchtower) included "a recurring log of criminal acts committed by minors that could be supposedly traced back to reading *Schundschriften* [pulp literature]."[9] Charges against film mirrored this socially conservative sensationalism in both their form and content, with critics such as Victor Noack linking an insatiable appetite for film to criminal acts in service of a burgeoning cinema addiction.[10]

Yet cinematic technics distinguished the dangers of film from their racy textual predecessors. While many reformers would argue that dramatic films promoted "a lascivious eroticism" and that "travesties of misery and hardship, poverty and sickness produced tortured thoughts about the injustice of the world," it was the way that they did so that posed the greatest peril.[11] Cinema threatened not only the integrity of individual desires and the education of youth but also the coherence of social institutions. And it did so by collapsing the crystalline structures of signifying practices upon which the ideals of social and psychological cohesion were built.

It is precisely the idea of integrity, at the level of individual, subjective autonomy, that demands a reengagement with such critics—critics whose theoretical interventions have otherwise been relegated to a history of retrograde techno-catastrophizing and doomsdayism.[12] For all of their irritable moralizing, these conservative sentries of older cultural and pedagogical systems did not respond uniformly to the rise of cinema. Instead, their arguments traced subtle evolutions in the nature of cinema as a source of psychosocial influence and a technical possibility that machines were able—through their bare management of mechanical intervals—to signify. In this way, these critics demonstrate a radical shift from a purely technical, psychophysiological subject to a semiotechnical subject.

The earliest commentaries on cinema's potential dangers focused primarily on the physiological overload caused by concentrated exposures to bright, fast-moving, flickering images. As filmic technologies and techniques evolved in the 1910s to disguise the machines at work in creating illusions of movement, however, reformers shifted both the target and the methodology of their criticism. Concern with purely neurophysiological effects gave way to psycho-symbolic critiques, even as critics continued to draw on the vocabulary of older nerve theories. It was no longer a question of how the cinematic machine acted on the bodily machine. Instead, a deeper worry emerged that the artificial psychological space produced by cinematic technologies intervened in distinctly human psychological functions and subject formation.

In the 1910s, *physiological* critiques mutated into *psychological* critiques—something that has been obscured by the dominance of modernist "nervousness discourse" (*Nervositätsdiskurs*).[13] Fixation on the traumatic acceleration of experience under conditions of electrification and mechanization in Wilhelmine and Weimar Germany developed during the 1980s and 1990s alongside a recuperated interest in the Frankfurt School.[14] "Nerves," in this view—whether shattered, frayed, or overexcited—functioned metonymically to designate an ill-defined but pervasive techno-social conflict between machines and humans that marked the beginning of the twentieth century. The relatively novel idea of a neuro-electric mind, itself understood as a machine overtaxed by the maddening pace of mechanical stimuli from cinema, streetcars, and telephones, entered popular consciousness at the end of the nineteenth century but would not remain merely a machine for long. More frightening was the prospect of machines able to warp the contours of the human semiotic universe: machines that no longer presented themselves as fairground gadgets or as gadgets at all.

Familiar visions of modernism focused on the dystopian (as well as utopian) possibilities of what the arch pessimist Oswald Spengler referred to as the "empire of the machine" tend to overemphasize the jarring, furious, dehumanizing, and interruptive conception of machines.[15] Critics within the reform movement, on the other hand, saw in the increasing smoothness and diegetic sophistication of the cinematic dispositif something perhaps more damning than the shocks of bright lights and high-speed traffic accidents. In their view, the modern experience represented by the cinema was radical not because of the discretized, mechanistic, and fragmentary conditions it produced but on account of the stable psychological continuities that emerged from such conditions.

The purpose of this chapter is not to add further to an already rich body of texts in the "nervousness discourse" but to suggest that the earliest engagements with the psychology of film by psychiatrists, psychologists, doctors, and analysts, which very often came in the form of conservative screeds by reformers, reveal an anxiety about not only the possibility that machines could *signify* but that human signification might also rely on similarly technical processes. That the psyche even came to be hypothesized as a scientifically observable unity that could be methodically disassembled and measured was itself a source of worry that was transmitted to arguments about the psychology of film at the end of the nineteenth century and the early twentieth century. Inner life was continuous and polysemic, filled with rich and layered strata of meaning that were not reducible to individual stimuli. A cinema that could capture or reproduce such states was more dangerous than the frontal assault of any machine.

Experimental psychologists in the nineteenth century sought to break down human experience into constitutive parts. That they did so using proto-cinematographic mechanisms, which discretized experience into measurable units, created an immediate parallel between the conception of the mind as semiotic machine and the cinematograph as movement machine. As an "attraction," the earliest cinema offered a mere source of stimulus, whose hierarchy of cogs and shutters governing limited internal interactions among parts were an analogy for the mechanical ordering of mental operations. Once the "attraction" of films was diegetic rather than a mechanical curiosity, however, the invocation of its physiological effects became much more complex. As Jonathan Crary so decisively demonstrated, the optical apparatuses used in nineteenth-century scientific psychology were "the outcome of a complex remaking of the individual as observer into something calculable and regularizable and of human vision into something measurable and thus exchangeable," which was related to a "broader process of normalization."[16] This was the effect of reducing the "observer to a supposedly rudimentary state" using "sequences of stimuli or images" that liberated "sensation from signification."[17] Yet the possibility recognized by the reform movement involved a reenchantment of such machines. Those demystified sequences of stimuli were reassembled in the cinema of the 1910s to manufacture semiotic continuities that were seen to dispossess viewers of their control over signification.

From Physiology to Psychology

Critics within the reform movement almost always coupled charges about the insidiousness of filmic content with the scientific authority of psychophysical language. Film engineered physiological circumstances that made the viewer more susceptible to the influence of content. These new conditions were thought to simultaneously produce sensorial and intellectual enervation and to facilitate the delivery of imperceptible messages through suggestion, simulation, and hypnosis—as well as simply damaging the normal functions of sensory organs. As the psychologist Robert Gaupp commented in 1911, "By itself the cinematograph harms and destroys nerves through the temporal concentration of psychic processes."[18] The rapid succession of images, he argued, denied the viewer the time for "contemplation" (*Nachdenken*) afforded by reading, which, in addition to the primary effects on the eyes and mind, represented one of the "assaults on our psychic life [*Seelenleben*]"—turning the content of the narrative into "catastrophic suggestions to the will-less, addicted psyches of common people."[19]

Suspicion about film's role in the disruption of psychological processes was tied to a methodological and theoretical overlap with areas of scientific inquiry, which were quite frequently concerned with the physiological outcomes of repeated exposure to various media, such as novels and films. However, as Gaupp's text makes clear by framing disturbances of the nerves and physical processes as problems of contemplation or reflection (Nachdenken; literally, "after-thinking"), sequences of mechanical operations could not be the sole source of psychic autonomy.[20] Physiological well-being was a condition of possibility for preserving psychological autonomy but not autonomy itself. Nachdenken connotes a cultural technique, whereby what is experienced is retroactively submitted to a second-order thinking that makes sense of or unifies multiple discontinuous elements. It is a specific logic, bound to practices of reading that systematize inputs as support for a whole—a kind of recursive or second-order position that allows a series of parts to signify as a whole.[21] While Gaupp believed the audience to be denied the technique of Nachdenken—no longer able to return to passages of text to unpack their meaning—the idea that it could nonetheless structure the psyche (even if negatively) through "suggestions" signals an early theorization of the relationship between machine logic and mental operations that was not merely the reduction of the mind to a machine.

Worries about nefarious mechanical influence and psychological suggestion arising from technologies of entertainment, informational transmission, and mediation occurred within an echo chamber theorizing the effects of modern life.[22] These cultural anxieties have been a wellspring of materials for contemporary scholarship on the culture of nerves and electrification at the beginning of the twentieth century and the end of the nineteenth century. Indeed, cultural prognostications regarding the degenerative influence of media have a lineage of well-established precedents in fin-de-siècle Europe. Perhaps the most famous of these was Max Nordau's *Degeneration,* in which he decried the diminished capacity for "attention" (*Aufmerksamkeit*) related to a "growing nervous excitability."[23] This is a line of thinking that has received significant and various "attention" of its own in the past thirty years. What was unique to film criticism amid the riot of techno-dystopianism around 1900 was its role as a vehicle for reconciling mechanical models of the psyche with metaphysics of the soul. On its face, film criticism seemed to reproduce a popular form of cultural mania related to technology and its influence on human capacities. More importantly, however, it surreptitiously constructed a model of the psyche that theorized it as both symbolic and mechanical, discrete and continuous.

At the point that film had enough of a cultural and industrial standing to warrant investigations into its specific operations, these problems of continuity were paramount. An area in which this was most apparent was on the issue of blurring, flicker, or "ghosting," which has since been theorized as the fulcrum of cinema's analogy with and influence over the functions of the psyche. The status of a phenomenon like flicker as something to be eliminated from cinematographic presentations and as an imperfection of the cinematograph makes evident a transition from physiological notions of psychic influence to psychological ones. It was only once longer narrative film became more or less the norm that referring to the ideal function of the cinematograph was also to refer to the proper relationship between physiological states and continuous psychological (i.e., "normal") states.

What flicker located was not only the necessity of the breaks and pauses for the generation of perceptual and diegetic continuities but also the necessity of their erasure. No doubt discontinuities between single images, and later between shots and scenes, were critical for the comprehensibility of moving images. But the breaks themselves were not to be legible. The change in the understanding of flicker from a physiological disruption to a diegetic disruption indicates a corresponding change in the understanding of the relationship between physiology and psychology. When flicker was believed to pose only a physiological threat, by damaging the nerves, retina, and the brain, film's relation to the psyche was purely a mechanical problem. To see evidence of the mechanical breaks and intervals that made an illusion possible was thus not a psychological problem but one of stress on the psychic machine. As soon as those same breaks and pauses were treated as *interruptions* to the seamless space of diegesis, cinema's significance for mental and psychological continuity changed entirely.

At least with respect to early cinema, a sweeping move from the first films, whose effects were theorized as directly affecting the nerves, to later films, which impacted the viewers' internal symbolic economy, does not bear out. Initial responses to film fixated on cinema as purely a mode of technical stimulus, causing physiological overexcitement in the viewer, who was conceived of as a complicated series of mechanisms for managing energetic inputs and outputs. The very "illusion" of movement in cinema, attributed to "afterimages" (*Nachbilder*) or "blending" (*Verschmelzung*) around 1900, was seen as a failure of the perceptual mechanism.[24] It was only as a faltering psychical apparatus that such visual continuities of movement could be achieved. That the phenomenon of apparent motion was treated as a failure to perceive the individual stimuli as separate instead of as movement reaffirmed the mechanical nature of the psychical device in much the same way that Heidegger famously described the malfunction of a hammer.[25] The operational technics of a physical device, which exists both as a cultural concept and purely material entity (*Seiendes*), only becomes conspicuous upon its failure to perform as it normally does. At that point, its use and future hammering are distinguished from its stark materiality and we can see it for both its pure existence and its cultural abstraction such that each signifies as independent of one another. So too with basic cinematographic operations. The apparent motion that formed the basis for the cinematic experience was not based on the ability to assemble distinct inputs continuously but defined the psychic machine's *limitations* in recognizing discontinuities. One could not see the individual frames as individual frames—and this was by design.

By 1912 it was "subject to no doubt that the eyes are easily fatigued through the flicker of images and in some cases are harmed by the flicker of images," but that was not the primary source of concern.[26] As Karl Marbe acknowledges in a section largely about the "avoidance of flicker," there had already been a history of attention paid to how best to design the cinematograph for the purpose of making the projection smoother, clearer, and less physiologically straining.[27] Previous considerations that contended primarily with the design of shutters no doubt dealt with what Robert Stigler at the University of Vienna called the "discontinuous" in cinematographic "presentations."[28] What was missing in early appraisals, and what a review of Stigler's article hinted at, however, when it noted "unfortunately, once again theory comes limping along behind praxis," is that the theory of continuity as a mental state corresponding to cinematographic operations had not yet fully emerged in the literature.[29] Flicker became a principle topic of interest as it indicated a failure of the cinematograph to allow for a space of diegesis that freed the viewer from an exhausting attention to the jarring physiological response to films. It is only once the success of a film was tied to its ability to render invisible its own mechanics and to open a space of diegesis that flicker was reframed as a break or rupture rather than merely physiological strain. As Carl Forch observed:

> The flicker of cinematic images. It is a fact of experience that the alternating stimulations of our sensory organs are at a certain point no longer perceived as distinctly separated individual stimuli, without which a blending of individual stimuli [*Verschmelzen der Einzelreize*] arises as a unified [*einheitlichen*] stimulus once they gradually work upon us in evermore rapid succession. This occurs to a greater extent the more rapidly the individual stimuli reach our

> sensory organs. Between the distinct perception of individual stimuli and blending there is an area in which we discuss the perception of the flickering effect of light. This flickering now plays an important role in the praxis of cinema. It fatigues the eyes of the viewer and significantly disrupts the impression of moving images. Designers of projectors [*Vorführungsapparaten*] must above all seek to eliminate the sources of flicker, though under the circumstances the projection operator [*Vorführer*] must also step in, as the tendency for flicker is different for different films, even when using the same apparatus.[30]

Strictly speaking, flicker was not a property of the cinematograph but a perceptual state linked to certain conditions of physiological stimulus. With their "faster shutter speeds, new media circumvented the lassitude of the human retina," and the human subject, who had been "at one time the guarantor" of "scientific knowledge," was "discursively constructed [*diskursiviert*] as the subject of fatigue."[31] The tendency to regard flicker as a part of the machine's operations indicates the presence of background presuppositions about psychological phenomena, and particularly the "illusion of movement." Cinema was a stimulus machine acting directly and perceptibly on a human stimulus machine, whose response to it was understood in terms that were mechanical—as fatigue. Because studies of the perception of movement had fallen into the domain of psychophysics, at least since the 1880s, the model of the psyche employed in the understanding of film's influence on psychic development was often positivistic. It failed to essentially separate between the cinematographic machine and the psychological machine. This remained true even at the point that there was a move in the 1890s to design experiments based on the "self-observation of test subjects during reaction time experiments," which insisted on a conscious, distinctly proto-cybernetic form of second-order observation.[32]

Fears about the psychological implications of film, in contrast to worries about its damage to the nerves, for instance, were the result of the medium's disappearance as a conspicuous form of mediation. Once the rickety, blinking discomforts of poorly calibrated intervals between images, bad lighting, and slow frame rates were replaced with brighter, more regularly presented images, which also substituted spatial and temporal continuities for narrative ones, the nature of attacks on films likewise changed. The relative invisibility of the cinematographic medium's mechanics around 1913, when compared with earlier iterations, changed the character of invocations of scientific psychology on the part of film critics. At the same time, the diminishing conspicuousness of cinematic machines simultaneously amplified the contention that exposure to films transformed the nature of thought.

Rhetorical bombast that marks early attempts to psychologize the mechanics of the cinema often belies an uncertainty about the principles of psychic unity in the empirical, scientific theories on which they were relying. This was an empiricism, if one is to generalize, that sought to mechanically formalize the laws of perception and psychic autonomy according to a regime of instruments. However, it did so amid an ever-widening schism over the meaning and place of "empiricism" in matters of mind. Lorraine Daston and Peter Galison have characterized this divide according to a transition from a "mechanical" to a "structural" objectivity that occurred between 1880 and 1930.

> Objectivity, according to the structuralists, was not about sensation or even about things; it had nothing to do with images, made or mental. It was about enduring structural relationships that survived mathematical transformations, scientific revolutions, shifts of linguistic perspective, cultural diversity, psychological evolution, the vagaries of history, and the quirks of individual physiology.[33]

What is at stake in both disputes over the nature of psychic coherence and early invocations of psychology in antifilm polemics during the 1910s is a worry about the *exteriorization* of operations in an apparatus that determined the order and meaning of thought. Indeed, as the medium of cinema became increasingly recognized for its narrative effects—following the elaboration of visual devices for diegetic continuity in longer, multishot films of the early 1910s—film became the subject of *psychological* instead of merely *physiological* concern. This suggests that it was not only exposure to flickering images in dark rooms that premised anxieties about the strain on eyes or neurological overstimulation but also that the organized rise of opposition to film was based on the detection of a deeper distortion of the psychological structures that imparted order to thought. While general anxiety about the attention-shattering fugue of an electrified and accelerated life in cities has long been the subject of historical appraisals of Europe around 1900, criticisms of film reached an early climax just as cinematic features were becoming longer and more coherent, not more fragmentary.

Order of Appearance: *Schein* and *Sein*

It is by now a commonplace in histories of film that the average shot length (ASL) decreased as part of the expansion of narrative films, enabling filmmakers to produce more complex and unified storylines through editing.[34] However, there has been much less attention paid to the fact that critical reform literature on cinema took as its object a longer-format narrative medium that bore only trace resemblance to jerky and wild one-act and early trick films. As evidence for the correlation between the development of longer, more diegetically complete films and the growth of a psychocultural critique of cinema, the average length of films between 1905 and 1906 was between eighty and three hundred meters and contained only a few shots, largely based on the varieté format, while it was not uncommon by 1915 to have films longer than one thousand meters with a wide variety of shots.[35] The eruption of journals dedicated to cinematic reform and the pedagogical impacts of film on psychological and moral development paralleled this evolution, with the most famous print prostheses of the cinema reform movement such as *Bild und Film* and *Der Kinematograph* existing as its extensions between 1907 and 1915.[36]

The very first cinematographic presentations of "actualities," and what Tom Gunning refers to more generally as the "cinema of attractions," already instituted rules of continuity that were of significant import for theories of psychic ordering.[37] In Germany these were met with speculation about a troubling movement from "being" or the "real" (*Sein*)" to "appearance" (*Schein*), signifying an opposition between the illusion of movement produced by the operations of cinematic apparatuses and the presumed coherence of nature connected to positivist notions of objectivity. Sein was the province of the real, in which an image was chemically bound to what it depicted, while Schein, by contrast, constituted a mere appearance distinct from the logic and order of the states and objects being represented. Sein could be understood as the province of technics, while Schein was a form of semiosis. Film was thought to introduce a break between the two, maintaining an impression of a connection to the world while forfeiting the substance of such a connection. At the same time, cinema was also believed to institute an order to the appearances that conjured an inner, psychological sense of reality that combined the images of the real (and thus not mere representations) with a highly variable, fictional logic, akin to personal fantasies constructed from mental images. Such fantasies, however, when fashioned from seemingly objective images using machine technics, were not personal at all; they were standardized.

In 1896, just after the first Wintergarten-Varieté presentation by the Skladanowsky brothers and in response to the Lumière brothers' first cinematographic performances in Paris, Maxim Gorky considered the psychological costs of new cinematic technologies, "as our nerves are more and more excited and become weaker, ever more strained, and in the process react less to the simple 'impressions of being' [*Eindrücke des Seins*], and lust ever more after extreme, unusual, intense, and outlandish sensations."[38] The change associated with mechanical forms of visual entertainment locates a hermeneutic upheaval. Psycho-physiological conditions of perception were altered such that the source of fascination with film was separated from an expectation that it present a veracious picture of the world. It was not that "self-recording machines" and "the anti-hermeneutic systems" that culminated in cinema "ultimately established their own domain of reality" but that they were seen to create semiotechnical *subjects* by means of the *objective*.[39]

The belief that films astonished audiences with their power to present a faithful excerpt of reality was already in question with the recognition that the craving it inspired in audiences was not for familiar experiences. That the "sensations of being" were not thought sufficient to maintain interest in film indicates that the logic of representation at work in cinema was not interpreted as bound to the logic of that which it represented. Films no longer captivated their audience on the basis of the world they supposedly reproduced or the magic of seeing cinematic machines work. Film's diegetic autonomy, which was so antithetical to the presumed virtues of the medium (as a view onto the undisturbed real), was not simply the result of an evolving narrative closure in the absence of text, nor did it function like a pure attraction to merely "display its visibility."[40] These were technologies that imposed a new order on images that was at odds with the world from which they were taken. As a result, it became a darling for discourses of modernism hung up on the asynchronicities of perception and thought under conditions of mechanization. Their operations, even where diegetic, were produced through objective, quantitative differences achieved through physical breaks and cuts rather than qualitative differences that were the putative foundation of unique, individual experience.

In general, the circumstances of perception and thought as conditioned by emerging media technologies submitted consciousness to an underlying serialization and quantification that destroyed the qualitative richness of earlier experience. In 1903 Georg Simmel famously characterized a crisis of signification tied to the pace and ubiquity of capitalistic transactions in big cities. This imposed a totalizing fungibility and thereby eliminated the textured relationship of people to their surroundings. Everything was mechanical, quantifiable, and substitutable. As a result, the city-dwelling individual developed a blasé attitude, mirroring the equivalence of currency exchange.

> Through the mere quantitative intensification of the same conditioning factors this achievement is transformed into its opposite and appears in the peculiar adjustment to the blasé attitude [*Blasierheit*]. In this phenomenon the nerves find in the refusal to react to their stimulation the last possibility of accommodating the contents and forms of metropolitan life. The self-preservation of certain personalities is bought at the price of devaluing the whole objective world.[41]

The perceived detachment of systems of signification from the "objective world" was linked to a cognitive insularity that would be deemed pathological, or at least problematic, even where it was seen as a necessary adaptation.

In the case of the urban cinemagoer, the situation was further complicated in that the "objective world" of "Sein" was viewed as precisely what films *should* offer. Thus, the prospect of a subjective identification with or immersion in the mechanical sequences of films, decoupled from the logic of the world they supposedly captured, posed a real problem for the understanding of how the viewers were formed with respect to viewing. It was not the case, as the apocryphal and storied panic of audiences fleeing the theater during the 1895–96 presentations of *L'Arrivée d'un train en gare de la Ciotat* would imply, that it was a confusion of the real with the appearance—but, quite the opposite, it was a profound division of the two that premised criticism.[42]

Roughly ten years after Gorky's prescient review, the critic A. Günsberg remarked that because "animated nature" was film's proper domain, "It makes present to us the 'world of being' [*Welt des Seins*], not the 'world of appearance' [*Welt des Scheins*]," explaining that at least in cases of fantastic paintings of real places, the medium was recognized as a "medium" (*Mittel*) only capable of representing a whole as a whole rather than mobilizing the parts *reassembled* as a whole.[43] The trouble with films was not that they were finely sequenced photochemical traces of real events and objects, which created a sense of immersion or contact with the real; many critics still bemoaned the jerky, irregular, visually exhausting nature of films, which were more a form of sensorial abuse than a seductive diversion. It was that they threatened to mechanically depose the spectator as the source of reason by making semiosis technical. If the psyche according to scientific psychology produced a coherent order from an array of discontinuous sensorial inputs that bridged between a seamless external real and the synthetic unity of consciousness, film seemed not to imitate this interiority but to supplant it. The real was continuous, consciousness was continuous, and stimuli, like their digital successors, were discontinuous. The nature of such continuities was incommensurable. The all-important protocols of the mechanisms by which they were placed in contact determined their relationship to one another.

In the same year that the psychologist, psychophysicist, and inventor of psychotechnics, Hugo Münsterberg, published his 1916 *Photoplay* outlining the analogies between film and the operations of the psyche, another short book by the Viennese "social philosopher" Richard Guttmann was published, titled *Cinematic Humanity: An Attempt at a Fundamental Analysis.*[44] Unlike Münsterberg's *Photoplay,* which treated certain similarities between cognitive faculties and filmic devices (such as the relation between the flashback and memory) as mere parallelisms and therefore as representations of an unexamined model of the "normal" psyche, Guttmann's analysis provided a set of terms critical of the intervention of cinematic apparatuses in the development of the psyche.[45] Although early writing about cinema tended to limit its speculation about the psychological effects of film to established psychocultural techniques like "attention" and principles of middle-class morality (*Sittlichkeit*), Guttmann ascribed a deeper role to the medium in the evolution of individual and group psychology. The fact that Guttmann's text—unlike Münsterberg's—has received almost no mention in the history of film criticism is telling. It adds further to the impression that the oft-invoked relationship in early film criticism between thought and film has not led to a subsequent interrogation of the problematic exchange between semiotechnical models of the psyche and their cinematic counterparts.

Guttmann's moralistic text, while at times highly objectionable, is in some ways typical of populist musings that characterized the Kinoreformbewegung and a tradition of technophobic laments predicting the disappearance of the imagination. Yet the genre of his book conceals a more substantial reckoning with the technological conditions involved in cinema's definition and transformation of psychological capacities and psychological modeling. By the time Guttmann was writing, which was already somewhat late in the context of the reform movement, there was some consensus that the conditions of cognition had changed dramatically as a result of media technologies. Guttmann isolates the dangers of the cinema by elaborating the distinctions between "fantasy" (*Phantasie*) and "reality," and "processes" (*Vorgänge*) and "content" (*Inhalt*) of the psyche in a way that illuminates a specific form of relationship between technics and the organization of the psychic apparatus—or at least a certain fear about that relationship. Not only, as he quips, do the stories in films of the period handle psychological problems "as if the director had copied it out of a psychoanalytic dissertation," but he suggests that cinema doubly participated in the development of structures of thought by transforming both the order of the objective ("reality") as well as the operations of fantasy.[46]

Both rationality (which defined one's impression of "reality") and a capacity for fantasy distinguished humans as a species and as individuals. Despite their seeming opposition, the difference between fantasies and one's sense of reality was not the nature of each's content. It was the "processes" of the content's ordering. At the level of the species, he claims that "fantasy cultivates [*ausbilden*] new psychic contents and processes from the vast complex of memories and elements of mental images. In the most varied manner, these contents and processes have external effects and, alongside the intrinsically fixed drives, constitute the individuality of the individual."[47] Furthermore, "the mechanisms for the capacities of mental imagery and memory function the same in all people."[48] Fantasy is thus identified as an important second-order capacity that mediates contact with the world from which past and present perceptual inputs are taken, acting as the structuring agent in the formation of psychic processes that distinguish the individual as more than a mere storehouse of empirical inputs. It is the operation by which a psyche's systematic relations to the world are personalized, which is to say, made meaningful. Imagining a person without this capacity is nearly impossible, according to Guttmann, and, importantly, as one verges toward a "zero point" in this faculty, they increasingly become a "depersonalized living machine" (*unpersönliche Lebensmaschine*).[49]

Guttmann's choice of the term *living machine* rather than a term like *animal*, which would emphasize the *absence* of a distinguishing human faculty, implies an *overrationalization*. It is through exposure to new technologies that a hypertrophy of the rational faculty occurs and the uniquely human is exaggerated to the point of threatening its status as human. A psyche vacated of fantasy is a machine, at the same time *more* and *less* than human: more in the sense that the rationalized body is turned into a highly calibrated empirical instrument; less in the sense that the failure to organize the memories and representations available through perception according to an individual, internal logic depersonalizes them and eliminates the process of subjectivization. It makes humans instruments for the register and storage of stimuli instead of subjects. Further, Guttmann's description of the role of fantasy and the peril of its absence strikes a note unmistakably similar to the arguments by later gestalt psychologists against the psychophysical endeavor to establish what Wilhelm Wundt had called "psychical causality."[50] Psychophysics' fantasy of a mechanized psyche and an empire of total discretization vacated of anything incalculable could never come to terms with the experience of inner life taken as a whole. Nor could the psyche configured by cinema be described as anything more than a machine.

Like Lukács, Guttmann ties the *how* problem of cinema's psychological surrogacy to the problems of positivism found in experimental psychology. As support for his distinction between Sein and Schein, he praises the neo-Kantian scholar Hans Vaihinger and his theory of the "as if" (*als ob*).[51] Guttmann writes:

> In order to emerge from eternal contradictions, humans use a stratagem. They take appearance [*Schein*] for being [*Sein*]. A major useful and purposive mechanism of life is the maintenance and deployment of illuminated knowledge [*Erkenntnis*] *as if* it were the truth. Otherwise one no longer progresses in the godless world. In order to achieve an end, we make somewhat artificial assumptions because we lack elements of absolute truth. If the goal is achieved it is certainly irrelevant whether we knowingly must make do with erroneous postulates—fictions—or whether we could have used fundamentally flawless and absolutely true principles—axioms. Hans Vaihinger has methodically and systematically illustrated this characteristic of human mental activity in his excellent *Philosophie des Als Ob*.[52]

The critique, considered separately from its invective tone, is a sophisticated one. Guttmann threads together the essential problems of psychophysics, cognition, and the contingency of both on the operations of the technological apparatuses that inform them. As he goes on to add, the "congruence of appearance [*Schein*] and being [*Sein*] had been achieved—with appearance, being disappeared. Appearance became the precondition of being."[53] Cinema provides the model by which—in a rethinking of the other theorists of the time—Sein becomes the arrangement of Schein. Semiosis becomes explicitly technical. Sein is therefore nothing but a certain regime of thought specifically tied to the continuities of diegetic space, in which appearances are arranged *as* the real. This is a distinctly digital conception, as the existence of digital objects admits of nothing beyond the binary sequences from which they arise. In a sense, then, there is a collapse of the traditional separation between the empirical and fantasy that is only made possible with the cinema—one that is positivistic and fantastic in equal measure. This would explain Guttmann's claim that film functioned as a "surrogate" for both fantasy and reality. The only distinction between the reality established by scientific measure and the inner subjective world was the protocols of their assembly. And those were established by the machines used to produce them.

Guttmann's reference to Vaihinger is a powerful one because the latter's theory of fiction is likewise an attempt to reconcile positivism and Kantianism (or "idealism" and "positivism"), such that the a priori continuities could be maintained in relation to the infinite array of disparate data points produced in experimental measure.[54] Or stated simply, it reconciled the universal and the particular, the point and the line, continuity and discontinuity, and perhaps even the analog and the digital. As Vaihinger argues in reference to the digital theorist Gottfried Wilhelm Leibniz:

> Leibniz realized that consideration of the point as an infinitely small line, and in general, the concept of the infinitesimal, is concerned with something paradoxical and absurd, but is nonetheless permissible as a rhetorical fiction treated as a fictive mode of presentation useful for invention.[55]

The very idea of continuity here is a space of fiction that both unifies the empirically distinct input and allows for thought. Cinema functioned within a larger sphere of concerns that extended well beyond the realm of entertainment and social representation. That it was beginning to assemble individual, photographic images into psychologically compelling visions of the world that did not or could not exist had much larger scientific and philosophical implications. Once film could produce an autonomous fictional space with which the viewer identified—and out of images whose cultural valence (as photographs) was one of objectivity—earlier worries about its purely sensorial effects were displaced into worries about its effects on ideas, imagination, semiotics, and the subject itself.

Vaihinger began the first chapter of his 1911 book with the claim that "scientific thought is a function of the psyche," arguing that the conceptual regularities that made sense of empirical inputs were ultimately only a specific mode of thinking.[56] He continued by arguing that "forms of perception and thought, and certain concepts and other logical constructs," were "created by the psyche for itself in response to external stimuli" but that "logical thinking . . . is an automatic appropriation of the outer world."[57] The only real difference between the mechanical instrumentation of science related to the definition of Sein and the interior space of subjectivity, or Schein, was "Technik" they deployed for producing the continuity defining each. As Vaihinger noted, "The psyche is a constantly self-improving machine" and "thought therefore, can be treated as a mechanism, a machine, an instrument in service of life."[58] When placed in the context of Guttmann's work on the effects of cinema on the psychophysiological machine, the relationship between cinematic mechanisms and diegesis reproduces the troubled connection between technics, semiotics, and subjectivity.

Guttmann's analysis of film's psychophysiological impacts was echoed by his contemporaries. Will Scheller, for example, remarked in 1913 on the centrality of "cinema psychology" (*Kino-Psychologie*) to the question of the "contemporary human" who "lives under essentially different conditions than the generation before him."[59] Such conditions were marked by the shift from continuities of text to mechanical protocols. Concomitantly, the nature of cinematic Technik mediated both the viewer's relation to the "objective world" as well as the relation to their own thoughts. Scheller insists that the new illusions of films "appear as if an ideal rescue" for a population that no longer had "the time and nor the strength of nerves" to engage "with abstract stimuli" that characterized texts.[60] Further, he argued that for this new generation, film presented a revised logic and foundation for experience of the sort described by Guttmann.

> Here one sees life without the oft deceiving costume of words [*Schminke des Wortes*], here actions are made visible with the shocking or exhilarating, frequently veracious, educational logic of unmediated necessity, here one's fantasy, chained to the conditions of his very being can run riot, if only passively. However,

> they have long unlearned active drives and actions. Here is the long anticipated, powerful illusion, carried out through the details of the everyday in the realm of a larger existential tension. Here is a pathos that is ungoverned by the meanings provided by concepts.[61]

Scheller gestures toward two contradictory tendencies in the interaction of cinema and the psychology of its viewer that are more thoroughly countenanced in Guttmann. With the advent of long-format narrative film, fantasy—both on screen and in the viewer—proceeded from the machine arrangement of events themselves. What had been a centerpiece of interiority was taken over by the mechanical and market-driven standards of cinematic presentation, which did not rely on hermeneutically rich and ambiguous associations of language but nevertheless had semiotic effects. The realization of the "powerful illusion" underlying fantasy, which had long been considered a productive domain of the surreal, instead appears as a mode of empiricism. Additionally, Scheller's account refers indirectly to the techniques of cinematic editing that were being formalized as conventions around the time he was writing. It is these, he argues, that allowed the "powerful illusion" to play out through a condensation of the trivialities of daily life. The editing techniques in question included parallel editing, shot/reverse shot, graphic matching, and cutting on action, all of which sacrificed temporal continuity to produce a diegetic one.

Of course, Scheller's discussion of fantasy was at odds with the dominant model of fantasy and the function of dreams found in Freud's *Interpretation of Dreams,* which offered the most elaborate meditation on the relationship between dreams, fantasy, and hallucination at the time.[62] As I discuss in chapter 5, cinema was a forbidden object in orthodox psychoanalysis, albeit a persistent interloper. Part of the allure and difficulty of cinema's affinity with psychoanalytic concepts and structures was that it offered a model for understanding empirical, mechanical operations and their connection to psycho-semiotic processes. As many scholars have already noted, *The Interpretation of Dreams* marked a departure from the thermodynamic psychic modeling found in Freud's *Project for a Scientific Psychology* (1895).[63] The importance of this theoretical turn is that the early work conceived of the psyche as analogous to a machine, managing an energetic economy through the creation of neurological pathways, while *The Interpretation of Dreams* shifted the source of psychic unity to a process of linguistic association. Freud's pioneering work essentially performed a conceptual maneuver similar to those of narrative films, effacing its mechanical origins through displacements, condensations, and continuities of a semiotic order. As Jacques Lacan notes:

> Contrary to what has been trumped up about a supposed break on Freud's part with the scientism of his time, that it was this very scientism—which one might designate by its allegiance to the ideals of Brücke, themselves passed down from Helmholtz and Du Bois-Reymond's pact to reduce physiology, and the mental functions considered to be included therein, to the mathematically determined terms of thermodynamics (the latter having attained virtual completion during their lifetimes)—that led Freud, as his writings show, to pave the way that shall forever bear his name. I am saying that this way never shed the ideals of this scientism, as it is called, and that the mark it bears of the latter is not contingent but, rather, remains essential to it.[64]

It was with this shift from scientism to symbols that the presence and influence of images in the psyche became problematic. In later work, the visual content and structure of dreams derived from thoughts during the course of the day and fantasies based on "infantile experiences."[65] To return to images was to regress to more primitive, unstructured material within the psychic apparatus. With this in mind, Freud claimed that "if we regard the process of dreaming as a regression occurring in our hypothetical mental apparatus, we at once arrive at the explanation of the empirically established fact that all the logical relations belonging to the dream-thoughts disappear during the dream-activity or can only find expression with great difficulty."[66] Stored images in Freud's early psychoanalytic writings were operationally prior to the formation of the autonomous ego and represented a chaotic and undifferentiated morass in the unconscious. Images acquired their sense through the associative linguistic machinations of the preconscious and consciousness. To return to such images during dreams was regressive in the sense that the dreamer was confronted with material that did not abide the elaborate linguistic structuring that defined the psyche as a closed system of reference. To think in images was not to think at all but to be abandoned to an incoherent inventory of residual material whose significance could not be established without the introduction of textual scaffolding.

On their own, mental images for Freud lacked the possibility for comprehensible self-organization, to say nothing of their ability to establish psychic autonomy. This was strengthened by the more general claim that the "processes of the system Ucs. are timeless; i.e. they are not ordered temporally, are not altered by the passage of time; they have no reference to time at all"; and instead, "reference to time is bound up, once again, with the work of the system Cs."[67] Images' native habitat was the unconscious, which did not even possess the order of temporal sequence. Logical structures of thought were weakened in the regression to primitive images and, as psychoanalysis' status as the "talking cure" suggests, it was language that recovered or imposed order on the visual content of fantasy and that premised psychic autonomy. Moreover, the independence of the logical mechanism from imagistic dream content, Freud claims, did not require additional empirical verification. It was self-evident to Freud that both the coherence of the psyche and the more specific order and meaning of images was bestowed by language, which accounted for the overdetermination of dream images that convey no singular meaning but a proliferation of possible meanings. As Jacques Derrida and Jeffrey Mehlman observed of its "logocentric enclosure" and the dominant analogies to text and writing in Freudian psychoanalysis, "starting with the *Traumdeutung* (1900), the metaphor of writing will dominate simultaneously the problem of the psychical apparatus in its structure and of the psychical text in its fabric."[68] Psychoanalysis could accept that images could document or capture the external real. But the "reality" of inner life, defined by ambivalences, substitutions, and veiled references, could only be governed by human language.

Guttmann's sneering comment that films of the period seemed as if the "director had copied it out of psychoanalytic dissertation" not only acknowledges Freud's prominence in his Vienna at the time but also points to the undeniable—if uncomfortable—resonance between film and psychoanalysis. Indeed, they had parallel evolutions: from a purely mechanical foundation to a semiotechnical practice that relied on, but simultaneously obscured, those foundations. The discomfort was the result of the images and technics from which cinema constructed its semiotic universe and that psychoanalysis buried silently in the unconscious.

The psychoanalytic trouble with machines and images was not lost on Guttmann. He characterized it as a challenge at the core of mechanical forms of empiricism resting on the dependence and antagonism between Schein and Sein. Schein was related to the ordered appearance of images and Sein to the photographic traces themselves. Film interrupted the traditional deployment of both. The photographic images in cinema could not be seen as unproblematically reproducing their referents, and the fictional diegesis they could manufacture when presented in succession did not derive from the images themselves or the world they were said to represent.

Where the order of the medium was concerned, film seemed to derive its logic not from "nature" as the appeal to photographic objectivity would suggest but from the technics of industrial organization, which disfigured and quantified nature for human ends. Early cinema may not have eliminated reading, but it was believed to reconceive of readers as products of a new industrial logic of representation. It was not uncommon for conservative reformers, who nearly all maintained an interest in pedagogy and psychological development, to claim, for instance, that "the cinematographic epidemic is starting to have the same consequences among our youth as modern pulp literature."[69] In this case, the reformer Max Brethfeld was writing on behalf of the inelegantly named Volksbund zur Bekämpfung des Schmutzes in Wort und Bild (People's Association for Combatting Filth in Word and Image), which looked to enlist cinematographic programming in service of educationally sanctioned subject matter after many German police departments had decided to forbid children from visiting the cinema.[70] Brethfeld's appraisal simultaneously draws upon an affinity between literature and film that treats literary and filmic content as interchangeable, while also hinting at real distinctions between each medium. Preoccupation with the "education value of material," including films of Niagara Falls, the attacks of torpedo boats, volcanic eruptions, and cellular protoplasm, were treated as specifically suited to the cinema, presumably because they could be easily comprehended in moving images, though it was mostly because they fit into a larger, loosely defined category of appropriate educational material.[71]

According to many pedagogues, the cinematograph as a "magnificent medium in service of the education of the people and children" had to avoid the "psychological unreality of the processes" or run the risk of "educational cataclysms."[72] Well-trained adults did not share the potential for catastrophic miseducation because the "educated adult is immediately able" to identify everything "manufactured and untrue," while children lacked the training to make such distinctions.[73] By designating adults who were not at risk from the influences of film as "educated," Brethfeld implies that education served as a prophylactic against the psychological effects of film. Such education was literary. Critics like Brethfeld believed that film changed the very nature of children's semiotic faculties, causing them to misrecognize the relationship between the world and themselves—a relationship that had been cultivated and maintained through a program of literary training since the eighteenth century. At work beneath the surface of an underexamined idea of education was a principle of technical mediation that allowed the viewer to differentiate the real and the purely psychological, recognizing that neither was independent of the means for its representation. The difficult concept of Bildung—which is explored in depth in chapter 4—involved a standardization of representational protocols that were thought critical to the formation of individuals as well as the larger political and cultural imaginary.

Such issues were also pursued by early films themselves. In a send-up of the sanctimony of cinema reformers, for instance, the film *How Cinema Got Its Revenge* (*Wie sich das Kino Rächt*) (1912) cleverly ridiculed popular arguments about cinema's social-psychological hazards. The relatively short film, produced at a point of increasing narrative sophistication in cinema and a rising tide of reformist outcries, ironizes a fictional exponent of the Kinoreformbewegung, Professor Moralski, whose efforts to denounce cinema eventuate themselves in the revelation of his own improprieties. Upon reading about the meeting of the "International Congress for Combatting Cinema" convening in "Dumbville" (Dummstadt), the head of the film production studio "Flicker" (Flimmer) enlists a young film starlet and a film crew to lure Professor Moralski into a staged extramarital tryst, which they secretly film. Later, Moralski is given the film, titled *The Paragon of Virtue at the Beach Resort* (*Der Tugendbold im Seebade*), to present to the meeting of the congress the next evening as an example of film's degenerative potential. Moralski's transgression is exposed when the film is presented to the conference, the members of the meeting are titillated and scandalized, and the film ends with a flier advertising the film's public release in theaters.

In addition to the metadiscursive commentary on the hypocrisy involved in the condemnation of cinema, the film also reflects on the technological training and production of its various audiences.[74] As one of the "earliest films to show 'film in film,'" the film demonstrates the second-order power of the medium as a constitutive pedagogical implement that "presents the double standard of the educated middle class [*Bildungsbürgers*], that seeks to guard it."[75] From the perspective of both the reformers skewered in the film and their filmmaker adversaries, film had the ability to determine something about the nature of the moral agents in question. Not only did the cinema transmit messages about morality, but its technical mode of presentation trained the capacities of a specific kind of viewer, who was fundamentally at odds with earlier educational ideals—something quite pointedly articulated later in the film. In contrast with "Uncle Josh" films, which affirmed the sophistication of the audience's viewing habits by ridiculing an uneducated rube depicted catastrophically mistaking films for reality, later films like *How Cinema Got Its Revenge* showed cinema to have become the dominant logic of a coherent subject position.[76]

The film opens to Professor Moralski declaiming to the International Congress for Combatting Cinema, holding up a film reel, drawing the attention of the audience (of which we are initially a part) to the unspooled filmstrip he holds in his hands. The nitrate strip's unprojected materiality stands as the object of his contempt, and the association's audience is depicted in clamorous approval. An intertitle follows: "Thus spoke Professor Moralski [*Also sprach Professor Moralski*] . . . this is how our people [*Volk*] are being poisoned by the filthy flows [*Schlammströme*] of immorality that the cinema pours over its audiences." In a parodic invocation of Friedrich Nietzsche's Zarathustra, as both a sage opponent of mean popular entertainment and also, paradoxically, a conservative defender of middle-class morality, the intertitle acutely caricatures the nature of attacks by the Kinoreformbewegung. Cinema corrupted its audience through its uninterrupted succession of images, flowing over them in a continuous stream—*Ströme* likewise being the word for electrical current as well—which infiltrated and overwhelmed psyches that had been "for a long time conceived of and represented as an electrotechnical system."[77]

Like the Ströme that accounted for the physiological vision of psychic function, the perpetual influx of stimuli participated in the formation of its viewer. The suggestion was not just that reformers thought cinema merely presented lurid images that affronted the existing sensibilities of the audience but instead that the mode of presentation shaped those sensibilities at their psychological foundations. It is the materiality of the film that Moralski offers to members of the conference as the source of the problem and that produces the Ströme that washed over its audience. The immorality he decries resides in the filmstrip, signifying the technical operations of film in general rather than a specific category of disreputable content associated with the images that remain unseen. Morality is conceived here as an effect of technics' educational practices rather than the selection of good content from bad content.

Moralski's condemnation does not lead one to the conclusion that viewers should be scandalized by what films depict but rather that viewers are constituted by the mode of depiction. This becomes clear as the film demonstrates its ability to distinguish and establish multiple audiences through the alternations of editing and projection. In the first shot of Moralski, we share the view of the audience at the meeting—the extradiegetic audience and the diegetic audience are synonymous through a shared perspective on Moralski. These two audiences are then differentiated from the hypothetical audience through the intervention of the intertitle, which identifies a universal audience at risk from exposure to film. Thus, the audiences capable of reflecting on the impacts of cinema, who are immune or less susceptible to its medial operations, are primarily identified through the act of reading—the educated critics of film are constituted as readers. Yet in the final shot of the sequence, the film sets the terms for its satirization of the reform movement by cutting to the clapping audience, with whom the extradiegetic audience is no longer identified.

In the film's own sovereign act of auto-distinction, the extradiegetic viewer is neither the passive, imperiled audience invoked by Moralski nor the reformers who support the censure and censorship of filmmakers. Instead, the filmic audience, as well as the producers, are both readers. This is reaffirmed throughout the film: the actress who seduces Moralski in the intradiegetic film sits in repose, reading a book, when she is informed of the plan to ensnare Moralski; word of the congress's meeting is brought to the producer by way of the newspaper (the *Fraktur* text of which is shown in a close-up); and the final scene cuts to a written advertisement for the extended run of the film in theaters.[78] News within the diegesis travels primarily by way of printed texts, unifying the internal informational economy through an implied textual exchange that is also made visible to the extradiegetic audience. However, the extradiegetic audience enjoys the last laugh strictly through the irony of the narrative's construction, to which only it is privy, and that requires an education in the operations of film viewership.

The traditional literary education that characterizes the association's audience, which they assume was threatened in the general cinema-going public, is shown insufficient for establishing and understanding the narrative effects of the film. Traditional textual semiosis is depicted as subordinated to the dominant medium, which, as in the case of Moralski, is demonstrated to have the power to rewrite his social and moral character through editing practices that transform him from a figure of moral esteem in the public eye into a deviant and a hypocrite. As a result, the film suggests that those who lack the ability to "read" films, and whose sense of personal narrative is marked exclusively by older semiotic regimes, become the miseducated punchlines of jokes by a more sophisticated cinematic viewer.

This is most pointedly underscored in the penultimate scene, in which Moralski is given a film reel depicting his own extramarital exploits to approve for its presentation at the next day's meeting of the congress. Examining the filmstrip, he fails to recognize himself as the antihero of the film, and therefore, he is shown to be incapable of both deciphering the semiotic content of films and of conceiving of *himself* according to the appropriate medial conventions. Technically, he reads the film the wrong way, examining it like a scroll, absent the projection mechanisms that render the discontinuous stills comprehensible as symbolically rich, semiotechincally unified moving images. He has been improperly educated as a cinematic subject to see himself cinematographically, and he suffers the consequences.

The film diagnoses a continuing discord within the psychotechnical theories of the early twentieth century. Beyond its cultural parody of reactionary moralizing on the part of reform associations, the film also gets to a fundamental concern provoked by the rise of narrative cinema, namely, the import of not *what* audiences read but *how* audiences still read. Encoded in the focus on the deterioration of the national moral fiber at the hands of narrative cinema and prescriptions about its educational use was a larger question about what kind of viewers were entailed in cinematic semiotechnics.[79]

Such technical transformations in how a symbolic inner life came about upended a belief in the unitary subject that had long been a fixture of philosophical and ethical inquiry. Heide Schlüpmann positions these theorizations of early cinema that questioned its role in producing intellectual and moral agents at the end of a philosophical tradition extending from Kant through Nietzsche. She describes film's attack on moral codes as a turn toward a simultaneous realization and destruction of a specific type of philosophical projection bound to a male utopian economy of desire, one that offered an intersection of the real and the imaginary very similar to what Guttmann described. Moral philosophies, according to Schlüpmann's argument, are bound by the representational economies that produce them. The individual, as a projection much like one found in the cinema, functions as an elision of many sequences into a single space of signification. How the ideal moral agent is imagined thus depends on the social and technological means for representing it. And, as a result, cinema's competition with text as the means for depicting social realities introduced a profound shift in the philosophical and moral imaginary.

> The cinema is formed [*bildet sich*] from bourgeois culture out of a moral utopia based on the "guidance of the body." Its forms emerge as involuntary imaginings from a male body and its desires. These forms only truly become real in connection with an audience that is physically confronted with this lost way of life and this morality. In this moment of realization, however, the utopian imagination of a different morality is lost; a morality guided by the body and its desires, its relation to the future, the projective.[80]

Early film emancipated morality as a by-product of training from a certain kind of subjective idealism, according to Schlüpmann, through projections that were "not projections of physical circumstance from internal image to the exterior" but "the *appearance*" of a utopian "reality" associated with "imagination" (*Einbildungskraft*) that had long been a point of mediation between perception and ideas from the "bourgeois universe."[81] Playing on the term *Einbildungskraft* paired all the senses of completion, education, and the symbolic imaginary of Bildung with the power (*Kraft*) to render such things internally. Film did not, therefore, produce a semiotic distinction that reinforced the barrier *between* inner life and the objective outer world instituted by silent reading practices but instead manufactured a vision of a fantastical inner world *as if* it were an outer world.

Schlüpmann's largely psychoanalytic study identifies early cinema as the theoretical turning point of a perceived change in the concept of morality and its corresponding "education process" (*Bildunsprozeß*). Further, there is an acknowledgment that "because film is both photographic and performed, imagination is not merely acted upon by the physics of light, but also by human psychophysics."[82] She incisively notices that "the early cinema was a cinema of imagination," and correspondingly "projection had not yet split into the technical apparatus on the one side and psychic mechanism on the other, reified and concealing the contents of the imagination."[83]

Yet it is precisely in not having been reified but instead supposedly clarified as an object of scientific inquiry that the cinematograph achieved its cultural significance as a determining factor in the production of a continuous psychic space.

In philosophical discourses, the test of moral principles, especially after Kant, was frequently determined by way of counterfactual projections. Positing fictional circumstances in which there is some moral ambiguity functions to test the validity of moral precepts in a concrete yet altogether imagined situation, while also bolstering the reader's sense of subjective autonomy by fostering an ability to project or imagine themselves as a conceptual unity in invented circumstances. One can think here of the oft-repeated dilemma of Kant's 1797 reply to Benjamin Constant in "On a Supposed Right to Tell Lies from Benevolent Motives."[84] The appalling absolution of Kant's categorical prohibition on lying, which has remained a source of endless dispute, is demonstrated by imagining a situation in which someone is confronted with either surrendering a person to murderers who come to the house looking for them or lying (a "lie of necessity" [*Notlüge*]), about which Kant insists that one is obligated to tell the truth. As a textual or rhetorical practice, such an exercise is relatively straightforward: one describes a logically possible scenario, designates it as fictional, then requires the audience to consider it *as if* it were real for the sake of determining whether the principles guiding one's original judgment are sound.

In narrative films, the practice was somewhat more complicated and located a technological rift in the tools for "projecting" a moral imaginary and the more general conditions for moral agency. In both cases, there was a technical element to the production of a projective, symbolically coherent agent who could be transported into various imagined situations. Because moral arguments against film already focused on the misuse of the supposed power of cinematic "realism" and the use of the objective in service of the fictional, the counterfactual stood as a test case for the psychosemiotic potential of film. While literary fiction has long been defended as a moral educational tool that "can be regarded as thought experiments that encourage conceptual discrimination of our virtue schemas through the imaginative deployment of structures of studied contrasts that function argumentatively," the essentially nonfictional technics of filmic depiction posed problems for its status in moral education.[85] The operating assumption about the literary imaginary was that a subject identified with the space

of narrative through the act of reading through the maintenance of a space of signification that allowed for multiple levels of correspondence with the true, real, or objective. Not so in films.

A robust capacity for Einbildungskraft was central to notions of how to properly train autonomous subjects, allowing individuals to develop a coherent, complete, abstract representation of themselves.[86] Moral calculus relies on the ability of a person to extrapolate to a hypothetical representation of themselves that cannot, therefore, be unmediated. In this way, film was thought to pose the risk of a double mediation. It threatened psychic autonomy through its reconfiguration of contact with the "real" by simulating the stability of external objects and events. It also jeopardized the recursive, semiotic landscape of fantasy, which internally structured the viewers' relationship to their own thoughts and allowed them to emerge as a moral agent. By *externalizing* the source of order, and therefore meaning, film made a "living machine" out of what had been a subject.

Less than a decade later, this process would be viewed as fully actualized. Béla Balázs, Guttmann's more famous contemporary among the circle of Vienna critics, would claim that the "inner process of accounting for oneself has been externalized" and "mechanically fixed" in such a way that it was no longer that "one films as long as one is conscious" but that "one is conscious as long as one films."[87] Highlighting the mechanical uniformity of this mediating role, Guttmann deployed the concept of a "surrogate" in cinema's relation to both fantasy and reality, which strikes one as odd, unless it is the order of image presentation that determines their difference and similarity. In other words, if film acts for Guttmann as a surrogate for both reality and fantasy, both of which are constituted by an inventory of perceptual images and recollections, then what differentiated them and the place where film was believed to intervene was in the all-important sense or coherence lent to them through their ordered discretization. It was the sequences and intervals that mattered. As Guttmann writes:

> The lively image is not the living image. It merely attempts to reproduce life. It is a *surrogate of reality.* Here one likewise reaches the limits of "scientific" cinema. The cinematographic experiment will never be able to replace the real and its logic through the progress supported by its dialogue in facts.[88]

By 1916 inner life was seen as fully programmed by the mechanisms of film. Guttmann argues, for instance, that dreaming serves the latent demands of fantasy and that most people can no longer satisfy the basic needs it satisfies, requiring various "surrogates." Both the "cinematic dreamer" and those intoxicated by cinema (*Kinoberauschte*) live in a permanent moment provided by the film, the experience of which involves "nothing characterized as human-made content," leading to a yawning abyss of unsatisfiable desire that he calls an erotic problem.[89] In distinction to some of his reformer contemporaries who worried about the *what* of cinematic depictions, this eroticism had less to do with content and was concerned more with the structural *how* of desirousness that emptied out viewers whose "will and active consciousness have disappeared."[90] Through the technical surrogate for dreaming, Guttmann contends that the viewer's relationship to herself, her fantasies and drives—which Freud had located as one of the primary sources of psychic autonomy—had disappeared as the typical functions defining psychic interiority were exteriorized.

As the psyche was believed to be divested of its power over the protocols of image arrangement and meaning making, the programmer became the programmed. Nothing was safe from the march of discretization. And as we shall see in the next two chapters, the core humanistic enterprise of reading was one of the first targets of attack. Although we are now largely comfortable reading texts that are entirely run on the hidden binary functions of microprocessors, the mechanical discretization of text starting in the nineteenth century shook the foundations of humanistic inquiry and, with it, abiding ideas of what it meant to be human.

3

Discrete Reading

Approaching the beginning of the twentieth century, the objectives of experimental psychology merged with pedagogy in a way that had been previously unthinkable. Theories about what constituted effective readers and how to cultivate them, which had long been an established topic of research and pedagogical theory, were imported into the psycholinguistic endeavor of determining what reading was and how it could be scientifically tested. Indeed, pedagogical objectives had never been far from the work of experimental psychologists. Finding methods to isolate and quantify the physiological operations that formed the basis for consciousness and perception was the bedrock of scientific psychology. But these operations were meaningless in the absence of a larger subjective unity that formed the telos of educational programs.

The rise of the mechanical interval as the defining measure of scientific practice set psychology on a collision course with long-held traditions of subject formation by challenging the semantic and metaphysical unity of text. As Bernhard Siegert writes, "*Culture* still serves to conjure up the sphere of art, good taste, and education (*Bildung*) in a Goethean sense—in other words, it alludes to the indispensable ingredients for the formation of a 'whole human.'"[1] The sense of this wholeness was largely trained through encounters with texts, whose narrative and semantic coherence was reproduced in their readers. With the discretization of reading as one among many practices of the physiological machine, the belief in such unities became tenuous and difficult to maintain.

We are by now very accustomed to the intrusion of digital tools into the sacrosanct space of readerly practice. Digital humanism and "distant reading" have made their virtue a quantitative approach to text, whose conceit is to reveal patterns and structures among and within texts that cannot be easily seen without the aid of computation and large data sets.[2] Equally familiar are the critiques of such methods and their very premises, which are seen to advance dubious statistical instruments, to fetishize computational tools and data, and to miss the literary forest for its quantitative trees.[3] At a more basic level, however, these turns to quantitative analysis required that texts become decomposable into more basic elements that could be recognized, compiled, and processed by computers.

Early figures in the development of textual recognition systems such as Gustav Tauschek in the 1920s and 1930s and the cryptologist David H. Shepard in the 1950s encountered this hard divide between the continuities of humanistic enterprises and the discretization required for machine reading as well. As Zeynep Çelik Alexander writes, in the earlier of the two models, "Tauschek's reader sought forms that were intelligible to humans" and "recognized the 'semantic value'" of texts, whereas Shepard "recognized no ghosts in the machine," operating instead by "discretizing images into fragments, breaking down the 'semantic limits' of a pattern, and analyzing it statistically."[4] The increasing move toward discretization that would enable later optical character recognition (OCR) technologies, the vast digitization of texts with Google Books, and ultimately powerful neural networks like GPT-3, capable of convincingly generating texts sensitive to distinctions in tone and genre, emerged from a pitched battle around 1900 about both texts and their readers. The project of breaking down the psychophysiological act of reading, and with it, readers, into measurable units according to the intervals of proto-cinematic machines pitted older notions of subjective continuity produced by systems of education against the standards of scientific inquiry marked purely by the starts and stops of machines. Techniques and technologies of cinematic narrative would eventually present a new and threatening horizon of educational practice that promised new subjective unities (discussed in chapter 4). But initially, the psycho-cinematic regime of discretization had to first disaggregate the central fixture of educational training: reading.

Avant la Lettre

In 1910 even the early pioneer of experimental psychological methodologies, Wilhelm Wundt, articulated a broader vision of psychology's role in not only studying subjects but also producing them.[5] Wundt expressed a host of misgivings about the idea of experimental pedagogy, which he thought supplanted proper psychological methodology with methods that served unverified assumptions, importing practices and norms of teaching and examination without first interrogating their foundations. The idea of "practical psychology" was not to support existing pedagogical programs but to introduce experimental advances to the study of applied psychological tasks such as memory and recall, all of which seemed to rely on quantifying the duration of activities under experimental conditions. However, the distinction between the goals of experimental pedagogy and the practical application of "pure" experimental psychology often overlaps in his writing. As he makes clear, the advances of experimental psychology are indisputably relevant to pedagogy, though experimental psychology seeks to probe deeper questions about the nature of the psyche and cannot just be plugged into a pedagogical framework.[6] What he acknowledged in attacking the uncritical applications of experimental methods to existing expectations about reading and education was that the very faculties to be tested and trained had to first be experimentally determined. In reading Wundt, one gets the sense that he found the aptitudes as defined by older readerly models of education irrelevant to a newer regime of testing and training.

Eighteenth-century pedagogical and linguistic theories had localized practices of reading and language development as fundamental to notions of ideal subject formation, and therefore to education. Johann Gottfried Herder opened his 1772 work, *Abhandlung über den Ursprung der Sprache,* with the assertion "already as an animal the human has language," suggesting that possessing language was coextensive with being human.[7] For Herder, "humans are the only speaking creatures [*Sprachgeschöpfe*] that we know of and distinguish themselves from other animals through language."[8] However, as concerned the study of language as a defining element of human subjectivity, he cast significant doubt on the ability to physiologically discretize human faculties, claiming:

> In the event that physiology comes so far that the science of the soul [*Seelenlehre*] can be demonstrated—which I very much doubt—it would supply this phenomenon with a ray of light from the dissection of the structures of nerves [*Zergliederung des Nervenbaues*], which also perhaps divide into ligatures separate, too small, and dull.[9]

Even in the event that an exhaustive physiological account for linguistic functions could be achieved, Herder was skeptical that the parts would equal the whole: "without language there was no humanity," and because language defined humans as such, it was the continuity of language that accounted for the unity of the psyche, not the physical mechanisms that evolved to produce it.[10] Countering Étienne Bonnot de Condillac, and earlier French thinking on education more generally, language may have been man-made, but it nonetheless made man. The continuities of language encountered while reading were essential to the continuities of inner life and the ability to become a nameable individual with a unique history. This principle that "language facilitates the progress of thought and the development of intelligence" remained a bedrock and even "commonplace" of theoretical and applied pedagogy through the beginning of the twentieth century.[11]

Even after writing a lacerating 1767 diatribe against moralistic educational literature whose aims toward Bildung he found laughable, Herder maintained that the "first words that we babble" both as a species and as individuals "are the foundations of all of our knowledge."[12] In a subsequent fragment concerning the relationship of poets to their audience, he considered the second-order possibility of "seeing and hearing one's self in reading."[13] Herder envisaged poets and not self-proclaimed pedagogues as the stewards of education. This was the case not least of all because poets gave expression to unities that revealed a larger continuity in the world in opposition to the scientific pedagogues who broke down meaning into rhyme, meter, diction, spelling, and alphabetization, which on their own were not sources of insight.

Bildung may have been a matter of reading, but it was not as a function of the sequences associated with individual physiological processes. The pedagogues Herder ridiculed emphasized mechanics over meaning and therefore, according to him, misidentified the nature of reading's relationship to both what it expressed and whom it educated. Education was not limited to reading, but reading provided the structure for knowledge, experience, and chance that gave shape to both the individual and humankind through the structures of meaning making.[14] This belief in the ontogenetic repetition of phylogenetic developments was a fixture of philosophies of education beginning in the eighteenth century and continuing through social Darwinist philosophies of the late nineteenth and early twentieth centuries. Text, practices of reading, and the ideational unities they produced created multiple scales of continuity from the meaning of the text itself, to the reader's subjective autonomy, to the intergenerational development and transmission of ideas. The "true Bildung"—starting from "the Bildungs philosophy of Rousseau's, Herder's, Pestalozzi's, Schiller's and Humboldt's"—

was a "consummate, well-rounded unfolding of the human essence in the shape of those individuals who understand their natural and historical living environment and who can become active in it."[15]

By the time Herder was writing, the mechanics of language associated with emerging practices of pedagogy were already tied to physiological inquires that would evolve to define the next century. Soul and physiology, letter and word, grammar and meaning were all bound to one another in the workings of language that would be discretized by later psychophysicists—something Herder was already keen to avoid. What Herder anticipates, particularly in his suspicions about the "dissection of the structures of nerves," is a scientific dismantling of both the thinking subject and their linguistic faculties that would not be fully pursued until the second half of the nineteenth century. Herder's reaction to the possibilities of isolated empirical study of language and thought was echoed by his contemporary interlocutors, such as Johann Georg Hamann, who in 1771 "bitterly denounced" Dietrich Tiedemann's treatise *Versuch einer Erklärung des Ursprungs der Sprache* for its empiricism, criticizing his "mechanistic view of language, in which language is nothing more than an assemblage of grammatical parts."[16] Because linguistic unities were the "foundations" of thought and inseparably bound to the production of autonomous, educated individuals, parsing language into its formal elements was viewed as equivalent to mechanizing the mind.[17] While the "beginnings of a scientific pedagogy in Germany go back to the eighteenth century" with the attempts to rationalize the tenets of education associated with Joachim Heinrich Campe, Johann Bernhard Basedow, and Ernst Christian Trapp, it was not until the 1880s, following the work of psychophysicists and physiologists like Gustav Fechner, Wilhelm Wundt, and Hermann Ebbinghaus, that there was a "framework for introducing experimental methods into pedagogy."[18]

The idea that language could first be learned as discrete elements, which were then assembled into syntactical and semantic unities, implied a corresponding psychological disunity, challenging both the residual attitudes about the divinity of text as well as the primordial distinction of humans as creatures natively blessed with language. It was equally a challenge to Enlightenment and institutional religious pedagogy. The notion that humans did not already possess the inherent capacity for language and textual representation but only acquired it piecemeal also meant that meaning and all attendant hermeneutic processes were mere operations.

Ernst Christian Trapp, the first professor of pedagogy at Halle, proposed to learn reading and writing together holistically.[19] Commenting on Campe and Basedow, he wrote:

> There is no agreement about whether children should universally be made to spell or equally to read, or when one is made to spell, whether they should spend a long or a short time. One can go a step further and doubt whether it is entirely necessary to learn the individual letters in advance to learn to read.[20]

The status of text, and reading as a rote operation, was subordinate to meaning and mental autonomy, which produced the subsequent associations that could be systematized. The connection of the apparent unity of text to psychological unity persisted as an artifact of Enlightenment pedagogy prior to the assault of empiricism. As late as 1818, the religious pedagogue Joseph Theodor Abs maintained the necessity of this union, claiming:

> Reading and writing are one and the same activity of the soul. Dissolving a word into its constituent parts and forming a word from divorced sounds that essentially belong together, just as every spiritual product necessarily requires the union of receiving from the outside and creation from the inside.[21]

The objectives of these educational reform movements to bring both of the "strictly divided cultural competencies of reading and writing" together served the higher purpose of placing them within the concept of "productive mental activities."[22] The desire to pedagogically enforce the inseparability of reading and writing, and words and letters through which the reader was trained, indicates the theoretical intimacy between how language was instructed and what kind of subject resulted. Practices of reading could not fundamentally transform human nature but could nevertheless warp it. With the entrance of scientific psychology in the nineteenth century, these psychological unities were evermore finely decomposed into measurable units, which worked to disaggregate into sequences rather than to cultivate irreducible metaphysical unities.

Following Trapp, the imperative for a scientific understanding of reading was initially to find the rather cybernetic-sounding "difference in the unity."[23] As Bernhard Dotzler notes, reading in the spirit of Kant "came out of the reform pedagogy of Campe and Basedow," which had to be "learned by heart and not through spelling."[24] He continues, writing that "precisely the reformed reading instruction that teaches 'reading by heart' implants in one's head that rather than dwelling on spelling they instead through reading form a 'new novel' for themselves."[25] Forms of reading provided structural armatures for the training and elaboration of internal mental organization that were wedded to larger units of meaning—words, sentences, or books. Psychological spaces may have been reproductions of textual media, such as novels or poetry, but this assumed that semiotic continuities could not be atomized in the arrangement of letters, which did not maintain a substrate of meaningful unity.

This was famously captured in Karl Philipp Moritz's illustrated 1794 ABC book, which paired drawn tableaux of objects related to letters with sentences that remarked on the reader's ability to make sense of those scenes using the text. So, for instance, the entry for the letter *B* would include a picture of a book and the sentence "the book makes young children smart." Yet the book, according to Moritz, did more than make a child smart. It also differentiated levels of psychological competence. As a pedagogical statement, the book made its stakes clear: "Those who cannot read only look at pictures. Those who can read, however, also understand the words" (*Wer aber lesen kann, der lieset auch die Worte, die unter stehen*).[26] The play on "unter stehen" as both "located beneath" the text but also the source of "understanding" makes a large claim for a simple children's book. To "only look at pictures" was to miss the significance of the pictures, and as a matter of instruction, lost the possibility of developing the corresponding internal structures of an educated subject.[27] Those who merely saw were passive, machinelike aggregators of stimuli. Those who read were thinkers who brought "unter" and "stehen" together as an "understanding."

This same privileged status of semantic unities is thematized in Moritz's most famous and expressly "psychological" novel, *Anton Reiser*, in which the main character Anton's exposure to reading and spelling manuals plays a role in determining his development as a primarily reading subject. Of the two manuals given to Anton by his father, *Instructions in Spelling* (*Anweisung zum Buchstabieren*) and *Instructions against Spelling* (*Abhandlung gegen das Buchstabieren*), Anton chooses the former, and with great hardship learns to read through spelling difficult biblical names such as "Nebuchadnezzar," selected precisely for their antiassociative effect. Proper names, and particularly difficult ones from "dead" languages, paradoxically acquire an antihermeneutic property by resisting associations or being embedded in commonly spoken phrases. It makes the words graphic rather than auditory, antisubjective, and empirical, building internal narrative and memories from the basic mechanical operations of the language. In distinction to the former manual, which treated learning to read through spelling as "harmful" and "psychologically pernicious," the latter imbued Anton with what would later prove to be a troubled, even pathological form of interiority (*Innerlichkeit*).[28] The failure to distinguish between objective and psychological operations by making the functions of language that formed the inner world of personal experience mirror those of hard empiricism fostered an unhealthy capacity to withdraw and substitute the real with the imaginary. Just after Anton learns to read, and before he undergoes a period of illness attributed to his reading, Moritz writes:

> Through reading a new world was all at once opened to him, the enjoyment of which could somewhat compensate for all of the unpleasantness in his real world. . . . He was thus displaced early on from the natural children's world into an unnatural ideal world where his mind [*Geist*] was alienated from a thousand joys of life that others with fuller souls could enjoy.[29]

Reading was thought to cultivate an alternative psychological space for Anton but one that was at odds with empirical, physical reality as it "displaced" (*verdrängt*) (a word used later by Freud to refer to "repression") the natural world into an ideational one. By learning to read according to a method that followed the logic of empiricism—breaking down semiotic unities into their component parts—Anton likewise could not be a "full soul." Anton's reading divorced him from the world. For this reason, Friedrich Kittler has commented that "Reiser's discovery led to signifieds or ideas, the general equivalent of words. Compared with the alphabetical hodgepodge of Biblical names, which are pure signifiers without translation, ideas were as enticing as Basedow's *rai-sins* or *stra-ber-ries*."[30] The two consequences, according to Kittler, were that "signifieds sweetened the pain and violence of alphabeticization" with such an extreme intensity that Anton, "unlike Rousseau," can remember what should have been repressed, namely "how he learned to read."[31] And secondly, it means that he "soon spends days living on nothing but air and signifieds."[32] In both cases, to treat words as technical spelling protocols was to misunderstand signification and therefore the relationship between reading, subjectification, and education. The fullness Anton lacks is the result of the brutal alphabetization of words—proper names severed from context—that constituted his training.

Questions about the role of language acquisition in erecting a boundary between objective world and inner world was a crux of early pedagogical disputes. Moreover, such questions indicate the degree to which problems of subject formation and psychology were already problems of technological training. Following Johann Friedrich Herbart's coup against Kant, who claimed that psychology could not be the object of science, both language and psychology rapidly became an area of scientific study, extending well beyond the negative predictions about empiricism leveled by Herder.[33] A symptom of this new mode of empirical thinking was a shift toward physiological and mechanical sequences and away from metaphysical unities. Individual parts of speech came to occupy a new significance in education at the same time that individual physiological functions came to dominate the study of psychology.

On the Clock

The rise of scientific psychology in the nineteenth century was a matter of timing, or more precisely, being timed. The central aim of nineteenth-century "analytical experiments" in the brand-new field of psychology was, according to Henning Schmidgen, "to disassemble complex issues into elementary components and to more closely determine quantitative components," and subsequently, "to be able to once again synthesize that complexity."[34] This is a field that grew out of experiments measuring human reaction times to stimuli as well as observations about the electrical propagation of nerve signals. Following advancements in the design and experimental application of the electromagnetic chronoscope by Charles Wheatstone, Matthäus Hipp, and Adolph Hirsch between the 1840s and 1860s, and eventually Wilhelm Wundt in the 1870s, the study of psychological unities entered the domain of mechano-electrically defined intervals.[35]

Chronoscopes—the central device for measuring response times—were initially designed and deployed to create an external, objective measure of ballistic projectiles that moved too fast to observe, or to establish the "personal equation," correcting biases in human astronomical observations.[36] Later, however, the instrument was used by major figures in psychology such as Wilhelm Wundt, G. E. Müller, Oswald Külpe, Sigmund Exner, and

Hugo Münsterberg to quantify the time that elapsed between a stimulus and a test subject's reaction to it.[37] Münsterberg, who was the first student of Wundt's to dissent with the master, conducted experiments on subjects' perception of time intervals (*Zeitsinn*) under variable conditions, such as changes in rhythms and attention.[38] About the limitations and objectives of these types of experiments, he wrote:

> Every experiment involving periodic functions of consciousness for the clarification of psychological phenomena starts from the distinction between consciousness and the contents of consciousness. The latter is psychophysically explicable: for every change in the contents of consciousness there is a parallel change in the physiological substrate. Consciousness on the other hand is the absolute physical precondition of being in general. Every change of consciousness as such is therefore psychophysically inexplicable and belongs entirely to a spiritual metaphysics, the acceptance of which is tantamount to the eschewal of the consequences of psychophysics.[39]

Münsterberg's appraisal of the epistemological scope of psychophysical experimentation cleverly reframes the stakes of consciousness. Psychophysics could not make claims about the fundamental nature of consciousness but instead only about the operations by which its contents were organized. Yet it was precisely the symbolic contents of consciousness that had previously distinguished the mind from rapidly developing machines. The question of what consciousness was thus became uninteresting, or at least unaskable, as the only area of plausible research redefined all semiotics as technics. Content was operationalized and quantifiable intervals supplanted irreducible qualities.

The increments by which the psyche came to be understood were instituted by the chronoscope. The variable tones test subjects heard, the controlled illuminations they saw for fractions of a second, and the pictures from which one was supposed to conjure mental associations were all reducible to a record of the opening and closing of an electrical circuit. Differences in duration indicated complexity—the longer a stimulus took to process, the more complicated it was assumed to be. Inquiry into the ontological status of the psyche as a primordial unity was relegated to a history of scholasticism, brummagem philosophy, and occultism according to scientific psychology. To claim otherwise was its own kind of heresy for Münsterberg and his new brand of psychophysicists.

The chronoscope, and mechano-electrical apparatuses more generally, mediated between the empirical universe in which the stimuli had an absolutely definable value and the inner world of experience, expressing the difference between the two as a measure of delay. Chronoscopic experimentation redefined subjectivity as latency. It did not matter to psychologists like Münsterberg whether "march music" stirred feelings of patriotism, or which "memory images" (*Erinnerungsbilder*) were recalled by rapid light stimuli.[40] Such issues were merely matters of delays as defined by mechanical intervals. The textured field of significations that had given inner life its uniqueness was flattened into fungible modes of quantification as defined by a modified clock. Kittler argues that this development in the 1880s was the result of the "technological differentiation of optics, acoustics, and writing" by which "the fabrication of so-called Man became possible."[41] In the reduction of psychological functions to the measurable difference between output and input as defined by an experimental apparatus, the essence of humans

> escapes into apparatuses. Machines take over functions of the central nervous system, and no longer, as in times past, merely those of muscles. And with this differentiation—and not with steam engines and railroads—a clear division occurs between matter and information, the real and the symbolic.[42]

Kittler here is essentially restating what can be seen as a precybernetic, pre-Lacanian form of the distinction announced by Münsterberg about reaction-time experiments. This is what Münsterberg called the difference between "consciousness" and "the contents of consciousness," the former being an "absolute physical precondition" that was "psychophysically explicable."[43] However, once psychophysical experimentation set about making reading the object of its observation, the symbolic was not separated from the empirical but was reimagined as an operation within it. The foundations for a cinematic nexus between mechanical discretization and semiotic continuity were not far away.

Prior to what André Bazin designated as "the evolution of film language," written text was submitted to the rules of film—before cinema was readable, reading became cinematographic.[44] In the 1880s, the intervals as defined by a Hipp chronoscope were paired with the tachistoscope, a device that allowed the experimenter to present subjects with a controlled, brief stimulus that could be seen in a narrow, illuminated visual field for a predetermined duration, often for a fraction of a second.[45] The initial design, first mentioned in 1859 by A. W. Volkmann, was a horizontal, tablelike apparatus, using the fall of a weight to quickly displace a plate covering an opening, behind which a paper displaying text or an image was concealed, allowing a controlled, measurable interval in which the stimulus became visible.[46] Later iterations of the instrument, following James McKeen Cattell's watershed redesign of the "fall tachistoscope" for Wilhelm Wundt's Leipzig laboratory, were frequently vertically oriented and included a litany of design modifications and corresponding changes to the devices' names. These included spring tachistoscopes, pendulum tachistoscopes, projector tachistoscopes, rotation tachistoscopes, mirror tachistoscopes, central tachistoscopes, and Cattell's own design of a rotating cylinder that allowed successive exposures to various visual stimuli.[47] Cattell's version of the device, whose specifications and diagrams have been endlessly reproduced, examined, and praised in experimental reports and articles, had the advantage of using the fall of the slide to trigger the electromagnetic timing mechanism at the moment it revealed the stimulus. This eliminated the problem of using sparks that changed the light conditions of the experiment and also included a variety of response mechanisms, including lip-key registers that recorded the moment the mouth began moving to vocalize the stimulus.[48]

In the case of the lip-key register, the brain was reconceived as a series of circuit gates running between the textual input and the verbal output—linguistic functions being reduced to the time it took the signal to be transformed by the mental machine, which was actually plugged into the apparatus. In this way, "the tachistoscope became paradigmatic of an ideal experimental control," generating "data that allowed a quantifiable image of the psychophysiological capacities of the subject," repositioning the "perceiver in a relation of *subjection* to an objective world newly decomposed into autonomous and abstract stimuli."[49] By measuring responses, intentionally engineered to be too brief for reflection, the experimental setting produced a possibility of "pure sensation *without* perception."[50]

Where Jonathan Crary and others have assimilated such experimentation into a modernist discourse on "shocks," occurring beneath the threshold of perceptual attention, introspection, or consciousness, one could argue that the existing subjective unity was not disrupted, but a new mental continuity underwent a novel theorization. The insistence on "shock" as the defining psychological category of this experimental milieu simplifies the conditions of research and psychophysical theory to a subject's encounter with a generalizable machine writ large, when in fact the specific operations of the apparatus entirely revised the understanding of the processes by which subjective unity arose in the first place. Experimental subjects were still readers, and reading was still the putative bedrock of subject formation, but not because the text bore the trace of some substrate of individual unity. It was because the text instituted a sequential, operational order that produced mechanical unities in much the same way that Franz Reuleaux described the total, gestalt-like function of well-engineered machines from which working continuities emerged as a sum greater than the multitude of discrete movements.

Letterboxing

The year 1885 was an important one for reading. Hubert von Grashey, the director of the Würzburg psychiatric clinic, published his paper on aphasic patients, arguing that in normal cases, reading occurred through the rapid scanning of individual letters, which were quickly converted into "sound images," then became word images that activated motor operations, better known as speech.[51] This theory, which came to be known as "spelling theory," built on the work of Carl Wernicke and Ludwig Lichtheim. The Wernicke-Lichtheim model isolated words and letters as basic units of language rather than larger semantic unities like sentences, and also located the problems of aphasia in the disruption of hierarchies of distinct neural pathways, which thus serialized reading as a physical order of operations.[52] Because this process was not localized in a single brain center, as Sigmund Exner had claimed, reading was transformed into a technical, operational practice.[53]

Aphasic patients with brain traumas were not lacking the proper language centers, only the proper protocols for deciphering its sequences. The inability to reproduce associations with words was a problem of linkages, not the absence of unities. Although the so-called spelling theory had an incredibly short life span, the age-old logic of reading had been fully displaced. Also in 1885, Cattell administered tests of sequential exposure to stimuli on a rotating cylinder to show that words and letters were recognized with nearly the same speed as letters, but a mania for discretization had already taken hold. Even as he wrote that "words and letters are not apperceived individually one after the other, but according to a psychological process as a whole group," their inputs were understood as discrete, and only "apperceived" (in other words, arranged) later.[54] Uneasiness about this empirical coup in matters of reading—and by extension education and inwardness—was articulated in 1900 by the high priest of psychophysics himself, Wilhelm Wundt, in a review of the broad field of literature on tachistoscopic reading experiments: "Apparatuses are truly not people—whom one loves despite their flaw—rather tools [*Hülfsmittel*]."[55] No doubt, Wundt was primarily arguing for the enhancement of devices to increase their precision, but it also points to his divergence with the extreme positivism of the moment and an ardent belief in the scientific value of subjective introspection as a part of empirical research.[56] Apparatuses may have been "tools" and not people, but they nonetheless provided the framework for explaining people's cognitive coherence, particularly once the study of reading was mechanized.

Interval-based experimentation instituted a theoretical divide already in evidence in the two reading manuals given to Anton Reiser by his father (to spell or not to spell), although the difference in method concealed a deeper change in the notion of what reading was and what it produced. As Kurt Danziger remarks, the "experimenter of the early [1890s] trusted, first of all, in his instruments," and it is no exaggeration to claim that the tachistoscope was "of more importance than the observer."[57] However, it was also not hyperbole to claim that the tachistoscope was also more important than the test subject as well, as reading was transformed from a unique human ability into a serialized operation.

In 1898 the Kant scholar Benno Erdmann and his wunderkind technician, Raymond Dodge, once again overturned the hypothesis that reading was a letter-by-letter operation.[58] In the process, however, they demonstrated the degree to which reading had come to be seen as a function of a psyche that was already conceived as an interval machine.[59] Using a mirror, and later a photographic apparatus, to observe the optical fixation points of test subjects reading texts, they noticed that eye movements while reading did not proceed continuously from left to right, scanning each letter individually. Instead, reading a single line involved a regular alternation between "periods of rest" (*Ruhepausen*) and "movement," which conspired to create the impression of coherent mental "representations" (*Vorstellungen*).[60] As it turned out, while reading did *not* pattern itself after the successive letter-by-letter fall of type hammers, as Kittler argues, it also did not imitate the semantic and psychological continuities attributed to reading that marked theories of the eighteenth and early nineteenth centuries.

Erdmann and Dodge concluded instead that the intellectual and semiotic continuities experienced while reading were the result of serialized, discontinuous inputs, mimicking the workings of the tachistoscope. Written text was a discrete technology, whose semiotechnical function for shaping thought occurred as quantifiable alternations of starts and stops. The electro-mechanical nervous system into which these inputs were fed was, conveniently, not conceived that differently. According to Erdmann, "Spoken languages are natural products of our thinking, alphabeticized texts [*Buchstabenschriften*] the artificial products of thought."[61] Thoughts could also not be simply transmitted as thoughts. They were both generated from and transmissible according to a kind of assembly protocol. In a view quite similar to Münsterberg's, the qualitative character of thoughts and the singular, internal experience of having them was not, for Erdmann and Dodge, the result of the "contents of meaning" (*Bedeutungsinhalte*).[62]

Meaning was a kind of epiphenomenon or emergent property of mechanical alternation—at the level of perception, cognition, and text. It was, as we shall see in the next chapter, a matter of thirdness or signifying for difference, stops, and breaks. For this reason, they claimed that "thought" could be found in "the data of our perception, memory, imagination, and abstractions."[63] The syntax of language from which meaning arose, and in turn, thought, was not an abstraction tracing the boundaries of metaphysical categories but the medial, in this case mechanical, logic by which language was presented, assembled, and perceived. Thought was material, divided into quantitative units defined by the apparatuses used to measure it. Reading was not, therefore, an invariable human capacity but a historically specific technique for organizing the data of perceptions, which did not on their own constitute thoughts. Just like any data set, perceptions demanded a series of functions to make sense of their relationship to one another. In previous generations, this had been represented as a kind of inborne, native property distinguishing humans as thinking creatures.

The core experimental problem of how one synthesized discrete data from interval-based machines like the chronoscope into meaningful conclusions mirrored the problem of the scientific psyche in the difficult relationship it envisaged between psychophysiological systems and the fullness of experience for which it was responsible. The governing scientific paradigm of psychophysical research demanded that both problems be solvable in mechanical terms. This was made all the more explicit in the tendency to study reading using constellations of letters forming meaningless syllables, beginning, again in 1885, with Hermann Ebbinghaus's study of his own memory capacity.[64] Among his other conclusions, Ebbinghaus found that the relationship between forgetting and time was logarithmic, with the most precipitous decrease in retention occurring during the period immediately following exposure to the letters. More importantly, however, his experimental method, which made reading and memory a computational faculty of mechanical storage and reproduction, was explicitly *antihermeneutic.* One did not read for meaning in these conditions, but instead meaning was the result of a technics that systematized exposure to stimuli. Mental states could be analytically decomposed into meaningless minimal significations with the tachistoscope, but likewise, as Kittler remarked, "Mathematical equations can be solved in either direction."[65] The process was reversible. This is a suggestion with powerful implications, as it meant that the same device that dismantled semiotic unities could reassemble them, only it would be called something else. It would be called a cinematograph.

With the introduction of chronoscopic instruments, the pauses and movements of reading resembled the stops and starts of the tachistoscope, and thinking took on the character of the apparatus used to represent it. It assembled discrete quantitative inputs into coherent unities, this being the objective of empiricism in general. Reading imitated the intermittence of mechanical instrumentation, and thought was molded by the structures of reading, with syntax, following Reuleaux, being a mode of mechanical succession. However, the tachistoscope, as a monument of empiricism, was an analytic rather than a synthesizing instrument. The ultimate statement about the operations of thought as mechanical syntax, allowing for the comparisons with the cinematograph, arrived with Friedrich Schumann's redesign of the tachistoscope, which used an electrically driven wheel to control the presentation of successive stimuli.[66] This focused ever-more intently on the individual letter and the minimum exposure required to identify a letter accurately when shown in rapid succession as part of a word.

Research on the minimal conditions for meaning that built on the results of Ebbinghaus's "nonsense" were combined with another essential field of psychophysical research on afterimages (*Nachbilder*). The study of meaning was assimilated into a discourse on apparent motion (discussed in chapter 1) that used cinematographic instruments to show how the order and pace of stimuli presentation could produce a cognitive effect greater than the sum of the individual stimuli. Meaning functioned like an afterimage that resulted from melding or blending (*Verschmelzung*), suggesting that the apparent unities of thought, which had been technologically broken down into an empirical data set, could also be reassembled. As Schumann notes in a 1906 review of his results and those of his colleagues:

> Yes, even with very short exposures not a single letter of a word was actually distinctly seen, though nevertheless a whole—or at minimum partially correct—phonetic picture [*Lautbild*] was reproduced. Initially, test subjects in this case often risk not specifying absolutely anything. At first when one asks whether absolutely no word-image [*Wortbild*] appeared, they identify the word in question, but simultaneously clarify that it is impossible that it could be correct, as they actually only would have seen a totally blurry spot.[67]

It was this "blurry" (*verschwomenne*) quality experienced when the tachistoscope was sped up that reintroduced meaning in place of mere recognition: semiotechnics in place of pure technics. The appearance of unity allowed experimental psychologists to solve for consciousness, as Kittler had claimed, "in either direction."

It was Schumann's generosity in lending his tachistoscope to Max Wertheimer for his 1912 study of apparent motion that marked the definitive point of embarkation for gestalt psychology and, with it, film theory as articulated by Münsterberg and Arnheim.[68] And it was this instrumental innovation in the empirical study of reading that made the subsequent suggestion by Béla Balázs and Christian Metz that cinema was a form of reading more than a mere analogy. While there were precursors to this kind of theorization present in the earliest responses to devices that produced "stroboscopic illusions," experiments on moving images were most often concerned with the insights they could offer about a standard nature of perception rather than how perception and cognition were based on or structured by such devices.

As the worries of the reformers detailed in chapter 2 made clear (and that gathered steam in the years directly following Wertheimer's study), cinematic machines were thought to divest viewers of a control over the logic of their own thinking. At the same time, they were also believed to institute mechanical forms of psychological autonomy, even where it was deemed pathological.[69] One senses the deep conceptual tensions about the development and nature of the psyche, which was simultaneously drawing upon divergent models of completeness, interiority, and objectivity. In one way, the force of the reform movement's objectives derived from a received cultural understanding of the well-adjusted thinker as the product of a literary education, in which psychological coherence was synonymous with a novel- or poetry-reader's sense narrative. On the other hand, the vision of progress and objectivity used to legitimize the indictment of cinema as a physiological and educational hazard was inextricably bound—through psychophysics—to instrumentation that reproduced the operations of film. This is how it becomes possible for a prominent figure of the reform movement like Adolf Sellmann to lament the systematic "fatigue of the nerves" uncovered by psychophysical "investigations" of the "flicker of images" while also celebrating literary education. The Geist may have died, but the machine remained intact. Sellmann writes:

> We would like to deepen our objectives of educating the people and to fulfill them with the appropriate spirit. Do not cinematographs, however, in all their many ways and through all the spiritlessness they offer make one superficial and spiritless? Can we rigorously awaken contemplation [*Nachdenken*] and powerful feelings when the filmic images' already astonishingly fast succession leaves no time for contemplation and the reverberation of feelings? Prof. Schubring said, not unjustly (*Frankfurter Zeitung* Nr. 149, 1912): "Since 1870 we have become evermore superficial and now apparatuses are coming about that still more systematically spread this poison. A consequence of cinema is the fact that, for instance, no more books are read, as anyone accustomed to these forms of entertainment finds it boring to sit at home and enjoy a book."
>
> In films there's such adventurous romance and such wild fantasy that the content of drama causes the regular visitor to gradually lose every quiet, clear sense of reality and to compose a totally erroneous and fantastical picture of the world for themselves . . . In a linguistic sense it is also certain that our contemporary cinema is still not a medium for the education of the people [*Volkserziehungsmittel*]. In most cinema our German language is abused in the most disgraceful way.[70]

The questions posed in this section of Sellmann's book, which the quoted article from the *Frankfurter Zeitung* demonstrates, constituted a larger cultural consideration about the persisting technical foundations for Bildung. This would not be the maniacal optimism of Thomas Edison about the obsolescence of books that will be discussed in chapter 4. What is interesting, however, is that the language used to wager a defense of older medial forms is decidedly psychophysical. As Sellmann's use of the quote makes clear in its identification of an ever-greater superficiality linked to the introduction of new technics, there was a systematicity in the challenge to traditionally educated subjects. This was a challenge associated with cinema's potential to rival books in the presentation of "fantasy" and "romance," that is, its maturation of a semiosis beyond mere impressions of movement.

As many of the fiction films of the early period in cinema, such as Joseph Delmont's *Der geheimnisvolle Klub* (1913), which was based on Robert Louis Stevenson's short story "The Suicide Club," were adaptations of literary works, the attack on a lack of reality was not on the function of film's fictionality but on the technical modes used to establish it. The "picture of the world" generated by film was paradoxically fantastic and erroneous, which indicates that the capacity at stake in accessing a true picture of the world was a matter of technics, not contents. Film's reduction of the world to mere appearances that left it, following Lukács, with a body and no soul occurred irrespective of the fact that in certain ways the images were thought to be more objective. What was important to critics like Sellmann was the "sense" of the real, namely the protocols by which things were made meaningful.

The operational nature of cinema upset the ontological underpinnings of subject formation and education that had persisted since the eighteenth century. Kittler notes of the Romantic pedagogical exercises of Johann Hermann Pestalozzi, for instance, that they taught the rudiments of signification through an incremental building of "discrete quanta of letters," and that Herder's educational program emphasized "imperceptible grammatical training by minimal signifiers."[71] At the same time, such a world of objects and the subjects that perceived them were seen as unitary and continuous, indivisible in some essential sense. The attendant notion of language and educational training to produce such a subject could not be one in which the procedures of reading superseded the meaning of writing in its propaedeutic importance. The form of classical education recuperated by members of the Kinoreformbewegung to stem the tide of order obsessed, mechanically informed cinematic technologies resisted a more universal discretization. The ideal psyche was postulated as an autonomous and gapless coherence that could only be found in holistic understandings of language and reading as the foundation of narrative.

Ultimately, the arguments about films' peril for psychological development, "reality," and "Sein" were not about the representational fidelity of the medium to the appearances in reality; if that were the case, then an education in photochemical traces would be paramount. Cinema was merely "Schein" because its supposed indexical powers belied the absences and Ruhepausen that were the foundations of the experience of continuity it inspired and which critics feared as a new source for subjectivity. Later in Sellmann's book, he goes on to add an important ad hoc etymology for the term *cinematograph* in support of this understanding.

> The name cinematograph, which actually means "writer of movement," shows us clearly and distinctly that we are on the right path with our claims. Precisely here the cinematograph is magnificently capable of accounting for a lot in a short time. The descriptive word or the fixed image altogether fail, in part because they cannot describe this life and these movements to us.[72]

Neither the image nor the single word were thought adequate to the task of describing life and movement, which were both marked conceptually by a notion of continuity. As the "writer of movement," the exteriorized ordering entailed in the editing and projection of movement failed, according to Sellmann, to capture the unitary nature of the world and in turn failed to produce a unitary psyche. At the same time, there was a conflation of this sense of reality with a naive understanding of scientific objectivity, leading nearly all early critics of film to invoke psychophysical theories of nerves, reaction times, and measurability that were already the basis for film. In this sense, the real as unitary and coherent and the objective as discrete and measurable generated a widespread and persistent fear that the cinematographic psyche was only an illusion of continuity made possible by the discontinuous logic of a machine. As the next chapter considers, this made the prospect of salvaging older principles of education a rather difficult one.

4

The Technics of *Bildung*

Humans are born. People emerge through socialization and education.

—Niklas Luhmann, *Das Erziehungssystem der Gesellschaft*

Education has traditionally been a practice of seeking closure. It codifies a set of techniques that train, discipline, and form students into autonomous subjects that can be plausibly treated as having a sense of agency, interiority, and a connection to a social universe. But how does one achieve closure? As every contemporary advice columnist probably knows, a definitive point of total absolution is impossible. Closure is merely an assumed point of externality—whether real or imagined—from which something or someone comes to function (or signify as functioning) as distinct from its surroundings. It is a practice, technique, or operation by which other practices, techniques, and operations can be viewed as a part of a stable unity. In the case of education, that unity is called an individual or person.

In the version of semiotics advanced by Charles Sanders Peirce, this can be understood as deeply related to "thirdness," which was a kind of outside, a "betweenness or mediation" that guaranteed the ability of objects as represented in systems of signs to maintain their distinction, and thus to become meaningful.[1] For Peirce, it was "the essential nature of a Representation and of a Symbol" and a "general principle" that was "operative in the real world."[2] Thirdness was the vital operation that allowed things to be seen not only in relation to other things but as autonomous and distinct. It was what allowed the discrete to become continuous, and in fact, as Peirce also claimed, "continuity represents Thirdness almost to perfection."[3] To produce and reproduce such continuities at the level of the individual was the objective of education and training—something not at all limited to human classrooms.

How and whether a system composed only of discrete operations could recognize itself as distinct and autonomous has remained a core puzzle of the information era that has persisted with the development of artificial intelligence. With no essential metaphysical property or categorically distinct form of materiality to differentiate entities, some form of emergent reflexivity or recursive operation was necessary to stake out the line separating the system from its environment. According to Heinz von Foerster, "cognitive processes create descriptions of, that is information, about the environment," and their ability to recursively recognize those descriptions—defined internally by the management intervals—was a mode of auto-distinction or autopoiesis.[4] This was something potentially common to both minds and machines, and an essential task related to what Marvin Minsky (who designed perhaps the first neural net in 1951) derisively claimed, along with Seymour Papert, was what "cybernetic jargon" had "grouped under the heading 'learning.'"[5] Orit Halpern has written of the pioneering cybernetician Gregory Bateson's "decision-making apparatus," for instance, that the problem of machine intelligence was not the fact of computation but "a problem of training, a question of how machines or people might adjust, change, and learn about the world; to be able to learn becomes the marker of intelligence."[6] The artificiality of the machine was less significant in determining whether it was genuinely intelligent than its ability to recognize and signify for its own internal distinctions.

"Learning," "education," and "training" were all processes by which a machine, whether physiological or mechanical, came to organize distinctions into meaningful wholes. It was as much true for first-wave "good old fashioned artificial intelligence (GOFAI)," neural networks, and machine learning as it was for older theorists of Bildung, albeit pursued with very different means and models.[7] Both the deep learning of recent neural networks trained on unlabeled data and the supervised machine learning guided by "training data sets," despite their obvious "artificiality," ultimately reckon with a question that troubled pedagogues following the mechanization of the psyche beginning at the end of the nineteenth century: how do abstract semiotic unities emerge from purely discrete operations? N. Katherine Hayles describes this shared terrain in semiotic terms.

> Successfully adapting to the changes enabled lifeforms to develop increasingly sophisticated cognitive skills, culminating in symbolic abstractions by humans. But humans, in extending their cognitive capabilities through computational media, built symbolic abstraction into them at the foundational level of the logic gates. The challenge for computational media is to build up from this deterministic base

> to increasing capabilities for handling uncertainties and ambiguities, which they can achieve through a variety of means.[8]

The gateway to the tense analogy between human and artificial intelligence was not a by-product of computational machines imitating—morphologically or otherwise—human cognition. Rather, the comparison only made sense because the human psyche was already viewed through the prism of machine operations starting at the end of the nineteenth century. This was the point at which psychologists, educators, and philosophers had to show how the psyche, having recently become a discrete state machine, could result in something like an autonomous human. As this chapter explores, cinematic mechanisms offered the bridge between older ideas of education that were essential to a belief in autonomy and the revolution in scientific psychology that dismembered the unities of cultural practices like reading and, with them, the educated subject.

Second-Order Cinematics

A provincial educators' tutorial from 1796 that revised guidance to teachers on the appropriate structures, methods, and topics for teaching also suggested for the first time that students should read "from economics books" and compose essays in order to become good citizens and achieve a "pure command in a pure mother tongue."[9] It was the seeds of an autopoietic reading subject who not only conceived of the world through text and articulated an individualized relationship to text through text but importantly also learned a "lived" language (a "mother tongue"). Heinrich Bosse notes that this was not just a matter of learning to read or of alphabetization: "the point is to write oneself, to read oneself [*selbst zu schreiben, selbst zu lesen*]."[10] At the end of the eighteenth century, Herder also contended that textual operations were not secondary but constitutive. He wrote that one sees "things in the world as the words of a large book."

> No lad proceeds one letter after the other, and so the question is: how is it that the letters get called the word that is obtained? Neither will a lad, once he grasps the sense of the word, seek the meaning outside of or behind the word, but rather in it, and by means suitable to himself.[11]

The acquisition of specific reading protocols, even for a theologian, was not a neutral vehicle for the delivery of purely transcendental meaning but a highly personalized and personalizing form of technical mediation. It was not an attempt to "ground meaning beyond the text—either in a transcendental subjectivity, in convention, in mental representations"—but instead a recognition of "discourse itself," texts, and reading practices as the basis for subjective cultivation.[12] And it was through these pedagogically refined acts of reading, recitation, and writing that an "autopoiesis, in which the subject in its approach to linguistic signs, constitutes itself."[13]

In distinction to notions of autopoiesis developed during the latter half of the twentieth century within what is often referred to as second-order cybernetics, the units of reproduction from the word to the artwork to the self were preconstituted unities. Writing about the neurophysiological problems of systems of consciousness, the biologists Humberto Maturana and Francisco Varela noted, for instance, that "a simple unity only has the properties with which it is endowed by the operations of distinction through which it becomes separated from a background."[14] This is how one might broadly conceive of the educated subject of the eighteenth and early nineteenth centuries. By contrast, a subject formed from systems of discretized operations that developed in the late nineteenth century began to look like what Maturana and Varela would call "autopoietic machines," whose "operations specify their own boundaries in the process of self-production."[15] In an unlikely step from the Romantics to the information age, it would be proto-cinematic mechanisms that would prompt this change. Where the discretization of reading discussed in the previous chapter broke down texts and inputs into constitutive mechanical operations, the cinema offered a program for their reassembly into something that could signify as a subject.

It is understandable, then, that when those concerned with the educational horizons established by film returned to eighteenth- and early nineteenth-century conceptions of literary training to assess film's impact on ideal spectators, there was a tension internal to their arguments at the level of technics. More than any other idea, Bildung was mobilized at the end of the nineteenth century and the beginning of the twentieth century by pedagogues, scientists, and theorists of film as a teleological master concept to organize the relationship between ontogenetic and phylogenetic psychological development, education, and technology. This was a concept based on reading. The way one learned to read determined what kind of person emerged as the abstract unified system of an individual and, as a result, what kind of social unity was possible. In each case, the answer stemmed from a foundational semiotechnical question: how are the distinct technical operations by which one is trained organized to produce a signifying whole? How, for instance, does one visually scan letters to understand that one is reading silently inside one's own head, which is perhaps the very source for the concept of "one's own head"? This was a question that would become troublingly explicit with the discretized mechanics of psychophysical instruments that made way for cinema, which highlighted the technically determined but nevertheless open-ended nature of subject formation.

Practices such as reading or watching films were in fact constitutive of the semantic, narrative, and conceptual continuities that were related to, and necessary for, educating and conceiving of individuals. In his extended study of Johann Wolfgang von Goethe's *Wilhelm Meister,* which could be described as the paradigmatic *Bildungsroman,* Friedrich Kittler writes:

> Techniques [*Techniken*] of textual interaction and of socialization are linked. In Goethe's novel the new literary studies formulates just that. That which is at the level of narration constitutes the plot. The invention of the individual and childhood cannot simply be presupposed. They are themselves created at the level of discourse. This certainly does not mean that the novel would come to be a reflexive consciousness of its texture. It means that socialization and literature around 1800 were subjected to a historical a priori. The one could not be without the other. Only in their socialization of the individualized reader could writers and figures from texts be interpreted as continuous individuals, as authors, and characters. Only the discourse network [*Aufschreibesystem*] of literature can determine individuals, and the new socialization techniques, which suffice without legal formalization, ensure existence and dissemination.[16]

The smooth ideational unity of the self was bound to practices of reading, whose connection to mechanical, educational protocols was less and less evident the more normalized those protocols became. Such protocols "found or invented continuous entelechy," and without a "discourse network the myth of Bildungs path remained empty and unclear."[17] In other words, without a semiotechnical moment of signification that made sense of technical practices as a part of a larger whole, the continuously self-fortifying (and autopoietically self-reproducing) boundaries of the educated self could not be tended or even emerge in the first place.

Cinema prompted a forced confrontation with the semiotechnical movement between the discrete technical practices of education and the perpetual reemergence and affirmation of the educated individual. If the "key property of the modern individual" was a "continuity" established through various practices of literary Bildung, then cinematic continuity principles were paramount.[18] However, continuity is not, paradoxically, a continuous principle. Pedagogical, cultural, and scientific discourses on Bildung offer a unique window onto the theoretical interdependence of educational ideologies, the psyches they sought to produce, and the media technologies they employed and from which they derived their understanding of subject formation. Pedagogues designed educational programs that used various media to train pupils for the purpose of cultivating individuals who were both psychologically sound and socially integrated. Thus, the invocation of Bildung in writing about film was also an insight into the technics at work in the conception of the psyche. Even where the virtues of reading were extolled, pupils after 1900 were already seen as primarily viewers, reconceiving of even readers as cinemagoers.

The narrative of a devolution toward cinema was part of a grand technohistorical arc. Each stage in the development of mechanical reproduction technologies was viewed as an escalation of dangers to the education of its audience. Ernst Schultze, a well-known university librarian, author of moralistic treatises on culture, and eventual professor of economics, downplayed the eighteenth-century worries about the "extraordinary increase of demands on readers," noting that "until about the end of the nineteenth century, public opinion had scarcely become aware of the imminent danger, because desire to read [*Leselust*] harmless books had been staunched."[19] The "dangerousness," however, increased in each successive generation of pulp literature alongside the pace of reproducibility.[20] At one level, the complaint was about a capitalist mode of production that, through increasingly efficient mechanization, represented a convergence of artistic and industrial production such that aesthetic value became a matter of quantification. Of this technologically manufactured art in the age of its mechanical fungibility, Theodor Bäuerle wrote:

> Indeed the possibilities of technology [*Technik*] are nowhere near exhausted with presses and books. There is the vast, beautiful

> territory of art. What was for a long time accessible to only a few people—our great works of art—technology has reproduced and offered to the masses for cheap. A stream of pure joy and the noblest pleasure has thus been directed to the people. Indeed, with the same machines filth [*Schund*] and kitsch in all its varieties has and will be produced. Whatever doesn't fill the display windows under the guise of "art" and offers itself to curious looks! Business is business. Perfect reproductions of the most beautiful, finest artworks sit next to their unworthy sisters.[21]

Nearly twenty years before Walter Benjamin wrote "The Work of Art in the Age of Its Mechanical Reproducibility," conservative pedagogues and social critics already saw themselves standing past the apex of industrially dominated artistic creation, drawing many of the same conclusions that would become hallmarks of the Frankfurt School.[22]

The standardization of exchange, currency, and book printing and the globalization of literary production, particularly with pulp from the United States, increasingly replicated the industrial act of reproduction in the act of reading.[23] According to Schultze, during the Goethezeit there was an inimitability to a book at the level of its materiality, such that neither good nor bad books were determined "as today through capitalistic forms of production."[24] With this in mind, Schultze remorsefully questioned the popular teleology of technological progress: "Unfortunately, we must rid ourselves of the illusion of previous centuries, that all progress in the art of book printing, like every invention of technics [*Technik*] in general, serves to promote culture."[25] The cinematograph, however, was not seen to merely accelerate the problems encountered in training literary minds in the age of the rotary press but to entirely replace literary models of Bildung. As Bernhard Siegert notes of the "disfigured senses," marred by cinematographs, "the powers of media and Bildung are no longer one and the same, the reign of writers and thinkers over the entire discourse is done; done are their self-assigned pedagogical executive powers over the reading materials of their subjects and vassals."[26] In place of these guilds built from a belief in the unique aptitudes of students and enchanted realms of specialized knowledge to which they were granted access was a form of democratization through mechanical standardization. All was made equal, but only through the pure equivalence of psychophysical instruments that paved the way for the cinema. What the cinema offered, then, was a model for arranging those mechanical starts and stops into something that once again resembled an educated subject, albeit one that bore little trace of previous centuries' contemplative reader.

Continuing Education

Wilhelm von Humboldt, who devised the precepts of higher education around which many universities in Germany and the United States are still organized, imagined Bildung as an open-ended process of knowledge accumulation that "resolves itself solely through the connection [*Verknüpfung*] of our Self with the world to the most general, fullest, and freest interaction."[27] The operations of the medium by which that "connection" was established therefore determined everything about the nature of the education. Humboldt's emphasis on the "fullest, and freest interaction" naturally imagined textual operations—polysemic, overdetermined, and requiring an imaginative faculty. Such a conception assumed a richly populated world of semiotic play into which students, themselves with inner lives formed by the clean contours of ideas and concepts, further populated their interiors.

One of the more prominent countermodels was offered by the forerunner of experimental psychology, Johann Friedrich Herbart, who believed in an idea of "educatability" (*Bildsamkeit*), which was an innate potentiality of transformation enacted through the process of Bildung.[28] The force of empirical, instrument-driven psychological study that Herbart brought about did not allow for preexisting unities. Everything was a process subject to incremental quantification, including the unities of nascent subjects perhaps most of all. If the psychic apparatus could be understood as a series of measurable physiological capacities (as discussed in chapters 1 and 3), it could also presumably be formed and conditioned according to such methods. How reading, viewing, and thinking—hallmarks of the well-formed spirit—could be submitted to the uniform quantification of mechanical intervals, however, would remain a source of extreme contention. Cinema's constant, metered intervals challenged the play and indeterminacy of textual signification that had been viewed as crucial to developing the interiority that marked the "gebildet" pupil. The "interaction," imagined by thinkers like Humboldt, was not preserved in filmic representations, which were seen not as full and free but as fixed and orderly, even, or especially, where their topics were surreal and fantastical.

The success of the cinema during the period of its early maturation undercut long-standing nineteenth-century ideas of Bildung that persisted even as their technological foundations were believed to be in decline. Older battles about scintillating reading material waned as attention turned largely to fears that the very act of reading was being supplanted or transformed by industrial, interval-based training. In general, by 1909 there was a conviction that the "struggle against pulp literature [*Schundliteratur*] is currently fully underway," and by 1921 that the Berlin police censor "[Karl] Brunner's first intention—the annihilation of old pulp literature—[had] for the most part succeeded."[29] As focus turned from the printed word to the moving image, even the bad book was a good object in that it preserved the act of reading as the source of subject formation. Where remarks on the resemblances between the content of pulp literature and films ended, the incompatibility between filmic and literary training became apparent. "Defenders of cinema" were eager to point out that "the novel and the theater" often "deal with the same processes and many cinematic dramas are modeled on a recognized poetic value."[30] However, the "fundamental difference" was that "the photograph [*Lichtbild*] must relinquish the word."[31] For that reason, "the mental [*seelische*] deepening and the beauty of language, which ennobles even morally dubious poetry," was believed "entirely absent."[32] The profound interiority cultivated by the word gave way to machine-based stops and starts that found no essential difference between the apparatuses that received, produced, and measured visual stimuli.

Even as most films included intertitles, cinema gave up on the word as its central power and with it the closure of intellectual inwardness associated with the silent reader. Without the interpretive demands of a textual medium that buttressed the boundary between the reader and the world, the distinction between inside and outside was thought to become weak. As Walter Ong wrote of the psychological impacts of a long readerly epoch, "Writing and reading are solitary activities that throw the psyche back on itself"—that is, they are contemplative and individually fortifying.[33] But the problem was more fundamental than an opposition between text and image. The mechanics of a putative filmic education indeed trained viewers, though not as the contemplative subjects valued by the *Bildungsbürgertum*. The resounding pedagogical claim about cinema's role in the production of individuals was that "cinema is now the entertainer of broad social classes" but also "their teacher and educator."[34] Starker still was the charge that in contrast to the history of textual educational practices, the new media environment dominated by film destroyed imaginative faculties key to proper subject formation, leaving an indeterminate space of possibility about what the new cinematic pupil looked like. While "a bad book can misguide the fantasy of the reader," the filmic medium "annihilates fantasy," making it the "most dangerous educator of the people."[35]

More important than the hyperbolic claim that films eradicated the life of fantasy, however, was the fact that they did fundamentally restructure certain popular notions of how those fantasies were shaped into symbolically meaningful experiences. According to both critics and proponents, cinema did not produce the animated and shifting "connection" between the imagination of the viewer, the world, and text, as Humboldt had demanded. This was a rupture of signifying practice at the level of technics. Cinema seemed to possess a "technological accuracy that is free from the distortions of subjectivity," drawing on "a discourse established over the second half of the nineteenth century that linked the photographic image to objectivity," which countered the "questionable veracity of the textual."[36] In many ways, cinematic devices were still viewed as instruments of science and therefore of discretization, which posed major obstacles for humanistic notions of education.

Machines Learning

There was a permanent entanglement between the formation of an individual, their distinction from the world, representations of that world, and the ability to manipulate those representations internally. Wilhelm Dilthey, who schematically reconceived the history of Bildung for the twentieth century, dismissed the argument that "one thinks of fantasy as only vague, foggy, indefinite, boundless, but never in the characteristic completeness of reality," writing:

> What is the relationship now between the accumulated experience and the freely creative fantasy, between the reproduction of forms [*Gestalten*], situations, and fates and their creation? The association, which recalls existing elements in an existing connection to mental representation, and the imagination, which creates new connections from the existing elements, appear separated from one another by the clearest boundary.[37]

At issue is a technical question of autopoiesis. The representational means available to the imagination and the logic according to which "new connections are created" were defined through technologies. The interplay between these processes, and particularly the reciprocal, imperfect "reproduction" of imaginary connections, was also "at the same time a metamorphosis."[38] It was also the case for Dilthey that "reproduction itself is a Bildungs process."[39] In this view, individuals distinguished themselves from one another, the great artist from the lesser, or the realist from the surrealist, through the subtle differences between each autopoietic generation bound to the reading, production, and reproduction of text. This was a process upended by a devious binarization in film. The abject mode of enjoyment associated with the cinema purely manipulated Sein, sacrificing the imaginary at the altar of the supposed real, and training its viewers according to the uniform intervals of the projected image.

The traditional cultivation of an educated subject depended on specific conceptions of media techniques and, in particular, specific forms of reading. As Friedrich Schiller argued in a December 25, 1788, letter to Christian Gottfried Körner on the "relationship of art to truth," the "writer never deals with the *real*, rather always only the *ideal*."[40] In his famous essay on the role of poetry in spiritual education, Schiller claimed that while art aspires to and inspires unities, and nature itself is a whole, one must separate between the natural and the ideational unities that approximate them and that were the principle of individual autonomy. For Schiller, poetry, "understood as nothing other than that which gives humanity the possibility of its fullest expression," functions in "the condition of natural naivete," where all one's powers work as a "harmonious unity," as a "complete imitation of the real."[41] At the same time, under the conditions imposed by culture, in which "this harmonious concurrence" is "but an idea," the "exaltation of reality as ideal" or the "representation of the ideal is what makes one a writer."[42]

Without following Schiller down the poetic garden path, it is worth noting that at least since the eighteenth century, discourse about poetics doubled as a discourse about the education of proper modes of subject formation and, therefore, the form of mediation between the real and the imaginary. The poesis of autopoiesis was indeed a matter of formal poetic training. This point is made perhaps clearest in Schiller's epistolary meditations on education in the wake of French Revolutionary reception of Jean-Jacques Rousseau's ideas about the denigration of humanity through acculturation. For Schiller, as well as many members of the early twentieth-century resistance to film, the "sensitive disposition" depended on the "wealth of the imagination," which could not be derived purely from nature nor a physical, corporeal milieu.[43] The richness and power of imagination could be "robbed," so Schiller claimed, by the "dominance of the analytic capacity," which divided and limited the sphere of possible objects of contemplation.[44] For this reason, Schiller notes that the "abstract thinker" very often has a "cold heart" and "dissected" the "impressions that only stir the soul as a whole."[45] To protect the power of imagination (*Einbildungskraft*), whose apotheosis was in a figure of supreme individuality—the artist—one forfeits the "sphere of the real" to strive to "create the ideal from a union of the possible and the necessary."[46] Inasmuch as Schiller suggests that it is a province of preternatural genius, imagination was a trained faculty whose character was defined by the form of its articulation, whose medium specificity also dictated the vision of the psychological space it represented.

The abiding suspicion about cinema, given its seeming dependence on photochemical images and a logic of editing that destroyed the given coherence of space and time, was that viewers would lose their individuality through a combination of photographic positivism and machine intervals. A similar fear had already been expressed in a reaction to the first generation of associationist psychologists like Thomas Hobbes, John Locke, and David Hume, who, as Wolfgang Iser has shown, had proposed a passive, mechanistic model of the psyche that involved the mere combination and recombination of perceptual inputs.

> Historically, association psychology was responsible for describing this faculty in more detail. Imagination was seen as a form of explanation for the association of ideas, since received data could not of their own accord join together in more complex ideas. The problem was to explain how the combination was guided, and how it was possible to join disparate data. Attributing this function to the imagination meant equipping it with intentions, since the combination of data appears to originate in an intention. . . . According to this understanding, there was no way to explain how the imagination's productivity had come into the mind; and as the mind was nothing but a tabula rasa, imagination must be antecedent to the mind, not least because it could also produce pictures of things that

> did not exist as objects. Furthermore, the combinations that imagination brought about had no correspondence in reality.[47]

At the point that films for public consumption were longer and involved more engrossing narratives with a high degree of diegetic closure, the charge against the medium was that it substituted raw perceptual material with an already structured imaginary object. This was achieved by combining the "realness" of perceptual continuities with a narrative logic that was not the viewer's. The overtly mechanical nature of the filmic apparatus could thus be easily attributed to a mechanistic version of experimental psychology that, as Iser notes, had summoned the ire of defenders of the imagination. And as Kittler notes, the entire history of both film scholarship and psychophysical experimentation on movement could be essentialized in this problem: "Chopping or cutting in the real, fusion or flow in the imaginary—the entire research history of cinema revolves only around this paradox."[48] Evolutions in the machine language of the imaginary in the 1910s would eventually act as a defining force in distinctions between the real, symbolic, and imaginary by the late twentieth century, a fact captured by Gilles Deleuze, who commented:

> In an organic description, the real that is assumed is recognizable by its continuity—even if it is interrupted—by the continuity of shots which establish it and by the laws which determine successions, simultaneities and permanence: it is a regime of localizable relations, actual linkages, legal, causal and logical connections. It is clear that this system includes the unreal, the recollection, the dream and the imaginary but as contrast. Thus the imaginary will appear in the forms of caprice and discontinuity, each image being in a state of disconnection with another into which it is transformed.[49]

It is a testament to the psychological dominance of cinematic technics by the time that Deleuze was writing that the imaginary's divergence from the real was marked by symbolic discontinuities that *signified* for the real distinctions between the intervals. The real was "recognizable" by its "continuity," which is not to say that it is continuous. Rather, the semiotechnical regime of cinema, in which differences between discrete machinations were experienced as signifying for seamless realism, established a logic whereby discretization became the condition of unity. Whether the interval signified as a continuity or a discontinuity—in other words, whether evidence of discretization was emphasized—was what delineated the real from the imaginary after the rise of cinematic narrative. Of course, both the real and the imaginary could only be experienced by way of symbols, but it was a feat of semiotechnical evolution that the joining of two discontinuous moments could define continuity.

In the 1910s, the commonplace experience described by Deleuze in the second half of the twentieth century represented an immense challenge to notions of psychic and subjective closure. The erasure of the tenuous medial distinction between the real and the imaginary through interval-based continuities was seen as film's essential danger to psychological development and education as well as the reason for its immense success during the period of its narrative development. Film did not require the difficult suspension between signifier and signified, nor the learned detachment and identification that textual training enforced. It is for this reason that Schultze diagnosed the success of the cinema in 1913 as essentially an obviation of the difficulties of textual and dramatic representation. The success of film even in the face of a glut of mass-printed trivial literature could be found purely in the character of the Bildung required by its operations—the educated ability to make distinctions in a representational space.

> What made this triumphant procession possible? The extraordinary maturation of the senses in cinematographic presentations makes the reasons understandable to everyone. Following them requires neither higher education [*Bildung*], nor mental [*geistige*] exertion. Truly, there are absolutely no mental prerequisites for one to be able to take in what is on the silver screen as well as someone more cultured, so long as they have at minimum learned to read and write. What is more, the rapid and entirely effortless scene changes that are realized in the cinemas make it superior to theater. Another factor contributing to the superiority of the cinematograph over stage—which it quickly learned to fear as its rival—is that it only requires small staff which after only a few hours can be changed, while the theater requires a carefully trained staff that is more susceptible to fatigue.[50]

Film's demands upon the viewer diminished the intellectual strain and Bildung necessary for the identification with a fictional space because the representational ambivalence that characterized the theater and text was eliminated. Film simply showed what it showed and began hiding its diegetic operations in invisible functions of perspective, editing, and sequencing once the editing methods for producing narrative closure more fully evolved in the 1910s. Thus, the viewer was believed to remain unconfronted with the distinction between the real and the fictional that was inescapably foregrounded in texts and theater.

Separating the possible from the real was an attribute of the autonomous and "educated" reader, specifically attributed to an internalization of reading and representational practices in the audience's own formation. Schultze linked the cultivation of individuals and the fate of Western civilization at large to this internalization, which he then framed as a physiological effect of "wonderment," a concept bearing strong resemblance to the mode of fascination Gunning famously describes in the early cinema of "attraction." It was not just that unrefined, sensational material "trains the fantasy of the masses" using "the force or brutality incomprehensible to refined tastes" but that it played *only* on what was "externally visible."[51]

Even in cases of pure fiction, film cultivated a dangerous illusion of objectivity that did not demand that the viewer erect a stable boundary between the immediately visible and the possible to allow for the second-order, meta-level process of introspection. Unreflective audiences were seen to lack the Nachdenken essential to tending the border between the imaginary, immediate sensations, and an apparently realistic filmic projection. Paradoxically, the lack of inwardness was a cause of violent solipsism because the connection between physiological impulse and visual gratification was thought to be immediate and did not prompt one to think beyond the limits of what was right before one's eyes. Without the firm and trained distinction between signifier and signified and in turn between interior and exterior, society was doomed to become "anticultural" (*kulturwidrig*).[52] According to many pedagogues, cinematographic presentations were the high point of a technological immediacy that destroyed subjective space by eliminating contemplation of the means—or one might say "second-orderness"—by which fiction was produced. It established a direct line of excitation between the viewer and the events represented to produce a seeming unity of time and place that was not marked by the traditional distance of subjective observation and reflection. As Schultze remarks:

> The technical peculiarities of our age contribute immensely to rapidly propagating this addiction in all directions. In the past when one delighted in a sensational event, the excited only took hold slowly and did not invade every city and town. Today, newspapers, telegraphs, and particularly cinematographs, ensure that every craving for sensation, crudeness, or blood lust, spreads not just in one country, no, but across the entire world.[53]

As an antidote to the rapidity and presumed realism of modern media technologies, Schultze returns to quote Goethe's *Wilhelm Meisters Lehrjahre.* The passage he selects is from an episode in the third chapter of the second book after Wilhelm criticizes his own poetic and theatrical talents, burns his poetry, and sets off on a debt-collecting trip at his father's behest. In the town of Hochdorf, Wilhelm is convinced by a man with debts to his father to attend the performance of an amateur theater troupe in a barn. The production was "full of action" but one "without the depiction [*Schilderung*] of true natures," and Goethe notes that the "crude people are satisfied when they simply see something happen; the educated [*gebildete*] want to feel, and contemplation [*Nachdenken*] is only entirely enjoyable for the educated."[54] In the context of its citation by Schultze, the "gebildete" here can be viewed as those who have internalized the operations of a certain kind of textual mediation, one that insists on and makes apparent the separation between the representation and the represented, and, in turn, between the audience and what it sees. "True natures" and properly trained viewers are formed through the projection of a unified, imaginary space of fictionality that is more than the simple correspondence between what is presented and what is seen.

The frequent recurrence of the term *Nachdenken* in *Wilhelm Meisters Lehrjahre* is very often in relation to an elevated subjective state associated specifically with literary training. Thus, when Serlo, however much the fool he is in the novel, addresses Wilhelm's overly literal rendering of *Hamlet,* the conversation becomes one of the problems of representation and correspondence, and ultimately Nachdenken. Wilhelm's insistence on following the text of the play to the letter rather than interpreting its spirit is revealed to be a form of immaturity that misses the truth at the core of the play, and is a part of a series of conversations between Serlo and Wilhelm about the nature of the aesthetic unity and the proper internal relations to the events of a play.

Nachdenken was an educational objective central to the earliest Bildungs programs as well as those of critics of cinema like Ernst Schultze and Friedrich Paulsen, and cinema reformers such as Robert Gaupp and Adolf Sellmann.[55] More than an idle mode of contemplation, Nachdenken constructed a mode of thirdness, or the second-order point of observation in cybernetic terminology, that allowed the individual to signify as distinct. It is above all a technically defined psychological space. As "afterthought," Nachdenken forms a readerly practice that requires a pause in the act of transmission. On this point, early pedagogical commentators on film come together in a refrain that film allowed no time for "Nachdenken," as discussed in previous chapters. The pedagogical theorist O. Götze, for instance, wrote that the overwhelming immediacy of early films worked to both damage sensory organs (again through the "flicker" discussed in chapter 2) and prevent the development of contemplative, that is, second-order, faculties.

> As is well known, on account of the wild speed of film's procession a constant flickering, pulsing, and flashing arises. Our retina is forced to react with lightning-fast speed to situations that change instant to instant. Even if our eyes are capable of reacting to an endless number of impressions and to endure repeated damaging effects with lasting detriments, continuously looking at the trembling, brightly lit screen must undoubtedly adversely impact the eye as well as the nervous system [*Nervenapparat*]. . . . Even images that could offer mental enrichment rush past so rapidly that it is impossible for clear impressions to emerge. One is habituated out of allowing a stable object to enter the realm of ideas [*Vorstellungskreis*] through the gateways of the sense organs. The senses become dulled by fleeting vision and precision. In this way the child is educated to be superficial, absent-minded, and disorganized; the opposite of what education [*Erziehung*] such as schooling strives for.[56]

The ceaseless onslaught of rapid, mechanically defined periods of stimulus disrupted the core objective of education, according to Götze. It made the act of self-observation that organized the self into a single, signifying unity impossible. Götze's appraisal reflects the period in which he was writing, a period between the prominence of short one-act films and the flourishing of long-format narrative films. Accordingly, there is an ambivalence in his text about where the threat of film resides—whether in the mechanical, energetic economy of the physiological apparatus or the representational economies of psychological space. In fact, his argument is a semiotechnical one. It recognizes that the management of technical inputs into the psychic apparatus defined the symbolic space. Because there is no distinction between the two types of apparatuses—cinematographic and psychic—what takes place is a mere overwhelming of the inputs of one apparatus by the outputs of the other. At the same time, he is also describing techniques of narrative editing that introduce "incomprehensible scene changes" and temporal disunities that are too fast to be appropriately accounted for through older representational models.[57]

In Götze's estimation, the child "in his relatively limited capacities understands the images as excerpts from reality," and "his inner representational space [*Vorstellungskreis*] is contaminated by false ideas of intense strength."[58] This was a position that was often repeated by newly minted experts on the pedagogical import film, such as Sellmann, who was more measured in his survey of the diversity of medical and pedagogical opinions on the effects of the "flicker of images" and whether children should "ideally" come to know and differentiate "reality with their own eyes."[59] For Sellmann and others, such exposure was explicitly a question of Bildung, which was framed as a physiological, and thus mechanical, question about the speed, pattern, and nature of reflection, and therefore an argument about the convergence of symbolic and technical operations. Both of these factors were weighed as advantages of text in the cultivation of individuals as thinkers.

> Frequently, because of the constant movement and restlessness of film, there can be no conversation about deepening. The thoughts and feelings do not penetrate deeply enough into the souls of our children, because one impression hurriedly chases away and represses the next.[60]

Cinema is positioned here as a troublesome bridge between physiology and psychology in the training of students because it linked physical mechanisms to hermeneutical practices. Nachdenken in this view, then, represented precisely the division of physiology from psychology. It was a program of technical training that erected a subject by the very act of recognizing the differences between stimuli, representations, realities, and fictions, and reproducing distinctions internally.

The problems of Nachdenken, and therefore of Bildung, in the reception of film were essentially an early, psychologized form of what Jay David Bolter and Richard Grusin have described as "remediation" and particularly "hypermediation" in the period of digital technologies' ascendance.[61] The digital created a unique problem, in that its basic binary operations provided no natively intuitable form of symbolic engagement. The power of computation that has guided the theoretical transitions to posthumanism was in its ability to process all inputs rapidly as binary, which did not lend itself to easy human interaction. It required interfaces and languages that borrowed from other existing media regimes and allowed binary, machine language to be manipulated at the level of human symbols. This includes object-oriented programming languages, screen-based "desktop" visualization, and film-editing software that represents images as if they are a filmstrip. This gets to the heart of what is at stake in the educational battle over cinema, whose uniform, supersensory machinations seemed to present a vision of the real without also training people in the techniques for its representation.

André Bazin described the dispute over filmic realism as a part of "the guiding myth of cinema," namely "an integral realism, a recreation of the world in its own image, an image unburdened by the freedom of interpretation of the artist."[62] Unlike the traditional "artistic" and literary practices, such as chiaroscuro, synecdoche, or meter, all of which "reveal something of [their] nature," the evolution of film offered "stages of a technical development that little by little made a reality out of the original 'myth.'"[63] One had to find devices for re-mediating filmic reality effects—for showing the audience how the cinematographic projection was *not* showing the audience its means for producing the illusion. Again, as Bolter and Grusin claim, in the epistemological sense, "hypermediacy is opacity," and in the "psychological sense," it is the experience that one has "in and of the presence of media; it is the insistence that the experience of the medium is itself an experience of the real."[64]

In general, for pedagogues this was not a problem for literature because the distinction between the acts of reading and perceiving were already conceptually distinct. In fact, for reformers like Friedrich Paulsen, this was the mainstay of a moral education, which forced readers into discriminating acts of contemplation.

> I'm not worried when the realm of the sensual is touched upon; so long as the writer represents what is, he is within his right and has

> no duty beyond poetic truth. It is not a criticism of the author that things happen in a novel which we would say should not happen if they were to happen in reality. However, if he does not merely represent such things in their inner necessity and their necessary effects, if he expressly situates them as harmless and virtuous, and thereby represses the effects they have according to the nature of the thing, then he ceases to be a poet; he becomes a moralist. And it is the right of the reader to examine and reject this morality.[65]

Paulsen here and in the rest of the treatise addresses the polyvalent representational status of literature with respect to moral education that is the theoretical core of the abstract, educated subject: the ability to think one's self into various fictional, self-observing scenarios with moral import. Whether or not something abided by principles of bourgeois morality was determined to a large extent by the ability to transport a fictional—but nevertheless possible—moral agent into ethical limit cases. Indeed, this was the type of subjective continuity that older versions of Bildung sought to produce. And it was precisely this form of training in "poetic" truths that the specter of a cinematographic subjectivity haunted.

Sociotechnical Mechanisms

W. A. Lay, the Karlsruhe pedagogue, revered as the "leading German authority on the experimental study of teaching," or what was referred to as "experimental didactics," mobilized experimental psychology to show that fantasy was indeed key to psychological development.[66] He also, relatedly, sought to demonstrate that such development was of inestimable aesthetic and ethical significance and that it was bound to certain key functions of language. Lay described fantasy generally as the "capacity to be able to represent" things in a "lively, vivid, expressible" fashion.[67] This was not an unstructured mode of invention, however, but instead a technical logic of combination defined by psychophysical intervals of measure. Lay described it as an ability of students to reorganize textual elements to produce multiple meanings or to fill "gaps" (*Lücken*) within a text and between a current situation and a projected future.[68] He referred to this capacity with the seemingly paradoxical term *scientific fantasy*.[69] It was an ability that would be tested using methodologies closely connected to Ebbinghaus's well-known "combination method," which tested the time required for subjects to complete "a meaningful whole" from sentence fragments called "stems."[70] More than testing intelligence as Ebbinghaus had desired, such tests were believed by many, such as Guy Montrose Whipple and Emil Kraepelin, to test exhaustion, or in the case of difficult versions of the test, the "active or creative imagination of the literary type."[71] In each case, Lay's testing methodology linked fantasy to the speed with which one was able to introduce a logical ordering of individualized textual components such as "letters" and "words." Training this ability to unconsciously process the operations of the textual medium to produce meaning was the cornerstone of Bildung and signified a high degree of psychological autonomy connected to aesthetic and ethical agency.

As Lay writes, the "concrete" operations of "individual imagination" were as important for "ideation [*Anschauung*] and fantasy" as they were for "perceptions in reality."[72] Moreover, he claimed photography never "yields a copy of reality and no one, least of all the true artist, is able to reproduce reality as it is."[73] Truth of any essential nature was not to be found in a faithful reproduction. This was a theoretical atavism, however, in that it unintentionally recapitulated older visions of Bildung as a "beautiful humanity," and as an "aesthetic Bildung of the individual" derived from the ancient Greek notion of *Kalos kagathos* (*καλὸς κἀγαθός*) as maintained by "Herder, Goethe, Schiller, Jean Paul, Schleiermacher," while also simultaneously adopting the antimetaphysical approaches that emerged with the "development of physiological and experimental psychology" after Herbart.[74] In a sense, the problem for experimental pedagogy was to understand how the unique psychological continuity associated with ideas of beauty as well as moral agency could survive the death of irreducible metaphysical unities. Despite the emphasis on textual operations and the explicit prohibition on photographic representation, the answer, especially in 1910, appears to be cinema. The origin of continuity, meaning, and autonomy, both psychologically and semantically, were displaced from ideal unities into logic sequences, whose organization and presentation were now scientifically administered according to cinematographic mechanisms.

Of paramount importance for considering the relationship between Bildung and the innovations of interval management introduced with cinematic machines was the concept of equivalence and fungibility shared between ideas of democratization and empiricism. Viewed as an apparatus whose history and purpose were inextricable from its scientific origins, cinematic education of a broadened public had the effect of rendering social and political equality as mechanical, quantitative interchangeability. No interval was different from any other, except in terms of their magnitude. Where practices of reading thrived on the fundamental difference between the world represented by texts and the imaginary encouraged by reading—as well as the class distinction between those who read and those who do not—film went a long way to eliminating such distinctions. Scientific apparatuses, and claims to hard empiricism more generally, while often used as tools of oppression through ideologies of standardization, also substituted qualitative properties with quantitative measure. Everything was equal insofar as it could be measured according to mechanical intervals. Heide Schlüpmann hints at this in her attempt to establish an alternative history of the "aesthetic of the cinema."[75] She claims that, against the rationalistic projection of a unified transcendental subject, the history of film represented a reception of the natural sciences "in which the sublation of the negation of the individual occurred," and the sociopolitical democratization of filmic content was matched by the quantitative equivalence of its technological means.[76] A data point was not privileged above others just as votes are ideally counted as equal in a democratic election.

Democratization through technical uniformity undergirds Emilie Altenloh's famous 1914 study of the composition and motivations of early film spectators, which is considered the first sociological work on the cinema.[77] Throughout her survey, Altenloh praises the highly educated groups who preferred scientific nonfiction films for their insistence on the separation between the space of fiction, which was to be internal, and the external space of objectivity. This was a boundary that even Schundliteratur in its raciest incarnations preserved. In her section on "Kolportageliteratur," she writes:

> What rudiments that were left of this form from an earlier epoch had to give way, because the cinema adapted itself better than others to the special demands of the present. In an age in which life is so intense, in which every instant must have its own experience, and everything spirals together as if in a vortex, there is no longer any suitable grounds for Indian stories and penny novels. To allow the imagination to travel along the hero's path it is essential to have an undisturbed, quiet corner, a closed quarter, in which the racket of reality does not intrude.[78]

The nostalgic undertone of the passage is certainly not for a specific genre of pulp fiction but for the absolution of the distinction between the representational space of "reality" and "fantasy" that film forever vanquished. This was the distinction that made reading the vehicle for the production of inwardness against the undifferentiated mayhem of reality. In much the same way that experimental psychology was vilified for mechanically applying principles of empirical observation to the study of experience, and thus destroying the point of mediation between inside and outside, film as the popular extension of scientific psychology eradicated the partition between reality and inwardness.

Niklas Luhmann locates this operation of textual fictionality, and novels in particular, as a form of differentiation at the heart of both the production of a faith in the "subject" as well as the system of *society*. His systems theoretical analysis underscores the relationship between discrete processes and the continuity of a system that emerges through a kind of operational thirdness.

> The parallel resides primarily in the fictionality of the text and the uncertainty produced by the text itself. Fictionality means above all that no point-by-point correspondence with real events is expected, but at the same time obvious improbabilities do not get fantasized together. The novel must do this, even though everyone knows that it remains credible and that the reader can draw conclusions about their own life. And it has to create a tension that is both produced by and once again resolved by the text itself. In other words, the self-generated uncertainty must be disentangled without external (extratextual) references. In this respect too, the novel serves as a model for a self-explicating life story.[79]

"Point-by-point correspondence" was the trademark of a positivistic scientific ideology in which photographic and moving-image technologies had been vested with the power and potential of reproducing "real event" as "real event." Altenloh's pessimism about the sociological consequences of filmic fictionality stemmed from its jeopardizing of the narrative autonomy involved in educational subject formation.

The creation of an autonomous agent with an ethical imperative of participating in and maintaining social continuity was a part of the reigning concept of Bildung. In his definitive work on the conceptual history of Bildung, Reinhart Koselleck notes that the process of programmatic cultural and psychological individuation was in fact always inseparable from economic and social conditions in thinking about Bildung. With a distinctly cybernetic tone, he writes: "The integration of self-development into the socioeconomic or political or psychological conditions under which it alone can occur belong to the reflexive processing that likewise socially mandated all Bildung."[80] The means for organizing this "self-development" in a way that accorded with the demands of an accelerated industrial form of capitalist production thus demanded that the psychic and socioeconomic merge around 1900.

Industrious Viewership

The method for appropriately educating a discretized psyche suited to a newly mechanized world was issued by an emerging field of industrial psychology called psychotechnics (*Psychotechnik*). It applied psychometric testing to the industrial production that developed in the early twentieth century and represented a real convergence of psychophysical inquiry and popular cinema. Among other reasons for this nexus was the fact that the founder of psychotechnics, Hugo Münsterberg, was also among the first film theorists. In addition to, or perhaps because of, his pioneering contributions to psychophysics and his talent for experimental design, he identified an analogical relationship between the operations of film and those of thought. The means by which narrative cinema, in distinction to earlier films, established its diegetic space was through mechanical continuities that had previously been the province of cognition. The photoplay, mirroring the relationship between discrete physiological functions and the smooth contours of ideas, produced narrative unities through systematized discontinuities. As Münsterberg remarked:

> The photoplay can overcome the interval of the future as well as the interval of the past and slip the day twenty years hence between this minute and the next. In short, it can act as our imagination acts. It has the mobility of our ideas which are not controlled by the physical necessity of outer events but by the psychological laws for the association of ideas. In our mind past and future become intertwined with the present. The photoplay obeys the laws of the mind rather than those of the outer world.[81]

Editing procedures such as the cut-back, which replicated memory, or the close-up, which "objectified in our world of perception our mental act of attention," instituted a logic of succession that erased evidence of that succession to produce a concentrated feeling of "omnipresence"—the appearance of a supreme autonomy without gaps.[82] Moreover, Münsterberg assumed that the functions of the mind reproduced by the photoplay were those of a "normal" psyche. Against the claim that Münsterberg was primarily interested in how the "technical system of cinema" performed a "trick on the nervous system" and exploited the "nervous system and the brain," his comparative analysis provides little reason to think that cinematic operations were treated as atypical.[83] To suggest that film simply exploited a deficiency of the physiological apparatus in service of illusion was to deny the parallel between the ways the cinematic apparatus and the physiological apparatus both worked to produce semiotic and subjective continuities. Kittler efficiently captures this fact when he writes:

> As Münsterberg demonstrated, such transformations are inherently deadly for the mind [*Geist*]. Mathematical equations can be solved just as well from the left as from the right and the title "*Psychotechnik*" already shows that experimental psychological film theories are likewise media technical psychological treatises.[84]

While Kittler powerfully frames the history of empirical psychological research and industrial psychotechnical experiments in the evolution of film theory, Münsterberg's book proceeds in a direction opposite the one emphasized by Kittler. The point was not just that the mind could be reduced to mechanical operations but that cinema provided a heuristic for the connection between mechanical operations and the apparent symbolic space of mind. Furthermore, such operations were not the revelation of a cognitive substrate but an acquired program of training that eventuated itself in a media-specific form of psychic autonomy.

One of the prominent outcomes of Münsterberg's psychotechnical work was that it implied a variability of basic mental states and capacities based on practices of technical training. To reduce materialist theories of the psyche to the claim that they were "mechanical" is to ignore the revelation of the nineteenth and twentieth centuries discussed in chapter 2—that cinema was feared primarily for its ability to function semiotically. This was a central anxiety prompted by the strong resonance between cinema and the history of psychotechnics. As Kittler writes:

> First psychotechnics—this relay from physiological and technical experiments, from psychological and ergonomic data—made film

> theory possible (to say nothing of assembly-line work and combat training). Münsterberg can effortlessly demonstrate that motion pictures, for the first time in the history of the artistic world, are capable of implementing the neurological dataflow. While traditional arts process symbolic systems or systems of things, the film transmits to its viewers their own perceptual process. This is a precision that is otherwise only available in experiments—at the very least, not to consciousness nor language. Münsterberg assigns every individual camera technique to an unconscious psychical mechanism: the close-up to attentive selection, the cutback to *souvenir involontaire,* the special effect to the daydream, etc.[85]

The re-presentation of perceptual states *as* perceptual states in silent cinema demonstrated the degree to which the psyche and the cinema were already modeled according to the same principles. The physiological, conceived mechanically, was an epistemic space of discontinuity, quantity, and measurement, while the psychological was associated with the continuous, closed, and immeasurable. What psychophysics did for cinematic theory, and cinematic theory for psychology, was to establish the connection between the two.

What is perhaps missing from Kittler's account is not the opposition of the symbolic or hermeneutic with the technological but their inseparability in narrative cinema. Diegetic effects represented a specific outcome in the evolution of filmic technologies as part of a history of empirical psychology that offered an account of the connection between mechanical operations and problems of subjectivity. Despite the elegance of Kittler's tightly articulated summary, the diegetic techniques to which he refers were not present, or at least not developed with any sophistication, in the earliest films. Initially, psychophysics relied on a structural isomorphism between the order of measurable responses to stimuli and the shape of thought to which they were believed to be connected. Absent was an explanation for how the myriad psychophysical processes could be unified as something that reflected human experience. Writing about earlier psychophysical research (including his own), Wolfgang Köhler summarized exactly this obstacle as an issue of psychophysics resolved by gestalt psychology.

> Gestalt Psychology works with a principle which is both more general and more concretely applicable than that of Hering and Müller.

> These authors refer to the merely *logical* order of experiences, which for this purpose, are abstracted from their context and judged as to their similarities. The thesis is that when related physiological events are also taken from their context, and also compared as to their similarities, the resulting logical order must be the same as that of the experiences, . . . But experience as such exhibits an order *which is itself experienced*. . . . This is also an order; but, instead of being of the merely logical kind, it is concrete and belongs to the very facts of experience. This order, too, we assume to depend upon physiological events in the brain. . . . *Experienced order in space is always structurally identical with a functional order in the distribution of underlying brain processes.* This is the principle of *psychophysical isomorphism* in the particular form which it assumes in the case of spatial order.[86]

In his work—much of which was conducted with Max Wertheimer, who had used a tachistoscope as a kind of primitive cinematograph—gestalt psychology is identified as a solution to a deep problem in psychophysics: going from the discrete, empirical, and physiological defined by machines, to experience. Indeed, Reuleaux might have been pleased to see the far-reaching effects of kinematics on the study of human psychology.

The idea that cinema presented its audience with an accurate, even ideal image of how the mind worked, and one rooted in science, was built into Hugo Münsterberg's treatise *The Photoplay.* Beyond being among the first extended engagements with film theory, his work incorporated earlier results of experimental psychology to claim that the model of psychic operations offered by film was *not* a distortion. In *The Photoplay,* he briefly details a story of the evolution of narrative cinema that treated the maturation of cinema as a process of technological Bildung.

> It was indeed not an external technical advance only which led from Edison's half a minute show of the little boy who turns on the hose to the "Daughter of Neptune," or "Quo Vadis," or "Cambria," and many another performance which fills an evening. The advance was first of all internal; it was an esthetic idea. Yet even this does not tell the whole story of the inner growth of the moving pictures, as it points only to the progress of the photoplay. It leaves out of account the fact that the moving pictures appeal not merely

> to the imagination, but that they bring their message also to the intellect. They aim toward instruction and information.[87]

His description works through an internal comparison of the development of the individual psyche to the history of cinema's development toward diegetic closure, as if the cinema became autonomous in the same way that we might imagine the individual matures. This development is at once mechanical and narrative. For humans it was physiological, imaginary, and intellectual closure, and for cinema it was technological: the three-bladed shutter, more powerful light sources, and faster frame rates, as well as techniques of editing that stabilized narrative continuity. In both cases, the move was toward what might be thought of as a diegetic evolution; the individual was trained and personalized in her relation to the world and the cinema advanced a narrative capacity according to its own media-specific visual techniques.

The 1895 Louis Lumière film *L'Arroseur arrosé* (Watering the gardener) is frequently cited by film historians as one of the earliest instances "adumbrating narrative closure" in a one-act film.[88] Lumière's film does not create narrative continuity "through a connection between separate shots," as would be the case in Méliès's *Cinderella* (1899), but instead shows a "conscious control of the material being shot" that was "designed to capture the spectator's interest."[89] The short one-shot film depicts a boy pranking a gardener by sneaking into the frame from offscreen to step on the watering hose, then releasing it as the gardener looks down to examine the nozzle. There are indeed strong diegetic operations in the film, such as the visual splitting of the frame into areas the gardener can and cannot see, against the audience's omniscient spectatorial position, which creates a possibility for dramatic irony. Likewise, there is a beginning, middle, and end, which allows one to restate the events depicted in narrative succession. What is distinctly not present in the film, and Münsterberg means to underscore in the example, is the reliance on film-specific diegetic effects. These are montage and filming techniques—such as shot/countershot, close-ups, matches, and parallel editing—that would demand a cinematographically educated viewer.

The same cannot be said of *Quo Vadis?*, which was the well-known subject of "the first serious film review" by Kurt Pinthus and an exemplar of editing techniques that Münsterberg identifies as the premise for the analogy between cinema and psyche.[90] What Münsterberg designates as an "esthetic" property that allowed films like *Quo Vadis?* to "fill an evening" was the medium-specific forms of narrative closure marking filmic diegesis. As has been addressed in previous chapters, films of the early 1910s developed technological and editing techniques that transformed cinema into a matter of psychological rather than physiological concern. One could argue that overcoming technical obstacles to encourage absorption in purely narrative presentations was the process by which attractions could become an art. But it was also the process of subject formation. For Jacques Lacan, this involved overcoming the early developmental frustrations of the physical body to identify with a unified image signifying for an idealized self in the mirror stage.[91] However, it was also a much older idea of education found in notions of aesthetic education. That Münsterberg calls it an "esthetic" change draws immediate attention to cinema's involvement in a process of maturation, education, and Bildung that moved from purely physical realities to ideal unities.

Aesthetic training and the development of an aesthetic sensibility were a sign of completion, harmony, education, and therefore subjective continuity at least since the eighteenth century. As Schiller clarified in a footnote to a section fittingly called "The Coalescing Beauty" ("Die schmelzende Schönheit"), there is "an education [*Erziehung*] toward health, an education toward insight, an education toward morality [*Sittlichkeit*], an education toward taste and toward beauty."[92] And it is this final mode of education that has the purpose of "cultivating the totality of our sensuous and spiritual powers in the utmost harmony."[93] Moreover, such aesthetic unity was not of an irreducible kind. It was traditionally viewed as only possible through modes of representation, and therefore, through the continuities produced through techniques enforced by media, namely practices of reading. As Christian Gottfried Körner wrote to Schiller of *Wilhelm Meister*: "I think of the unity of the whole as the representation [*Darstellung*] of a beautiful human nature, which itself is cultivated through the gradual synthesis [*Zusammenwirkung*] of its inner dispositions [*Anlagen*] and outer relations."[94] According to the "pedagogical intelligence of the bourgeois," film upset the long-standing "conception of art" (*Kunstauffassung*) and threatened both the fragile cultural "group identity in the signs of literacy" as well as the "socially integrative, system stabilizing function" of the personal and cultural organization implied by aesthetic education.[95]

This residual overlap between aesthetics and education through a shared ideal of individual and artistic autonomy and completion was advanced well into the twentieth century, where it was scientifically discretized. Following Münsterberg's analysis of narrative film's development as a mirror for human cognitive faculties, he turns his attention to a more standard discourse on early film, reproduced ad nauseum by early commentators—namely the necessity of maximizing the potential of the filmic medium as distinct from other media.[96] Echoing Schiller, Münsterberg writes that the singular aim of the artist is to "remold nature and life so that it offers such complete harmony in itself that it does not point beyond its own limits but is an ultimate unity through the harmony of its parts."[97] Against the various principles of unity by which theorists and historians defined the aesthetic value of painting and drama, the autonomy of the filmic medium for Münsterberg was inseparable from the union of psychological and technological operations. He emphasized the creation of a uniquely filmic representational order that at once reaffirmed the interiority and individual autonomy of the viewer as well as the continuity of editing practices.

> If this is the outcome of esthetic analysis on the one side, of psychological research on the other, we need only combine the results of both into a unified principle: *the photoplay tells us the human story by overcoming the forms of the outer world, namely, space, time, and causality, and by adjusting the events to the forms of the inner world, namely, attention, memory, imagination, and emotion.*[98]

The principle of cine-aesthetic autonomy is functionally identical with the principle of psychological autonomy. Moreover, they are simultaneously narrative and mechanical, which had the distinct effect of elevating film out of a purely physiological discussion. If a "human story" forming an "inner world" could be accomplished through mechanical sequencing, the nebulous concept of Bildung, historically attached to forms of textual education, could be redefined according to the conventions of films. Through the end of the nineteenth century, the Bildungsroman stood as an "exemplary" fictional device for these objectives and the "most pedagogically efficient of novels" because it thematized and enacted "the very motion of aesthetic education" and had as its referent "the self-positing consciousness of the human."[99] The same could be said for films with the difference being that aesthetic autonomy, psychological continuity, and the distinction between interior and exterior were achieved through purely discrete operations on the sensorium.

For Münsterberg the film theorist, as well as Münsterberg the high priest of psychotechnics, there was little separation between technologies of education and the subjects they educated. Right after Frederick Winslow Taylor published his revolutionary 1911 study, *The Principles of Scientific Management,* Münsterberg's equally momentous *Psychology and Industrial Efficiency* also appeared.[100] Among the recommendations Taylor's industrial lodestar put forward was the necessity of substituting "science for the individual judgment of the workman," and a "scientific selection and development of the workman, after each man has been studied, taught, and trained, and one may say experimented with."[101] Despite being credited as an exponent of global industrial capitalism, Taylor was actually forced to defend himself in front of a special committee in the House of Representatives that argued that "the worker under the system of scientific management risked becoming a mere automaton."[102] Taylor also came under fire from other proponents and followers of scientific management and especially more labor-friendly counterparts in England. Edward Cadbury, for instance, listed among the potential "evils" of implementing new organizational and production techniques the ever-narrowing scope of tasks for "unskilled labor" and their function in the production process.[103] This restated congressional worries that the function of "judgment" has been eliminated from individual work, making it "monotonous and depressing" with the "division of processes being carried to such an extent that there is a narrowing of interest, and automatic machinery almost eliminates any demand for initiative and adaptation."[104] As a rebuttal to such charges, he replied that scientific management was "a *complete mental revolution* on the part of the workingman" as well as an "equally complete mental revolution on the part of those on management's side," and that "without this complete mental revolution on both sides scientific management does not exist."[105] The decidedly psychological character of the transformation was supported by Münsterberg and was viewed favorably by Cadbury himself when he wrote that "certain writers, such as Hugo Münsterberg," claim "that the problem can and should be handed over to the experimental psychologists."[106]

Though a "mental revolution" might have been the perceived result of Taylor's system when he was forced to reflect on its implementation, it was the theoretical core of Münsterberg's work from the beginning. Scientific management was just the practical application of experimental methods that were already the mainstay of work by experimental psychologists such as Münsterberg and Wundt. This becomes apparent in Münsterberg's simultaneous praise and criticism of the advancement of Taylor's principles in industry, where he claimed, for instance, that "followers of Frederick W. Taylor" had "made almost a religion out of his ideas," though, nevertheless, "nobody can deny that this revolutionary movement has introduced most valuable suggestions which the industrial world cannot afford to ignore."[107]

Münsterberg applied his immense knowledge of psychophysical experimentation to industrial organization, training, and testing in his work on psychotechnics. His primary concern—and that of psychotechnics more broadly—is to "analyze definite economic tasks with reference to the mental qualities which are necessary or desirable for them," and "to find methods by which these mental qualities can be tested."[108] This necessitated that one "construct experimental conditions" to be executed in a "measurable way," such that the "psychical part of the vocational work" is "schematized, and is simply rendered experimentally on a reduced scale."[109] To this end, one had the choice to either break up the industrial task into definite psychological elements that could be simulated and measured, which had "at its disposal all the familiar methods of experimental psychology," *or* one had to simulate the conditions of the mental states required for the task in their entirety.[110] For these "industrial tasks," it was "just this unity" of the "total process" that was the "essential condition," and therefore, "testing of the mental elements" would be "insufficient as if we were to test a machine with reference to its parts only and not with reference to its total unified performance."[111] In other words, technical questions had to be viewed as questions of semiotechnics, Bildung, and aesthetics. The "unified performance" of the machine was associated with "complex unified" combinations of "attention, imagination and intelligence, will and memory," and could be simulated by psychophysical measurement, trained mechanically, and described as a relationship between discontinuous mechanical movements and continuous results.[112] Moreover, these essential features of mental life that could be reproduced mechanically under experimental conditions were not only the defining properties of the educated subject but precisely those properties Münsterberg located as cinematic in *The Photoplay.*

The line of reasoning drawn from his psychophysical experimentation to cinema is strengthened in his work with streetcar operators.[113] In pursuit of "transportational safety" (*Verkehrssicherheit*), he was tasked with establishing tests for evaluating the accident-proneness of drivers based on their mental capabilities as a total cognitive disposition and training.[114] The preparation needed to avoid potentially deadly accidents was not a matter of whether one had individual shortcomings, was "diligent or lazy, honest or dishonest, obedient or insubordinate, sober or prone to drink."[115] Instead, it relied on a total, continuous psychological state that emerged—like subjective identification with cinematic narrative superseding any individual frame—from sequences of operations.

> These extraordinarily uneven aptitudes alone should be determined through laboratory experiments to avoid accidents by streetcar conductors. Then again, however, it does not reside in experiments with merely arbitrarily constituted apparatuses, but rather the method itself must first be put to the test through the comparison of real technical performances of the individuals. The apparatus was considered appropriate, because it yielded a characteristic variety of results between such train conductors who had established themselves as effective and those for whom small accidents were common. Only on the basis of this interdependence did it appear valid to recommend that the employment of electrical streetcar conductors be made dependent on these or similar psychological tests. . . . *It was even recommended that cinematographic images be used as stimuli for this purpose.*[116]

Such tasks demanded an integration of multiple cognitive mechanisms that could not be measured independently but presumably demanded an integration that could be tested cinematographically. To become the kind of psyche that could recognize the schematization of the tasks required to operate a streetcar when presented cinematically meant that one would have to be able to identify with the representational space offered by the images. No doubt the testing was conducted through psychophysical stimulation, but it was not a purely mechanical-physiological exercise. It also demanded that the stimuli be legible to participants at the level of representation—understanding, for instance, differences between street signs, distinctions between elements on the track, and making predictions about the trajectories of objects in their field of vision as they might potentially impact their future course. The inference was that the new experimental subject, who was also the worker under the conditions of a Taylorist division of labor, was a cinematographic one. The subjective unity in question was at once mechanical, sequenced, and testable. But it was also semiotic, representational, and autonomous—just like the cinema itself, which had brought these two previously disparate areas of investigation into contact.

Münsterberg was not alone in these cinematically informed observations. There had already been other filmic engagements with industrial efficiency, some of which were conducted by Taylor. The film-based experiments of the greatest historical importance, drawing upon the principles established by Taylor (but ultimately acting as a source of competition and irritation), were conducted by the engineer Frank Gilbreth and his wife, psychologist Lillian Gilbreth.[117] Among their vast contributions to the fields of scientific management and scientific psychology, their definitive legacy was established through their motion studies. One of the first and longest of these was published in a large book on methods of bricklaying.[118] The analytic method called a "micro-motion study" involved "filming a worker's operations against a cross-sectioned background while a chronometer within the motion picture camera's field of vision counted time."[119] Gilbreth would use a magnifying glass to examine the filmstrip and determine the length of time required for each distinct movement, then compare them to other methods he had filmed and synthesize an optimal sequence through editing. As Brian Price and others note, this was a source of ire among labor unions who saw these methods as tactics of management to speed up the pace of production. The Gilbreths countered that their methods in fact only made movements more efficient rather than faster and eliminated the subjective judgments of management. Whether or not their concern was genuine, both publicly advocated for workers, intending to rehumanize the industrial workplace and maximize the benefit to laborers. Lillian Gilbreth expressed as much when she wrote in praise of scientific studies of production:

> By separation of the individual work, not only is the man's work itself shown, but at the same time the work of all other people is separated. . . . The man has not only an opportunity to concentrate, but every possible incentive to exercise his will and his desire to do things. His attention is concentrated on the fact that he as an individual is expected to do his very best. He has the moral stimulus of responsibility. He has the emotional stimulus of competition. He has the mental stimulus of definiteness.[120]

The premise of her appeal was that by reemphasizing the individual within a production sequence, the dignity of work was recovered from the monotony and facelessness of industrial labor. In this view, individuality once again becomes a function of the degree to which industrial sequence is internalized as the defining feature of one's subjective identification. Fittingly, the motion studies submitted the idiosyncratic irregularities of human production to filmic study, recombining movements as if on an editing table, which were then to serve as a renewed source of individual "authenticity."

This was, however, only after one adopted the filmic organizational logic of production as the means and measure of the value of one's work. Claims about the humanizing—understood as "individualizing"—capacity of industrial film experiments were made in contradistinction to the observations of German contemporaries in the field of scientific management. Karl Bücher, who was long in conversation with everyone from Taylor to Münsterberg to Wundt, wrote, with respect to the rhythm imposed by mechanical work:

> The human worker is no longer the master of his movements, the tool his servant, his enhanced appendage. Rather the tool has become his master. It dictates the measure of his movements. The tempo and duration of his work has been stripped of his will. He is shackled to a dead and equally living mechanism.[121]

Mechanization of labor here is nothing less than an inversion of the relationship between cultural production and commercial production. As Bücher analyzes, prior to nineteenth-century industrialism, work was controlled, narrativized, and made a part of collective life through its regulation by song. However, after the scientific and filmic regulation of industrial production, the rhythm of labor and the rhythm and pace of vision were imposed by an apparatus. The expression of one's "individuality" was thus, as the Gilbreths argued, at worst a quantitative measure of efficiency, and at best a unique mechanical sequence. It was not simply that the symbolic unity of the self had been replaced by a machine. The case was seemingly much worse. Machines were theorized as now producing a symbolic unity that stripped the individual of all her previous magical or ensouled properties. It is no wonder then that one of the first genres to employ diegetic editing techniques was industrial film.

In the period between one-act varieté presentations and more developed narrative techniques in the 1910s, industrial cinema introduced forms of diegetic closure that were a function of mechanized labor. A convincing example of this is the 1902 Edison Films production *Loading Ice onto Trucks*. Of this film and others shot between 1901 and 1902 in Groton, Massachusetts, Charles Musser has argued that they were "principally actuality subjects" consisting of "several shots taken at approximately the same time and place," even if they allowed the producer to "perform an editorial function as well."[122] Yet what is interesting about this "editorial function" is that it was dictated entirely by the industrial process being depicted. So, for instance, *Loading Ice onto Trucks* begins with a worker shoveling ice onto an ascending conveyor belt, cuts to a scene from the top of the hill of loaded railway cars descending toward ships and trucks, then cuts to a final scene of the ice trucks arriving and unloading the now blocked ice to put on ships. The logic of the editing is provided by the industrial sequence. These cuts' diegetic function relies on a prior education in the processes by which ice was made and the order of industrial production sequences. What the film institutes mentally, by producing an identification on the part of the viewer (however minimal), is the Taylorist division of labor itself.

Ignoring the fact that the film is overloaded with self-reflexive cinematic tropes, such as the railroad and the conveyor belt—to which Kittler compared film in his analysis of Münsterberg, and Benjamin associated with the history of cinematic training—it creates a clean line of reasoning from industrial sequence, to film, to the mental function of the viewer. Not only does the film train the eye to see movement, but the mind is trained to reproduce its own education as a part of divided labor. This recalls Max Horkheimer and Theodor W. Adorno's much later observation of circumstances that found their origins with Edison.

> The familiar experience of the moviegoer, who perceives the street outside as a continuation of the film he just left, because the film seeks strictly to reproduce the world of everyday perception, has become the guideline of production. The more densely and completely its techniques duplicate empirical objects, the more easily it creates the illusion that the world outside is a seamless extension of the one which has been revealed in the cinema.[123]

In this respect, one could consider the entire history of film as a psychotechnical evolution toward an industrialized, semiotechnical form of

Bildung. One need only think of Louis Lumière's 1895 film *La Sortie des usines Lumière à Lyon* (Workers leaving the Lumière factory), showing workers unceremoniously exiting the Lumière factory, who would later become the audience for the very same film. Workers were trained as cinematic subjects and cinemagoers were trained to return to the factory.

Particularly in the case of Edison Films, the nexus between the training of cinematic viewers and the psychotechnical training of workers is more than a cultural metaphor. By 1906 the Edison Company had undertaken an effort to produce educational films for use in schools instead of theaters and had even developed a lab for testing the educational efficacy of films with schoolchildren.[124] By 1912 Thomas Edison had also developed a small-gauge 5.7mm film projector for educational use and a series of educational films about the Revolutionary War as well as a number of government films with heavy financial support from none other than Henry Ford.[125] On December 9, 1914, a fire, started by film stock, resulted in the total destruction of Edison's educational facilities and nearly all the educational films.[126] Despite the crippling misfortune of what Edison had called his "Educational Library," and what was arguably his "chief interest in the motion pictures," he continued to evangelize for the new medium as the future of training and education.[127] In a 1913 interview, he claimed that film would eventually replace books in educating the populous, and particularly the poor.

> The motion picture is the great education of the poorer people. It incites their imagination by bringing the whole world before their eyes. It sets spectators thinking and raises their standard of living. . . .
>
> Books will soon be obsolete in the public schools. Scholars will be instructed through the eye. It is possible to teach every branch of human knowledge with the motion picture. Our school system will be completely changed inside of ten years.
>
> We have been working for some time on the school pictures. We have been studying and reproducing the life of the fly, mosquito, silk weaving moth, brown moth, gypsy moth, butterflies, scale and various other insects, as well as chemical crystallization. It proves conclusively the worth of motion pictures in chemistry, physics and other branches of study, making the scientific truths, difficult to understand from text books, plain and clear to children.[128]

The sense of competing media-educational regimes was not only implied in Edison's actualities but was a primary impetus for his involvement in film in the first place. He aggressively advanced the idea of a "film library" to supplant existing libraries and found reading unsatisfactory for new demands and social conditions. Not only did film ostensibly change access to knowledge, but there was also a fundamental change in the status *of* knowledge starting in the nineteenth century. Knowledge as a matter of subject formation had become cinematic, not least of all because film had become synonymous with science, producing evidence of physical processes that were invisible without cinematographic technologies. More important than the subjects of the films, however, were the modes of learning entailed by the medium. That it incited the "imagination" by "bringing the whole world before [one's] eyes" and made "scientific truths" "plain and clear" suggests that film was seen as a form of unmediated exposure to the principles that undergirded the visible world and that could not be translated into text. This was different than an emphasis on firsthand observation because film showed the viewers something more primary than the event itself by assembling it according to a cinematographic logic that was equal measures real and imaginary. As a result, the internal logic of the film became the internal logic of the audience, unencumbered by the difficult hermeneutics required by texts. In a moment of mounting frustration in the face of skeptical questions about his educational objectives, Edison responded in an interview:

> Did it ever occur to you that people don't like to be educated by force? My suggestion of education by means of film was taken too literally. People had an idea that film education might be crammed down their throats. That was not my intention at all. The eventual picture—the popular film of the distant future—will have what we might call an educational tone. It will not be labeled educational.[129]

Edison's bristling rebuttal reinforces a sense of film's subtlety in the transformation of educational processes. One can only resist what is perceptible, and his notion that the popular films of the future would only have an "educational tone" meant that the viewers of the future would no longer be confronted with the propaedeutic effects of the medium because they would have already assimilated them.

The integration of industrial production and viewership as both modes of managerial efficiency and psychological engineering found obvious expression in partnerships between manufacturers and film firms. "Assembly" took on a number of meanings in these instances, referring to the creation of consumer goods and the individuals who made them. In the early twentieth century, in both Europe and the United States, it became popular practice to hire film firms to produce films depicting the wonders of modern industrial production and also to use films as training manuals for workers. The Edison Company, as but one instance, established a department of commercial films, headed by Fred Abbott, and in 1915 announced its partnership with Ford Motor Company—"Fordism" obviously being synonymous with rationalized, sequential, industrial production. About the films, the *Edison Kinetogram* reported that Abbott

> is in Detroit, with a party of Edison players working on a sociological film for the Ford Motor Company. The picture is to be educational in that it will show how the Ford organization takes the raw, ignorant foreigner and, through their settlement and allied institutions, makes him over into a highly desirable citizen.[130]

The nexus between film, industrial rationalization, and subject formation could not be more explicit, nor more racist and vulgar. The film was to turn the raw, unprocessed materials of new immigrants into not only socialized, integrated workers but also citizens. What the Edison Company had in mind for the film was nothing short of an industrial form of Bildung that worked to cultivate individuals through their participation in sociocultural institutions. One expects at the beginning of the description of the Edison project that what will be depicted in the film is the transformation of raw materials into finished consumer goods. However, in this description, the processes of manufacturing and socialization are not distinct, and film is conceived of as the ideal instrument for both. Here Benjamin's assertion that "what determines the rhythm of production on a conveyor belt is the same thing that underlies the rhythm of reception in film" seems not to have been an abstract theorization of modern life as much as an observational statement about real developments in industrial production.[131]

Industrial films similar to Edison's at the Ford Company were not limited to the United States but had become a standard practice in Europe by the mid-1910s as well. Carmakers were, not surprisingly, some of the most avid adopters of manufacturing films, perhaps because their products were also symbols of technological modernity, and their factories were early advocates of scientific management and assembly lines. The German automobile manufacturer Opel produced *Blick in ein Automobilfabrik* (1910), an often disorienting reenactment of the production sequence in the assembly of a car; Oskar Messter worked with Daimler to make *Der Werdegang eines Daimlermotors* (1912); and between 1917 and 1920, the Gaumont Film Company made *Aux Usines Renault* (1920), a documentary depicting steps in the manufacturing process from raw materials to finished product.[132] Like the Edison films of ice-cutting and the "naturalization" film at the Ford factory, these films were designed to capture the interest of audiences and instruct them in the processes by which industrial goods were produced. In these films, the human body remained "the most important reference point for industrial moving pictures," but as Martin Loiperdinger also notes of a film about a beer factory, *Hopfen und Malz, Gott Erhalt's! Ein Rundgang durch die Brauerei Binding in Frankfurt am Main* (1910), and echoing Karl Bücher, "it is immediately clear that the work rhythm is determined by the speed of the filling machine" and that "the workers conform to the machine."[133]

According to traditional film scholarship, these films would not be called "narrative," although they employ key elements of narrative filmmaking. They did not "reproduce the temporal course of a trip," instead using the "process of production from raw material to finished product as their dramatic framework."[134] The time of the process was also obviously "compressed," as Loiperdinger notes, meaning that the industrial causality of the manufacturing process was turned into a function of filmic narrativity. Industrial films required some level of subjective identification with the space of the film to produce a coherent logical sequence out of the spatiotemporally dislocated moments that the film linked together. They therefore seemed to train their viewers in a logic of production that was indistinguishable from their logic of spectatorship, turning their viewers into workers, and workers into viewers. There was always the possibility, however, that these new semiotechnical evolutions in the education of the machine psyche could go wrong. In the next chapter, we will look at how cinematic semiotechnics came to structure not just the formation of the healthy psyche but notions of pathology as well.

5

The Cinema of Afflictions

> It was odd, it had already occurred to him many times in these past days: he was thoroughly incapable of thinking what he wanted, he had no control over his thoughts. They ran as they wanted and despite his resistance, they were inclined to linger on ideas that tormented him. It was as if his brain were a kaleidoscope in which the alternation of images was controlled by a foreign hand.
>
> —Hermann Hesse, *Klein und Wagner*

Histories of madness in modernity have had their own fixations. Fascination with the nightless din of city life and the asynchronous pounding of machine rhythms lent itself to an all-too-literal metaphor of psychological illness as mechanical "breakdown." The machine age was marked by powerful regularities whose failures produced equally powerful accidents of unprecedented violence from which the psychophysiological machine was not exempt. In the famous opening passages to *The Man without Qualities,* Robert Musil captured the electrified milieu that gave rise to such comparisons between technological and psychological breakdown. He described the mechanical hum of an August 1913 day in Vienna that would soon give way to a truck accident.

> Like all big cities it was made up of irregularity, change, forward spurts, failures to keep step, collisions of objects and interests, punctuated by unfathomable silences; made up of pathways and untrodden ways, of one great rhythmic beat as well as the chronic discord and mutual displacement of all its contending rhythms.[1]

As if a scaled model of Brownian motion, the competing cadences of machines were analyzable only through their statistical regularities. Neither the city, with the vehicles careening through its streets, nor the subjects who experienced the riot of stimuli were irreducible entities. They were all seen as machines of varying scales, assembled from mechanisms regulated by their own harmonized intervals from which emerged a continuity—something unified, recognizable, autonomous, ontologically stable.

And then, as Musil describes, something breaks, "falling sideways with a crash."[2] A truck crash interrupts the apparent continuities and a crowd assembles. But no sooner has the bustle momentarily ceased than the accidental break has itself been assimilated into the mathematical uniformities defining modern life: "'According to American statistics,' the gentleman said, 'one hundred ninety thousand people are killed every year by cars and four hundred fifty thousand are injured.' 'Do you think he's dead?' his companion asked, still on the unjustified assumption that she had experienced something unusual."[3] Accidents were not essentially different from normal functions.[4] They could be explained according to the same principle of operation from which they seemed to deviate. This was as true for the milling machine as it was for the psychophysiological apparatus.

Musil, whose PhD examinations took on Hermann Ebbinghaus and Johann Friedrich Herbart, and whose 1908 dissertation was about the governing theories of the psychologist, physicist, and historian of science Ernst Mach, recognized the multitude of chaotic-seeming physical processes on which continuities were based.[5] Once all unities were viewed as emergent properties of machine intervals, aberrations also became quantitative, measurable, and patterned. The much-fetishized "breaks" and "ruptures" that have characterized a belief in the trauma of modernity were not fundamentally different from the droning and periodic eruptions of the machines that supposedly produced them.

The quantified, incrementalized character of supposedly irregular states was nowhere clearer than in attempts to come to terms with psychological anomalies. The effort at the end of the nineteenth century to create a definitive, scientific classificatory system for diagnosing psychopathologies was an attempt to come to grips with this interdependence between mechanical concepts of continuity and discontinuity. Technical psychological engagements with the question of mental illness sought to find the appropriate point of intersection between operations in the real and the symbolic spaces they produced. On the one hand, psychopathologies had to be measurable like all other psychic states, demonstrating a quantifiable deviation from the norm. On the other hand, one had to account for how the psyche, as an apparatus, could create imagined experiences that were semiotically coherent at one level but also deemed abnormal. This was ultimately an issue of how the technics of the psyche produced their semiotic landscape, as even the wildest hallucinations had some level of internal coherence. As Jacques Lacan observed in his reflections on the nature of psychoses:

> What difference is there between what belongs in the imaginary or real orders and what belongs to the symbolic order? In the imaginary or real orders we always have more or less, a threshold, a margin, continuity. In the symbolic order every element has value through being opposed to another.[6]

Where did continuity come from if the imaginary was believed to be determined by the regularities of intervals in a machine?[7] Indeed, the notion of a "psychological break" only occurred at the level of the imaginary, though from a materialist perspective the problem had to reside in the psychic machine. In one way, the machine was working just fine, generating symbolically rich interpretations of the outer world and an imaginary subject position from which it was viewed. Nevertheless, something was wrong.

In what has been called the "continuity view" or "continuity model" supported by many nineteenth- and twentieth-century scientists who thought "*morbid phenomena* were quantitative variations of 'normal' mental functions," psychopathology became "a branch of normal psychology."[8] The competing view, if one is to broadly divide between camps, found that there are "psychological anomalies in the insane to which there is nothing analogous in the state health."[9] Even among adherents to the continuity model, however, the "emergence of a discontinuity model of mental illness prompted redefinition" and even a redoubling of the "continuity model."[10]

The necessity of finding a model of psychological continuity that accounted for the differences between profoundly disrupted psyches and healthy psyches was most pronounced in cases of paranoid and schizophrenic delusion. What paranoid hallucinations revealed, and particularly those of persecution from imagined external menaces, was a compensatory mechanism developed for the purpose of rationalizing the frightening chaos of seeming psychic disorder. An intensely unpleasant inner world could be explained through the hallucination of malevolent forces external to a patient that functioned, if not to soothe, then at least to make sense of the seeming irrationality of the experience. The pathological mechanism (whether megalomania, hallucination, or persecutory fantasy) actually worked to *reassert* a psycho-semiotic continuity, even where it was clearly at odds with what would be considered "normal."

The question then became: what means existed—beyond a mere social consensus—for scientifically distinguishing between rational and irrational hallucinations in a way that drew a clear line between the "normal" and the "pathological" when, as Georges Canguilhem famously claimed, the emergence of the latter category in the early nineteenth century was "only a quantitative variation"?[11] By focusing on two psycho-cinematic case studies, this chapter argues that both the problem and the solution frequently entailed disguised commitments to interval-based semiotechnical models of the psyche. The scientific psychologist and Wilhelm Wundt student Oswald Külpe described, for instance, the difference between regular and irregular hallucinations as a matter of discretization and transmission.

> The hallucinations in which subjective impressions falsely become objectivized are thereby characterizable as abnormal, pathological phenomena, because the normal delusions do not pass into them continuously, but are instead separated from them by the gap [*Kluft*] of unnoticed distinctions between stimuli.[12]

Discontinuity characterizes the normal psyche, as the healthy person at some level acknowledges the mediation and latency involved in the production of the hallucination. There is a "Kluft" that distinguishes representational space from the "real" and forces confrontation with the medial means for producing the experience. What irrational hallucinations lack is the *discontinuity* that marked the *continuous* psyche. Further, there is a subtle indication here of the medial regime properly suited to the definition of the healthy psyche. The normal psyche is structured, as Freud would claim later, by "words and concepts," not images. Images were the raw perceptual material, which underwent a process of organization and signification that defined a psyche's relation to the world. Conspicuously unmediated images, whose fact of having been transmitted from the sense organs remained concealed, were therefore deemed pathological, even when, or precisely because, they produced the illusion of continuity.

Consequently, theories of psychopathology were forced to navigate the technological premises for continuity and its role in differentiating the healthy from the pathological on the basis of how discretization occurred. The most salient of such technological models in the 1910s was the cinema, which had the demonstrated ability to produce coherent psychological states from discrete images but also visions of supreme irrationality and psychosis. In the process of coming to terms with modern conditions for psychological abnormality, psychologists became not only some of the first theorists of film but also early adopters of a purely operational, and one might even say "digital," model of mind.

In both of the case histories the chapter considers—one explored by the early psychoanalyst Viktor Tausk and the other undertaken by psychologist and cinema reformer Robert Gaupp—pathological "breaks" were no longer seen as purely interruptions of otherwise autonomous, normal subjects. Instead, pathological and normal states alike were the emergent properties of protocols for managing discrete mechanical operations. It was only in misrecognizing or failing to acknowledge the mechanical intervals underlying the experience of continuity, whether subjective or cinematic, that a state could be said to be pathological. To believe in unmediated access to the real was by its very nature a delusion. This was an essentially digital problem, as it reduced the qualitative distinctions between healthy and sick, normal and pathological, experience and hallucination to a matter of discrete alternations. Its epistemological foundation during the 1910s, however, was film, as both the psycho-mechanical model of mind and the devices used to evaluate it were cinematic.

Case 1: Viktor Tausk

The dialectic between the machine and the human psyche has been a generative core of film theory since its beginning. One of the clearest articulations of this opposition was offered in 1922 by Dziga Vertov, who in his call for a cinema that captured "the perfect electric man" declared that the "psychological" interfered with the "desire for kinship with the machine."[13] Existing films, he argued, aped the conventions of older media and subordinated the "poetry of machines" to the obsolete symbolic unity of the "bungling citizen," who had emerged historically as a product of literary training.[14] The "poetry of levers, wheels, and wings of steel" was incommensurate with the poetry of the written word, and the cinematic viewer of the future—himself a reflection of the precise orders of industrial mechanisms—was fundamentally at odds with the older, silently reading subject of the Bildungsbürgertum.[15] For Vertov, the opposition between the visibility of the machine and the psychological identification of the viewer was clearly motivated by a Marxist program that regarded subjective identification as a superstructural deception masking the conditions of production.[16]

Not limited to a Marxist theoretical prism, such insights have bridged the chasm between "classical film theories" and the "psychoanalytic-semiotic film theorizing in the late '60s."[17] Just as Vertov concluded that "psychology" masked the revolutionary potential of the cinematic machine, the apparatus theory of the 1970s, following Lacan, identified the disappearance of cinematic mechanisms as the sine qua non of its subject effects and the source of an ideological "fantasmatization of the subject."[18] What had long prevented psychoanalysis's union with film theory despite a lifetime of courtship was an entrenched opposition between the psychophysical apparatus and the psychological space of signification—an opposition that Lacan himself ingeniously identified in Freud.[19]

For Vertov, the "electric man" was the future; for Freud, he was the specter of a psycho-positivistic past. But what such a psychic apparatus, for all of its speculative efficacy, could not explain was how a subject emerged as a unified "I"—moving from a mechanistic physiology to a psychology, from psychophysics to psychoanalysis, or, in the case of cinema, from "attractions" to films with which the viewer psychologically identified. Lacan wrote of this transformation in Freud's work with an explicit nod to cybernetics.

> The subject sets itself up as operating, as a human, as *I*, from the moment the symbolic system appears. . . . To put it another way, for the human subject to appear, it would be necessary for the machine, in the information it gives, to take account of itself, as one unity among others. That is precisely the one thing it cannot do. To be capable of taking itself into account, it would have to be something more than the machine it in fact is, because one can do anything, except get a machine to include itself as an element in a calculation.[20]

In psychoanalysis as in cinema, the machine was simultaneously a condition of possibility for and obstruction to subject formation. Indeed, in his 1899 *The Interpretation of Dreams,* Freud abandoned his mechanistic rendering of the psyche in favor of a symbolic one, just as the projector was being moved from the spectatorial space to a soundproof booth, hiding the noisy mechanisms responsible for the cinematic spectacle.[21] The affinity between psychoanalysis and film is, then, even more structurally profound than the simple proliferation of dreamlike sequences and psychoanalytic themes in the history of cinema implies. Cinema confronted psychoanalysis with an uncomfortable irreconcilability between the machine and the "psychological" that kept the two at an erotic distance until the mirror stage placed the real, material operations of a media technology at the center of the symbolic process of ego formation. The import of that innovation allowed the discrete, "disconnected" machinations of the psyche to be constituted as a "virtual unity," and for that same reason made way for a fruitful period of psychoanalytic film theory.[22]

Highly calibrated mechanical operations were clearly necessary for subjective identification with a narrative space, but their visibility had to be minimized or turned into a symbol governed by the rules of filmic diegesis.[23] As Friedrich Kittler observed, the "shutter and Maltese Cross" made "Lacan's *corps morcelé*" into a "matter of positive fact" that was synthesized as a subjective unity through the projected identification of the viewer.[24] Literature and poetry (against the poetry of machines envisaged by Vertov) had promised the subject a stabilizing sense of autonomy, one that had been previously "provided only in the imaginary space of reading" but was now, suddenly, "in the Real [*im Realen*] on screen."[25] At the same time, the attribution to film of this ego-forming power was rerouted back through language, so that Lacanian theories of filmic subject effects were wedded to the idea of film viewership as a form of "reading."[26] In Jean-Pierre Oudart's important essay "Cinema and Suture," for example, film was treated as a form of "énoncé" and its units of expression as "syntagms" governed by "syntactic procedures" that formed "semantic" unities.[27] Not only were the filmic procedures that enabled subjective identification framed linguistically; the very idea of "suture" transformed the technique for mending bodies into a textual operation regulating the syntagmatic workings of montage.[28] In short, the price of integrating psychoanalysis into film theory was that film was analyzed largely as a "textual system."[29]

Fifty years prior to the explosion of psychoanalytic film theory, however, Viktor Tausk, a lauded if controversial member of the Vienna Psychoanalytic Society, illuminated a path for reconciling the external, technological fact of cinema with its capacity for psychological identification in the absence of textual systems. In his now famous paper "On the Origin of the 'Influencing Machine' in Schizophrenia" (1919), he presented a psychoanalytic account of the mechanisms by which certain schizophrenic patients hallucinated persecution at the hands of complicated machines resembling magic lanterns or cinematographs that subjected them to a kind of cinematic spectacle.[30] His objective was certainly not to offer a psychoanalytic theory of the cinema, which remained a taboo object of investigation for Freudian analysts. But his intervention—against its own stated intentions—is arguably the first psychoanalytical theory of film.[31]

Tausk's paper made sense not only of the vexed relationship between machines and the semiotic operations of psychic life that harried Freud from the moment he abandoned his mechanical model of the psyche in 1895; it also did so for cases in which the affliction was cinematographic in nature.[32] Moreover, the mode of psychological identification that Tausk's paper describes did not rely—as did psychoanalytic theories of film from the 1970s and 1980s—on films being treated as texts. His paper can therefore be read as more than a psychoanalytic account of an idiosyncratic form of schizophrenia. It is an early confrontation with the media-technical operations of subject formation posed by the rapidly developing methods of narrative filmmaking in the 1910s.

Tausk's paper revealed a subtle shift in the medial regime governing ideas of subject formation, arguing that the influencing machine in question emerges precisely from a failure to develop the intellectual-linguistic faculty Freud believed responsible for defining the ego. Instead, it took its cue from maturing practices of narrative in early cinema. In fact, a model for the functions ascribed to the schizophrenic influencing machine was evident in the films Tausk was likely watching in Vienna. One film in particular, Léonce Perret's *The Mystery of the Rocks of Kador* (*Le Mystère des roches de Kador,* 1912), presented the possibility of cinema as a psychotherapeutic remedy for psychological rupture, showcasing its power to manufacture the psychological spaces that were denied to machines. By meditating on both filmic diegesis and psychological autonomy as the result of the same mechano-filmic operations, the film demonstrated the psychological ramifications of narrative cinema to which Tausk could only cautiously allude.

Movie Night at the Asylum

By the time Tausk presented his now famous paper on the influencing machine, case histories detailing hallucinations of persecutory machines and captivation by malevolent, invisible forces already had an established legacy in psychological literature. At the Bethlem Royal Hospital in London, John Haslam compiled the writings of James Tilly Matthews, who was committed to the asylum in 1797 and believed he was subject to a nefarious "air loom" apparatus, which among other things supplanted his thoughts with "magnetic impregnations," or administered control by way of "rays," pneumatism, or a fantastical inventory of recondite gadgetry.[33] Freud, too, despite some reluctance and difficulty submitting schizophrenia to the psychoanalytic apparatus, offered an interpretation of the Daniel Paul Schreber case based largely on his autobiographical writings, in which Schreber claimed that he was manipulated by God and "little devils" alike—the influence of his tormentors being exacted by means of "light beams" as well as complex apparatuses such as the elegantly named "head-compressing machine" (*Kopfzusammenschnürungsmaschine*).[34]

In this respect, the schizophrenic delusions Tausk examines in his paper are a part of a familiar psycho-pathological history in which fantasies of technological menaces provide a supplementary, even hypertrophic technological rationality to account for the experience of psychological upheaval. The breach in the psychological autonomy of the afflicted is explained through the introduction of a machine, which represents rationality par excellence. As a figure of order, discretization, sequence, and materiality, the schizophrenic machine is a metastasis of faith in technology and empiricism that relocates the seat of rationality to technological protocols that one believes present wherever the thunder of moving parts is heard from behind a burnished metal surface. In turn, the logic of thought is elided with the logic of the machine. Because the patient's internal order has been lost, mechanical order is deployed. Yet these machines are not timeless and the character of delusions of mechanical influence is determined by the logic of the period-specific storage and communication technologies that regulate general understandings of space and time, something Kittler keenly observed of Schreber, whose "paranoid machine" operated "like an integrated system of all the data-storage devices that revolutionized recording circa 1900."[35] This is also true in nonpathological cases, of course, as the normal workings of the psyche have been variously conceived according to technological heuristics such as ROM, RAM, telescopic lenses, telegraphic wires, search algorithms, mystic writing pads, and magic lanterns.

The schizophrenic condition Tausk describes is one in which patients suffer from the delusion that they are under the influence of, and often persecuted by, "a machine of a mystical nature," the construction of which they can only "hint at vaguely."[36] Nevertheless, they endeavor to explain its design through recourse to their "available technical knowledge," which Tausk attributes to the "progressive popularization of the sciences."[37] In its final stages, the influencing apparatus takes on an incomprehensibly complex character consisting of "boxes, cranks, levers, wheels, buttons, wires, batteries, and the like," most often operated by a male figure and usually someone of intellectual or medical distinction, such as a professor or physician.[38] One of the most remarkable effects of the apparatus is that it "makes the patients see pictures, appearing on a single plane, on walls, or windowpanes, which are not three-dimensional like typical visual hallucinations."[39] In these instances, the machine is generally identified as a "magic lantern" or "cinematograph," though Tausk soon abandons the cinematograph, and all later mentions of the projection technology refer only to a "magic lantern."[40] Beyond the type of projection device and the two-dimensionality of its images, Tausk provides almost no detail about the nature of the "pictures" the patients experienced when under the apparatus's influence, and we are left to infer from the pathological function ascribed to them what kinds of images they were. He tells us in broad terms that the appearance of the influencing machine "originates in a demand for causality that is immanent to humankind" and that its emergence is partially attributable to the "development of a delusion of influence [*Beeinflussungswahn*]" deriving from the rediscovery of "old libidinal images."[41] The images produced by the influencing machine, and the delusion of the apparatus itself, return to more developmentally primitive images in order to restore a fundamental sense of logical coherence that had been interrupted in the ego's developmental process. Yet a question persists about the machine's etiology and why the magic lantern or cinematograph recurred as a suitable means for supplanting the lost psychical order.

Deferring to Freud's 1914 analysis "On Narcissism," Tausk identifies this peculiar form of schizophrenia as a problem of narcissistic regression, locating the beginnings of the condition in a possible point of fixation during a stage of innate narcissism to which the patient later returns.[42] Prior to the ego's self-identification as a distinct psychical unit—a period of "objectlessness"—all stimuli are experienced as endogenous.[43] In order to guard against the appearance of undisguised fantasies and to preserve psychic autonomy, the ego of the child must somehow jettison foreign sensations and therefore project an image of his/her own body to account for feelings that cannot be explained through purely internal means. Called a "delusion of influence," the condition emerges from a disrupted sense of causality in which the sources of sensations or ideas must be invented. The ego then has to disguise the true nature of this pathological projection through a series of transmutations that turn the projected image of the patient's own body into a foreign and inscrutable machine. To describe the result, Tausk coins the important phrase "loss of ego-boundaries" (*Verlust der Ichgrenzen*): it is precisely because the patient is unable to properly invest external objects with a causal significance and to devise a frontier between the inner and outer world that he or she has to project the body as the origin of externally caused sensations.[44] In other words, the ego manufactures a pathological form of autonomy by transforming an estranged experience of the body into an image of an external, mechanical tormentor. Or, as Tausk writes, "The ego finds itself facing the task of mastering an insane outer world, and hence behaves insanely."[45]

Tausk was well aware that Freud had already offered a similar analysis of the mechanics of "projection" at work in the Schreber case.[46] Freud argued that the "most striking characteristic of symptom formation in paranoia" is what he termed "projection," in which an "internal perception is suppressed" and, "after undergoing a certain degree of distortion, enters consciousness in the form of an external perception."[47] Yet no sooner had he acknowledged the importance of projection than he immediately began to walk it back, writing:

> Having thus been made aware that more general psychological problems are involved in the question of the nature of projection, let us make up our minds to postpone the investigation of it (and with it that of the mechanism of paranoiac symptom formation in general) until some other occasion.[48]

Perhaps what is so threatening about recognizing the role of projection in a larger field of pathological symptomatologies is the realization that the discrete operations of machines might be sufficient on their own for drawing ego boundaries in the absence of external object finding—sufficient, that is, in the absence of language, which shores up the distinction between the ego and its surroundings by allowing the external world to signify internally.

The function Freud attributes to "projection" in the paranoid patient bears immediate resemblance to the way in which Tausk's patients seek to reassert ego boundaries by suppressing evidence of the difference between perception and hallucination—internal and external stimuli. But it also sounds a lot like Christian Metz's much later reckoning with the mirror stage identification of the viewer in the cinema, which confuses primary and secondary identification. On the one hand, Metz writes, the subject "knows he is at the cinema."[49] There is a stable semiotic space of the ego that experiences a secondary identification under conditions of darkness in front of an illuminated screen. On the other hand, the viewer identifies with "himself as a pure act of perception" like a child in a "sub-motor and hyper-perceptive state" that, unlike the original mirror stage, "returns everything but ourselves."[50] Both in terms of its primary nature as a perception and because the delusion has to obfuscate the body image by transforming it into an incomprehensible machine, the influencing machine initiates the same situation described by Metz. It does so as a substitute for a stable, preexisting ego governed by the workings of language. Indeed, the cases of schizophrenia that troubled Freud, and with which Tausk dealt so deftly, involved a failure of ego boundaries. But they also plausibly involved the successful reparation of those boundaries through images alone. Kittler observed that all media "dismember the narcissism underlying a unified conception of the body."[51] As the immense proliferation of early films about doppelgängers suggests, however, cinema also reasserted an ego unity where it was impossible to "derive [*herauslesen*] doubles—that is, possibilities of identification—from letters alone."[52] Cinema offered both a mirror image without a body and ego autonomy without language, stealing literature's pride of place in matters of subject formation.

The re-presentation of a psychological space in the absence of the body was a form of identification particular to film. Jean-Louis Baudry and Alan Williams describe the disruptions to identification with filmic diegesis, writing, "We should remember, moreover, the disturbing effects which result during a projection from breakdowns in the recreation of movement, when the spectator is brought abruptly back to discontinuity—that is, to the body, to the technical apparatus which he had *forgotten.*"[53] One gets the sense not only that the pathological image machine is adequate to the task of establishing ego boundaries and repressing countervailing material that might threaten to disrupt them but also that it does so cinematically.

In the single complete case history that Tausk includes, he describes how the apparatus evolves from an image of the body to obscure its own origins as a projection of the patient herself. The patient, Frl. Natalija A., a former student of philosophy, and therefore a woman possessing a mature linguistic faculty, is persecuted by an "electrical machine made in Berlin" that "had been prohibited by the police."[54] This forbidden machine produces two-dimensional images, and even an image of the apparatus itself, which are not visibly related to the repressed body relations from which they emerge.

> At the very beginning the patient reported that the limbs appeared on the apparatus in their natural form and position. Several weeks later, however, she explained that the limbs were drawn on the lid [of the apparatus]. I am now of the opinion that what I witnessed here was a significant developmental stage in the emergence of the delusion [*Wahngebildes*]. It clearly involves the progressive distortion of the apparatus, such that, part-by-part, it eventually loses all human characteristics and becomes a typical, unintelligible, influencing machine.[55]

The exteriorization of foreign sensations through a projection of the body is not sufficient on its own to produce an autonomous ego. It must be coupled with successive distortions that render the mechanics of the process invisible. For the illusion of influence to succeed and, in turn, to produce ego boundaries and satisfy the inherent "demands for causality" (*Kausalitätsbedürfnisse*), the apparent logic of the apparatus and its relation to the patient must become "unintelligible" (*unverständlich*).[56] This is different from suggesting that the workings of the machine are *illogical.* Instead, the transformation of the body image into an incomprehensible machine institutes a logic that is both impenetrable to "available technical knowledge" while also making sense of the ego's troubling experience and mollifying a general anxiety about causality.

Tausk argues that thoughts and images must first be assimilated into the "consciousness of ego unity" before they can become a part of the "automatic ego function" and that this cannot occur until "the intellect has advanced to the stage of memory representations [*Erinnerungsvorstellungen*]."[57] Here, the intellectual faculty is inseparable from the later capacity for concepts and language that presuppose the ego's distinction from the outer world. In order to generate the abstract linguistic associative networks by which representations or images achieve an order and significance beyond their mere inclusion in or exclusion from the inner world, the original images must be properly marked or cathected according to their relationship with a definite subject. Thus, Tausk's analysis reasserts a Freudian subordination of images to language with the assumption that images cannot become meaningful or participate in the ego unity until the intellect is developed enough to intervene and make sense of them. This requires that the images occur as "memory representations," meaning that it is the intellect and its deployment of language that gives them their temporal situation as memories, and likewise, their significance as uniquely a part of an autonomous ego. It is orthodox for Tausk to claim that the images are integral to the intellect's preservation of ego boundaries but not that they are sufficient on their own to invent them—and that is what makes Tausk's analysis so suspiciously cinematic and semiotechnical.

Editing the Ego

There is good reason to think that Tausk's interest in cinema was hiding in plain sight. Unlike Freud, who was unapologetic about his allergy to film, Tausk was an enthusiastic cinemagoer. Lou Andreas-Salomé confirms this in a February 1913 diary entry from her time studying psychoanalysis under Freud.

> Tausk, the boys, and I indulged ourselves in a somewhat similar pleasure at the Urania Theater. Indeed the cinema has played absolutely no small role for us—about which this is not the first time I have had cause for contemplation. Included in the many things one can say in defense of this Cinderella of aesthetic judgment are a couple of purely psychological considerations. One of these pertains to the fact that it is only filmic technologies that make possible the rapid image succession that comes close to approximating our own powers of imagination, whose erraticness [*Sprunghaftigkeit*] it also imitates to a certain extent.[58]

While the cinema represented a simple "pleasure" in which they periodically indulged as a kind of family outing, the entry suggests a more substantial, shared interest in film's technical approximation of psychic operations. The "purely psychological considerations" film solicits stem not only from an analogy between the illusion produced by the succession of images and the mental "powers of imagination" but also from the "erraticness" of both experiences. Films of this period, with their jerky imperfections and inchoate continuity editing, captured something of the hallucinatory character of the imagination and therefore a pathological form of ego formation. It does not require much extrapolation to claim that film in this account would provide a model for ego operations where the sovereignty of the imagination was uncontested by encounters with objects in reality, namely in the cases of schizophrenia. The entry substantiates a familiarity on Tausk's part with how films worked and perhaps even an interest in their affinity with mental processes that had been established by psychologists like Max Wertheimer and Hugo Münsterberg.[59] Such affinities would be repressed in his decision to write only of the older magic lantern and later to dismiss the relevance of its operations to psychoanalysis altogether.

Tausk was a faithful and talented disciple of psychoanalysis whom Freud described as "clever and dangerous" (*gescheit und gefährlich*), a fact perhaps not unrelated to his time spent at the Kino.[60] Freud's suspicions about the threat Tausk posed to psychoanalysis did not result from the latter's strident revolt. On the contrary, unlike that of Alfred Adler or Carl Jung, Tausk's fraught relationship with Freud stemmed not from a break with the master but from the strength of his allegiance. Given Tausk's avowed commitment to Freud and the latter's harsh censure, Tausk's paper lends itself to being read the way one reads "writers who hold heterodox views" and who in turn write "between the lines."[61] A coup against the standard Freudian understanding of the psyche is legible, even if it was inadvertent or actively repressed. To obscure the possibility that filmic images could reassert ego boundaries in the absence of language, Tausk goes to great lengths to hide the cinematographic operations of the influencing machine, which would undermine "Freud's method of detecting unconscious signifiers in oral discourse" and of interpreting them "as letters of a grand rebus or syllable puzzle."[62] What Tausk suggests is not only that media-technological operations fundamentally alter the function and understanding of the psyche but, more problematically still, that these operations could be cinematic.

The advent of long-format narrative cinema offered a powerful epistemic challenge to the medial logic of the "talking cure," reconfigured as a kind of "watching cure." While Tausk's double movement of theorization and disavowal regarding the nature of the cinematic device is likely a response to Freud's low opinion of the cinema and irritation at its nagging relevance, it is also an oblique recognition of the challenge such an argument for ego formation based on images posed to the foundations of psychoanalysis.[63] The technological operations of the hallucination, it turned out, were more important than the fact that one was hallucinating. The notion that a perceptual apparatus like the cinematograph could invent an autonomous psychological space exhumed a long-buried psychophysical model of the psyche by resolving an opposition between the machine and the psychological.

It has been long acknowledged that filmic narrative is achieved by substituting spatiotemporal uniformity with editing practices that rely on spatial and temporal discontinuities between individual images. The flow of perceived time is parsed into frames and shots that are then reassembled to create continuities according to conventions of filmic montage. Film is theorized as delimiting a continuous diegetic space not in spite of but because of its negative relationship to the "typical" experience of space and time, such that, as Stephen Heath noted, "fragmentation" becomes "the condition of a fundamental continuity."[64] Much like the two-dimensional images experienced by the patients in Tausk's paper, there is a distinction between the continuity of lived experience and the narrative coherence that arises though the continuous presentation of temporally dislocated, two-dimensional images in films. Viewed in this way, the serial presentation of images and their establishment of a diegetic space offer a relevant framework for understanding the potential reestablishment of ego boundaries by the schizophrenic image machine—and without recourse to the typical linguistic systems Tausk locates in the development of the intellect. The logic of images present in narrative films, which were maturing into a robust practice around the time of Tausk's paper, provide a timely counterexample to the presumed deficiencies of images in Tausk's commitment to a Freudian model of the psyche.

Tausk's treatment (or nontreatment) of the technical specificity of the influencing machine becomes a figure for his difficulties in reckoning with images' participation in the construction of ego boundaries and thus their potential role in structuring the ego. After commenting that the end-stage influencing machine is described by patients as either a "cinematograph" or "magic lantern," he quickly adds:

> From the very outset, we should disregard the magic lantern that produces the images, because its construction corresponds too well to the effects ascribed to it and demonstrates no error of reasoning beyond the fact that it does not exist.[65]

He continues by claiming that the "psychoanalyst cannot doubt for a moment that this machine *must* be a symbol," a fact he notes Freud had also emphasized.[66] In a telling reversal, it is more important to the psychoanalyst than the patient that the operations of these cinematic projection devices be consolidated as *symbols,* which belie their technological specificity and return them to the province of text. As a disciple of Freud, Tausk had to disavow the cinematic machine; he had to treat the workings of the image apparatus as a single symbolic element—the "machine"—that could be deciphered psychoanalytically. In a moment that seems to anticipate Freud's proscription, he notes: "Freud has explained in one of his lectures that complicated machines *always* represent the genitals in dreams."[67] His inclusion of "always," to the degree that it reveals his careful subservience, also indicates his awareness that the influencing machine did function as more than a symbol, though he was not at liberty to make that claim. The solipsistic lack of external reference among schizophrenics, which prohibited the development of a linguistic faculty capable of dealing adequately with symbols, appeared to render the simple symbolic interpretation of the influencing machine impossible.

Based on their involvement in the reassertion of some kind of ego boundary and their two-dimensionality (i.e., their distinction from regular visual input), one gets the sense that the images projected by the influencing machine are not arranged in a way that is "timeless," as is unconscious material as described by Freud, nor primarily structured by their insertion into the symbolic economy of the intellect, which Tausk already deemed insufficient for understanding its mysterious operations.[68] Freud attributed the difficulty in analyzing schizophrenics in part to the regression to old libidinal images prior to language, thereby isolating the problem of schizophrenia in *images.* As a result, any logic used to delimit a pathological psychological order would not have the "words and concepts" at its disposal that were believed to be essential for ego autonomy.[69] The surrogate logic would only have access to images. There is no doubt the magic-lantern-like hallucinations must do at least some of the work of maintaining ego continuity. However, it is the permanent cinemas of Vienna, not the fairground lanternists of the nineteenth century, that could explain how the schizophrenic could invent a psychological space of identification. Films shown in Vienna during the exact period of Andreas-Salomé's diary entry demonstrated an ability not only to produce subject effects with a diminishing reliance on intertitles but also to intervene actively in the process of subject formation and the reparation of ego boundaries.

Perhaps the most elegant metafilmic reflection on the process of identification described by Tausk was presented in Léonce Perret's 1912 film *The Mystery of the Rocks of Kador.* Shown to German-speaking audiences as *Ewige Zeugen* and opening in Viennese theaters only three months prior to Andreas-Salomé's reference to her visit with Tausk to the movies, the film was part of a burgeoning genre of psychological crime drama. It is the story of a young woman, Suzanne, who succumbs to hysteria after falling victim to her cousin's plot to defraud her of her inheritance and kill her lover, Captain d'Erquy. In the second part of the film, a Professor Williams is called upon to conduct an experimental treatment on Suzanne involving the "application of the cinematograph to psychotherapy." Thus begins the sequence of greatest interest, and one that captures the subversive significance of Tausk's paper for interpreting technologies' real and heuristic role in the development and understanding of psychic operations.

Professor Williams's method is to film a reenactment of the traumatic events that prompted the breakdown and to then re-present them to the afflicted patient, replacing the "talk" of the talking cure with a cinematic representation. The film cuts to the beach at the rocks of Kador and the site of the attempted murder, where the professor, acting as director and cameraman, loads film in the foreground. Importantly, the composition of the shot *does not* correspond to how it was originally presented in the earlier scenes of the events responsible for Suzanne's traumatic break. Instead, it shows the camera positioned in such a way that our original perspective on the scene is rendered legible to us—we see our earlier vantage point revealed from an extradiegetic position that is integrated into the unfolding diegesis. In other words, we are made extradiegetic witnesses to the creation of our own earlier identification with the subject position of the film while still remaining within the ever-widening boundaries of its narrative space. In Lacan's language, the cinematic machine does the one thing it "cannot do"; namely, it includes "itself as an element in a calculation" responsible for the production of an autonomous subject.[70] It makes a view of itself from the outside a part of its internal semiotic universe.

As the camera rolls and the captain reenacts having been shot on the shoreline, the film doubles down on the audience's commitment to the continuous space of the narrative by confronting us with the conditions for its production. Even the outside of the narrative is figured as a part of the diegesis, demonstrating the mastery of the filmic medium for manufacturing subject effects. We see, much like the appearance of the influencing apparatus in Tausk's paper, a fantastic exteriorization of the mechanics of our own experience, which, rather than having a demystifying effect, reinforce the logic of the illusion by expanding the scope of the diegesis to include its own outside. One might even say, following Tausk's analysis, that the film entails a narcissistic regression at the hands of a cinematographic machine operated by a psychologist who also happens to be a filmmaker.

The film then cuts to a laboratory doubling as a projection room, where together the captain and Professor Williams examine the filmstrip while assistants pull curtains, position the screen, and remove all indications of the constructed nature of the cinematic performance to come. Suzanne is led into the frame like an apparition divested of worldly agency, dressed in a long white gown, and is guided offscreen in preparation for her "therapy." Cutting on action to an empty, darkened room, the film shows Professor Williams seating Suzanne in a chair, clinically positioning her head to direct her vacant gaze toward the screen that bathes them partially in light emitted from beyond the frame. Williams withdraws into the background, effacing evidence of his influence, and the intertitle reads, "Look, Suzanne . . ." The therapeutic command of "listen" is replaced with looking. We then see only Suzanne's disembodied head, illuminated by the screen, and in a shot / reverse shot construction, Suzanne appears suspended in rapt attention to scenes from a trauma she *could not* have seen while unconscious on the beach. We understand this scene as Suzanne viewing a film rather than as the exteriorization of her mental state, in part because of the alternation of close-ups of her increasingly dismayed expressions with shots of her facing the floating images in the darkness, as well as our inference of a projector as the source of the light.

The mechanical conditions of possibility for both the diegetic and intradiegetic film are obscured. It is only the visual continuity effects of the film and the light of the intradiegetic projection that establish the causal connection between Suzanne and the images from Kador. In short, the film's own subject effects resolve the indeterminacy of her relationship to the projected images. As viewers already acclimated to the cinema, we know that these cannot be her memories, although this fact functions to strengthen instead of to attenuate the connection between cinematic and psychological continuity. Against a potential tendency to read this sequence as the therapeutic repetition of her traumatic experiences, it is apparent that the curative property of the cinematographic method resides in Suzanne's identification with the diegetic space of the film, which reasserts a narrative order such that the intradiegetic film *becomes* her interior state. Cinematic subject effects that neither replicate the seamlessness of lived experience nor re-present her actual memories nevertheless offer a restoration of psychological autonomy as a product of visual continuity, and Suzanne is healed.

Suzanne, however, is not the only spectatorial subject in question. In a moment reminiscent of the rube and Uncle Josh films from ten years earlier, Suzanne stands, desperately extending her arms toward the screen, as the lights come on, revealing the material conditions for the illusion but likewise, because we no longer see what she sees, suggesting that the narrative continuity of the images has been internalized. The comedic effect of rube films derived from seeing a supposedly provincial, film-illiterate spectator fail to recognize the filmic conventions of verisimilitude as a way of confirming the audience's own visual sophistication, or of training proper modes of viewership. In a similar fashion, Suzanne's affective response to the narrative space of the film, equated here with her psychological restoration ("She cries . . . she is saved"), thematizes and also participates in the elision of psychological continuity and filmic continuity. The cinematic reassertion of ego boundaries through the intervals of continuity editing, witnessed in a scene in which the mechanical origin of the projection is disguised, functions therapeutically to produce a subject position in Suzanne, even though, or especially because, it *could not have been her own.* It also serves therefore as an affirmation of the extradiegetic audience's own acclimation to the visual conventions of cinematic spectatorship, by showing us that the very ruse by which we are captivated is itself part of the film's subject effects. By allegorizing the success of filmic subject effects, perspectival stability, and narrative continuity as conditions of psychological coherence and autonomy, the film implies that Suzanne's restoration was actually a training in modes of cinematic spectatorship that were already integrated to the point of invisibility in the audience.

This mode of "subject formation" or "restoration" was, in fact, the adoption of, or subjection to, a male perspective, in the form of film spectatorship and psychoanalysis, both of which had histories of seeking to cure ailing women from overexposure to the nerve-shattering fugue of a modern urban experience and its man-made machines. Psychoanalysis substituted the narrative authority of inner monologue with the voice of the male analyst, and film responded to cultural anxieties about technological sensitivities that might morally compromise women—the term frequently used being "Frauenverblödung"—which, among other things, required special films suited to gendered educational demands. In each case, the threat and the narrative-structuring apparatus were male, dispossessing women of control over even their own illnesses. In all cases, however—from cinemagoers to analysands—the cultural implications were clear: cinematic semiotechnics had not only developed subject effects but had affected models of the subject, while successfully disguising its influence.

This was decidedly not the case for the magic lantern or similar devices favored by Tausk. By the time Tausk presented his paper on the influencing machine and Andreas-Salomé wrote of their trips to the cinema, magic-lantern shows, along with the spectacles of Johann Schröpfer's *Gespenstermacher,* lanterns of death, and traveling lanternists, were anachronisms preserved in the memory of a cultural consciousness occupied by cinemas with a permanent address and increasingly broad audiences. At the beginning of 1909, there were already sixty-two cinemas in Vienna; the Urania Theater, mentioned in Andreas-Salomé's diary, would add to the list in 1910.[71] The existence and multiplication of permanent theaters did not mean that cinema as an institution had legitimated itself aesthetically, nor that films of this time exemplified the narrative sophistication available in films from just a decade later. By and large, the films that Tausk saw at the Urania were not the short spectacles of variété performances but occupied a position with regard to their diegetic effects somewhere between what Noël Burch has called the "primitive mode of representation" (PMR) and the "institutional mode of representation" (IMR).[72] The "narrative discourse" of films characterized by the "primitive mode" was "located outside of the picture—in the spectator's mind or the lecturer's mouth."[73] By contrast, films from the period of Tausk's paper were much closer to later films that had fully integrated the "institutional mode" and its "unity-ubiquity of the spectator-subject," diegetic "closure," and "narrative self-sufficiency."[74]

What was recognizable in the cinema with which Tausk was familiar, then, was an incipient logic of technical succession, capable of sustaining narrative coherence in the absence of text, even if it was not fully rid of the "erraticness" described by Andreas-Salomé. In light of Tausk's decision to settle on the "magic lantern" as the apparatus most associated with the visions of schizophrenic patients, the reader is left to wonder: Why, in a paper that some have rightly associated with a climate of technophobic suspicions about machines, psychiatrists, hypnotists, and a general preoccupation with *new* technological menaces, does a magic lantern enter the picture?[75] The answer resides with the supposed psychoanalytically "primary" nature of the images with respect to their internal narrative logic.

In a magic-lantern performance, whether the phantasmagoric conjuring of Philidor or Gaspard-Étienne Robertson in the late eighteenth century or the dissolving dream sequences of Auguste Lapierre in the late nineteenth century, the projected images of the magic lantern required detailed oral narration or stage setting on the part of the lanternist to transform the slide projections into a story.[76] The theatrics and narrative interventions of the lanternist imposed a diegetic structure on the colorful series of images that was lacking in the images themselves, thus establishing the narrative space populated by the pictures.[77] Moreover, lanternists as well as early projectionists were often located in the spectatorial space of the projection and many times could be seen by the audience turning the crank of early cinematic projection devices, moving the slides, controlling the speed of the images' succession, or actively participating in the mise-en-scène.[78] As the projectionist was relegated to a booth, evidence of the operator's agency was effaced, reducing the attention to the material conditions for the production of the illusion of movement. This was a setting that was certainly familiar to Tausk from his cinema going, and one unsuitable to the explanation of a condition that involved a crisis of causality and estrangement from the bodily, and thus mechanical, relations between the phenomenal outer world and inner sensations.

The cinema of 1918, with its far-from-rudimentary semiosis and relatively well-disguised mechanical conditions of possibility, offered an example of narrative autonomy that was too sophisticated to function as a model for a symptomatology that was ultimately pathological. In returning to antiquated proto-cinematic technologies, Tausk signaled a commitment to a conception of ego boundaries that resisted the primacy of cinematic semiotechnics in the movement between the machine and the psychological, even while demonstrating their power to do exactly that. The apparent urgency with which he then claimed that the psychoanalyst could not doubt for a moment that "this machine *must* be a symbol" indicates the level of anxiety or suspicion about the prospect for a model of the ego that relied on images without resorting to language. His paper, however, seems to have proposed just such a model, lending credence to the notion that Tausk was indeed as "clever and dangerous" as Freud thought he was.

Case 2: Ernst August Wagner

Robert Gaupp, one of the preeminent critics of the German Kinoreformbewegung, was also a highly respected professor of psychology and criminal psychologist. To his contemporaries, his best-known work was perhaps his case study of the mass murderer Ernst August Wagner, conducted during his time as a professor at the University of Tübingen.[79] On the night of September 3, 1913, Wagner murdered his wife and four children, then traveled by bike and train to the town of Mühlhausen, where he set several barns ablaze before shooting twenty people with a pair of Mauser pistols, killing nine.[80] While he was reloading his weapon, villagers attacked and captured him and he was eventually taken to Tübingen, where he was admitted to Gaupp's psychiatric clinic to be analyzed ahead of the trial.[81]

What distinguishes the Wagner case, beyond Gaupp's role in the cinema reform movement, is Wagner's exemplary literary training and the degree to which it posed real problems for understanding his condition according to new models of psychopathology. The nature of this problem was two-sided. First, Wagner was a head instructor of German literature who, although regarded as "eccentric" in performance reviews, was nevertheless revered and, in 1909, was "officially lauded."[82] As we shall see, his commitment to the literary canon and his attempts to self-consciously construct himself as a part of an elevated body of literature was a metastasis of readerly ideals that Gaupp finds as the foundation for his psychological disfiguration. Secondly, however, Gaupp's own education as a psychologist was indebted to a tradition of psychophysical and psycholinguistic inquiry that frames his insights about Wagner's pathology as a contest between a readerly and a discretized, rational, semiotechnical psyche.

Gaupp began his career in Breslau as an assistant to Carl Wernicke, the famous experimental psychologist whose "spelling theory," work on aphasia, and role in reading experiments are discussed in chapter 3.[83] Later, in Munich, Gaupp became the senior assistant to Emil Kraepelin, with whom he wrote his habilitation, and who helped shift Gaupp's methodology from a view of psychopathologies focused on purely somatic measures to one that took up Kraepelin's taxonomy of pathologies, especially that of endogenous psychosis.[84] In Gaupp's diagnosis, there was "no doubt" that "Wagner suffers from paranoia," and his description could have been lifted from Kraepelin's account of *Verrücktheit* (paranoia), where he observed that "the sufferer is dissatisfied with his position, he feels neglected, believes himself already to have not been properly treated lovingly by his parents and siblings, but rather in many ways misunderstood."[85] Importantly, however, Gaupp differed from Kraepelin in thinking that paranoia was not psychogenic but instead an exogenous affective disorder.[86] His investigation of the case history thus looked for external influences that guided the emergence of Wagner's paranoia, and especially factors in his training that affected the logic of his self-conception and subject formation. In short, the observational period concentrated heavily on the technics by which Wagner's inner life was configured.

From his training with Wernicke, Gaupp also retained the practice of galvanometric testing, which assessed patients' mental associative networks using short, controlled exposure to words and phrases, measuring their response time. As a result of these two competing backgrounds, Gaupp's analysis sought to both detect the mechanics underlying the emergence of Wagner's defining personal narrative as a function of his lifelong literary training and to reconstitute this narrative according to the intervals of the psychophysical testing. The dissonance between these two approaches is particularly salient for determining the kind of pathology at work, because, as Gaupp's own student in Tübingen later noted and Kraepelin had already established, paranoia was a "delusion of reference" (*Beziehungswahn*), generally distinguished from schizophrenia through the logic and coherence of representational relationships that comprised the patient's inner world.[87] The logic of the nineteenth-century readerly ideal was not that of the tachistoscopic patient or the cinemagoer, and a paranoid was particularly well suited to revealing this conflict.

The extended period of psychiatric observation, which ultimately led Gaupp to find Wagner "beyond prosecution," was not unrelated to his thinking about the influences of film. His diagnosis of the formative conditions for Wagner's rampage was part of a broader history of psychology's cultural interventions that included the Kinoreformbewegung, in which the disputed conditions of psychological continuity were increasingly expressed as a clash between the media by which the psyche was trained and represented. Unlike the banal attribution of criminal behavior to exposure to new media by figures like Karl Brunner, the case of Wagner did actually hinge on the cultural techniques enforced by various technologies. So too would the looming questions of diagnostic categories that were the source of disagreement between figures such as Eugene Bleueler, Gaupp and his student Ernst Kretschmer, Karl Jaspers, Freud, and Kraepelin.[88] In fact, the core question that Gaupp pursues in his study of Wagner is not just whether Wagner is a paranoid or a schizophrenic but how sanity and insanity are configured as properties of the technological training.

At the near total exclusion of other attributes, Wagner is characterized as a reader. Moreover, Gaupp treats him as a text to be hermeneutically deciphered, close-reading his autobiography, letters, and dramatic writings as if they were Wagner himself. David Trotter argues that because "Gaupp's diagnosis did not meet with uniform acceptance" from psychiatrists and critics who maintained that Wagner suffered from a "mild form of paranoid schizophrenia," Gaupp's own paranoia about producing an "utterly coherent diagnosis" led him to find Wagner's delusions "utterly coherent."[89] However, as Gaupp's numerous publications on the dangers of film establish, his conviction about Wagner's fundamental soundness of mind stemmed not only from his "professional identity" being "crucially at stake" but more so from an underlying belief in a literary form of psychological continuity.[90] This is reinforced by Gaupp's insistence on diagnosing Wagner as a paranoid, since the literary subject who can be constructed from a text—who can be treated as synonymous with the act of being written—demands that language retain its faithful correspondence with a world it represents. As Louis A. Sass neatly summarizes, a characteristic of "schizophrenic language involves tendencies for language to lose its transparent and subordinate status" and "to emerge instead as an independent focus of attention or autonomous source of control over speech and understanding."[91]

For the paranoid patient, on the other hand, language is not divested of its correspondence and communicative function but is overladen with significance and overinvested with correspondences that may not exist. The paranoiac always finds more than is present in language, suspicious that an even greater field of meaning and more absolute level of correspondence hides beneath what is apparent. And the psychologist thus becomes a philologist, exhausting the patient as a text to be interpreted.[92] As a defense of text, especially facing the rise of cinema, Gaupp's program of analysis with Wagner became a kind of literary study, highly influenced by the fact that Wagner was well educated.

Wagner was not just a head teacher of German literature; he was a representative of literary Bildung par excellence. His project of becoming a literary figure himself was actually the most evident symptom of his psychological decline. He repeatedly proclaimed himself a dramatist and author of the highest order, who deserved to be recognized among the pantheon of German literary figures like Schiller and Goethe. In his autobiography and letters, he writes: "I consider myself the greatest contemporary dramatist (Stuttgarter Spaziergänge S. 280), as one of the greats (Biographie I, S. 71), as one who can stand next to Schiller (Spaziergänge S. 68)."[93]

In line with the standard paranoid diagnosis, Gaupp frequently refers to Wagner's "overestimation" of himself "as a poet" as a part of a typical "megalomania," which was also involved in an escalating suspicion of his peers, whom he believed to mock and defame him.[94] It is Wagner's disgust and his own megalomaniacal self-appraisal as a literary figure that formed the groundwork for a long-planned violence against his erstwhile neighbors. Yet part of what is so unusual about Wagner's case is that his Bildung was not just a process of subject formation but the form of subjectivity itself. The boundaries of Wagner's psyche were delimited entirely by text, which is why he could only find expression through writing, and could not distinguish himself from the literary canon with which he identified.

Gaupp uses the first hundred pages of his analysis to carefully reconstruct and comment on Wagner's personal development prior to the shootings, drawn primarily from collections of letters, plays, and Wagner's massive autobiography. As a young student, Wagner was described as a "quiet, orderly, decent" student whose "favorite subject was literature" and who had a "powerful imagination."[95] From early on, Wagner "had read a great deal," although Gaupp, ever the reformer, also notes that he also read a lot of "pulp literature [*Schundliteratur*] in the cheap 10 Pfennig volumes."[96] In line with Gaupp's reformer-style arguments, the fact *that* Wagner read was more important than *what* Wagner read, and Gaupp seemingly excused his youthful indiscretions and even highly disturbing sexual episodes with his "preference for beautiful literature" and his later dedication to "German literature."[97] The most immediate consequence of this lifelong immersion in literature and pedagogy was that Wagner comported himself well in the observation period and displayed an immense power of reference and rationality, even when rebuking himself in his memoirs as a fraud.

> It is true, I am a teacher, educator, shaper of the youth. . . . No, I was not a good educator. I was poorly educated and did not go far in educating myself, as you would like to believe of me. However, whatever I have not done in life, I have known all the better.[98]

This reflexive self-observation only adds to the sense that, as with his developed imagination, Wagner had a robust ability to imagine himself from the outside. He did not, like the patients described by Tausk, suffer a breach of ego boundaries. Against his own expectations, Gaupp is astonished by the man he finds in observation and comments that "immediately after he was led here into my examination room I saw right away that I had proceeded from false assumptions" and that "a serious, grief-stricken man of worthy demeanor faced me; polite, prepared in every way to comply, an educated person in his entire conduct."[99]

The frequency with which Gaupp reiterates Wagner's seeming psychological soundness based on his education, and the extent to which that troubled his diagnostic outlook, is telling. It insists on the sense of proper psychological interiority as a function of readership. As the cases Tausk discussed show, the ruptured psyche was indicated primarily by subjection to visual hallucinations, even if Eugen Bleuler and others had advanced subcategories of paranoia that involved hallucination.[100] If anything, the boundaries between inner world and outer world in cases of pure paranoia were *too* developed, a problem that can be seen as the outcome of fanatical silent readership.

The paranoid delusions tormenting Wagner and paving the way to the massacre in 1913 were a part of a literary fantasy, amassing a textual self as a bulwark against a world perceived as hostile. Wagner's identification with German literature was so total that the development of his personality was conceived of as a progressive canonization, reading and producing texts as inseparable from the cultivation of his identity. Words, and especially text, stabilized the threatening ephemera of personhood that had been endangered since childhood. Both the act of reading and joining the canon offered the ultimate form of personal indemnification. This expressed itself in rudimentary ways at first through feelings of deeply obligated promises "to keep his word once he gave it," exclaiming, "I am the fool of the word! How much misery does this vice yet have in store for me!" when he had broken an oath.[101]

The earnestness of this compulsive obligation to the word was symptomatic of the degree to which the architecture of his psyche was viewed as written text. This was underscored by another tendency that Gaupp mentions many times in his readings of the autobiography and assessments from administrators and teachers. In addition to having "read many books and novels," Wagner also "invariably spoke written German [*Schriftdeutsch*]."[102] Throughout his life, Wagner refused to speak colloquial, spoken German, which complemented what Gaupp calls his "pure truth-fanaticism" (*reinen Wahrheitsfanatismus*)—the conditions of truth determined solely through consecration as text.[103] Thus, in 1909 Wagner writes of the motivation for writing his autobiography: "So often I sit down to write this book and set out to deny my own Self. I write as if I were addressing Ernst Wagner as an objective biography. . . . I do not spare myself."[104]

In this melancholic idiom, which he often takes in his appraisal of personal failings, writing becomes both a constitutive and a negative act, annihilating the ambiguous indeterminacies of his inner life in favor of the perceived absolution of texts, where what is objective must be written. In a truly paranoid overinvestment in the power of mediation over truth conditions, the autobiography provides a necessary confirmation that requires Wagner read himself as a part of text.

Unlike a canonical autobiographical work like Goethe's *Dichtung und Wahrheit,* whose "Truth" (*Wahrheit*) is self-consciously left to both activate and develop the interpretive faculties of the initiated reader, there is no truly hermeneutical dimension to Wagner's writing. It is meant to simply make himself literature, therefore rendering psychology reducible to a hermeneutics without technics. Literature did not represent a vehicle through which to express one's inner state but became a substitute for an inner state. As he writes of the reason for his interest in literature: "I wanted to flee from my own 'histories' into a more bearable milieu. . . . I have more or less read the entirety of German literature and dared to establish a standard of excellence."[105] Thus, to express himself in conversation with Gaupp was for Wagner to cite himself: "I cite myself, me the once revolutionary."[106] As the text became a primary, rather than a secondary, manifestation of his psyche, writing became the practice of establishing and maintaining the tenuous boundary between himself and the world.

Recognizing this, Gaupp is transformed from an observer into a *reader* of Wagner, quoting page after page of his texts. This is made explicit in Wagner's response to a question from Gaupp and the head investigator, Ho., regarding a play he wrote about Nero. To read the play, Wagner claimed, would be "to read my soul [*Seele*]."[107] Wagner recognizes a danger in being read that accompanies Gaupp's hermeneutical practices. Namely, the logic of Gaupp's psychiatric method will not vindicate the literary soundness of his psyche; it will actually find him outside the canon, illegitimate, and a madman. For this reason, Wagner remarks "very politely" that he sees Gaupp as his "most dangerous enemy," as he can determine whether he goes to an asylum where they both know he is "not like those who are there."[108] Indeed, Gaupp does conclude that "beyond his overvalued ideational complexes [*Vorstellungskomplexe*]," Wagner's "perception" is "undisturbed," his "logical thinking" is "intact," and the violent actions are "unrelated."[109]

Yet how is it that Gaupp could so often remark on Wagner's psychological soundness when there was no question whether he not only went on the shooting rampage but had meticulously planned it for years? The answer is in the model of psychological continuity by which Wagner was diagnosed. This was a tachistoscopic, psychophysiological model that formed a picture of the patient through a series of discretized responses based on a program of reading experiments in which Gaupp was trained as a psychologist. It sacrificed the very historical and canonical notion of literary narrative continuity that Wagner had envisaged in writing himself and was the reason that he was terrified of being *read* by Gaupp.

The Discrete Truths of Text

The mechanically defined intervals of Gaupp's tachistoscopic word association tests were what, in part, made Wagner legible. However, they did not do so according to the ideals of a traditional readerly education. If Wagner's aim was to fortify and objectify himself by becoming readable to himself and others—a fact that impressed Gaupp and accounted for his "pure truth-fanaticism"—it required that he be read *as text.* He was forced to forfeit the logic of his self-construction, which remained entirely idiosyncratic and subjective. It is for this reason that when Gaupp asked him whether it bothered him that "his texts will remain evidence for the case files," he responded with contempt, saying, "That would be a disgrace, that would be a robbery."[110] This is also why Wagner claimed that the doctors had become his "most dangerous enemy," as their ability to "clarify" would not vindicate the readerly logic of his auto-fictional self.[111]

These were not literary readers but clinicians. Gaupp was trained in psychophysical assessments that, despite his literary predilection, did not preserve the logic of a psycho-literary narrative. Instead, Gaupp's reading of Wagner was paired with tachistoscopic tests that enforced the protocols of their own discretized mechanisms. Wagner feared that his "soul" would become readable to Gaupp, but according to a logic that was not readable to Wagner. The logic of text was his singular source of power in defining himself, as he could freely manipulate it in accordance with the literary conventions established by great canonical figures. To imitate them—as he did in his plays and autobiography—was to objectively legitimate himself by collapsing the process of auto-distinction in the process of canon building. This is most pointedly expressed in his autobiography.

> I have extended my life, although the torture has intensified with each day. But because letters are easier to kill than people, at the very least I want to overcome my wretched weakness with proper spelling.[112]

By spelling himself out correctly according to the rules of text, Wagner could exert a control over the production of his inner life and his place in the world that did not arise organically. Such a practice starkly contrasts with the case of Daniel Paul Schreber as described by Kittler, where the idiosyncratic, hyperpersonalized reasoning of a textual compulsion became the psychoanalytic man himself. Freud only had Schreber's text at his disposal and thus, by necessity, had to substitute the text for the man. Nevertheless, Kittler writes: "In describing the mind as information system, however, the psychotic text, which describes the system throughout its four hundred pages, is said to be the unmetaphoric truth."[113]

In one way, Wagner was the absolute opposite of Schreber because it was his panic to adopt and deploy the rules of language and literature established by the canon that served as the source of personal distinction. However, as Kittler notes of the informational era of scientific psychology inaugurated by Gaupp's teachers, in "'the age of Flechsig and Wernicke,' (Benn's Term), souls became nerve information systems, and cures became experiments."[114] As a student of Wernicke, Gaupp used precisely this method to make Wagner readable.

Gaupp and his psychiatric team attempted to find "indirect routes" to gaining clarity about Wagner's underlying condition through "experimental psychological" investigations that might determine deeper underlying "structures of reference."[115] To this end, Gaupp described the experimental design of a test of Wagner's linguistic associations intended to reveal the degree of his psychological coherence.

> Numerous words were called out. He had the task of verbally reacting to them with his very first impressions. The reaction words were written down and the reaction times measured. Experiments with the galvanometer were also employed, an apparatus whose specifics cannot be discussed, but whose essence entails that it can comfortably bring such excitations to optical-visible expression that

> otherwise escape simple observation. The experiments proceeded negatively with relation to the performed task (fornication with which animals?) but apart from that yielded a not uninteresting look into his *psychological structure*: his intellectual capacities, his bias toward logical, elevated associations, his preference for literary things, his ego-centric mode of reaction. In his case, all of these appear to powerfully underscore a relation to an abnormal person, strongly foregrounding his moral misconduct, the deep feeling of his suffering, his preoccupation with thoughts of murder and revenge, which all came to expression with these experiments.[116]

What Gaupp identifies in Wagner, and that which troubles the diagnostic move to a statement about his insanity, is that his "intellectual capacities" were at odds with clinical notions of psychological rupture. Using electrical impulses to measure the intervals between the presentation of the words and subsequent associations, Gaupp's psychometric analysis assessed Wagner's answers according to a temporal measure that was problematic for the distinction frequently drawn between the virtues of reading versus the hazards of film. As discussed earlier, Gaupp and others decried film's interference with "contemplation" (*Nachdenken*) as one of the primary attributes of the readerly psyche, imagining that the quick replacement and alternation of images found in films was both physiologically harmful and produced an unconscious order structurally different from that of texts. In line with this thinking, the galvanometric tests on Wagner were praised for their ability to bring to "optical-visible expression" that which remained invisible to traditional observation—precisely by eliminating contemplative, second-order reflections. It was not just the presentation of visual content in films versus the internalized act of reading that premised Gaupp's worries about the nascent narrative medium of film, though it was no doubt important to his criticism. It was also embedded in a suspicion tied to the psychophysical claim that mental processes could be modeled and simulated by compiling the result of discrete, uniform elements, which parceled the semiotic psychological terrain into mechanically definable units.

Gaupp's observation of Wagner externalized and incrementalized his textual and verbal associations as a function of the on/off mechanism of the galvanometer and chronoscope. It broke up a whole field of associations into individual responses that were then compiled to offer a diagnostic picture of his psychic life. The series of words to which he responded were intentionally presented without a meaningful syntactical sequence, and were then evaluated according to the response and period of delay with the intention of evading "Nachdenken." The logic by which the responses to a series of syntactically unrelated and meaningless words were reassembled was the opposite of what had been described as a healthy, educated, readerly mind. To arrive at the underlying "psychological structures" at play in Wagner's narrative about his own actions, the psychiatrists in Tübingen tested his reactions to individual words based on a proto-cinematic protocol—metered alternation between on/off, shutter closed / shutter open, frame 1 / frame 2. It was a digital framework, and one that equally perplexed later cyberneticians and systems theorists who sought to come to grips with how closure and autonomy could be achieved in a purely operational fashion.

The tests produced a vision of Wagner as a literate, rational agent that was incompatible with the larger narrative about his murderous actions, which troubled long-standing beliefs about subject formation. Gaupp's citation of the research leader, Dr. Busch, confirms this when he is quoted as saying, "Wagner possesses extraordinarily strong—undoubtedly to a pathological degree—sentimental ideational complexes [*Vorstellungskomplexe*]," though the pathology was located in the ordering, not the content, of these complexes.[117] Emphasizing the extraordinary nature of the dissonance between his apparent benchmarks of a moral-literary Bildung and his criminal behavior as a problem of "ideational complexes" points to an intuition about the importance of *how* such informational complexes are arranged rather than *what* they contain. Kittler observed a similar incompatibility in Freud's reading of the Schreber case: "The basic principles of the classical discourse network have thus deteriorated into being the defensive weapons of a mental patient. In the crossfire of psychophysics, the last bureaucrat is left with only the sediment of his education [*Bildung*], whose norms, however, are taken apart bit by bit."[118] The appeal to the foundations of a literary Bildung are marshaled for the purpose of creating the impression of repairing a classical conception of interiority, even while the basic ligatures of such internalized narrative forms are being digitized.

Everything Is True and Real

It appears as if the general concern was that discretized units can be reassembled to give the illusion of an autonomous, coherent unity. This was a model of continuity pursued through discontinuity that would have been impossible to achieve through Wagner's own canonical, literary-historical self-conception. The words were extracted from a semiotic whole that included a personal narrative about his life as a child and the literary training that conditioned his powers of self-conception. But the associations were not ordered according to conventions of written narrative and were instead operations of a deeper psychic structure arranged as if on the cinematic editing table (according to their duration). Psychological unity thus became a function of the unity of the data set. It replicated a "revocation of the word," which Lukács tied to the loss of "memory" and a "faithfulness to oneself" that was a property of film.[119] In describing film's divergence from the logic of reading and drama, Lukács accounts for the empirical operations of film in way that could double as an experimental protocol in the case of Wagner.

> These individual moments whose confluence brings about the temporal succession of "cinema" scenes are connected with one another immediately and without transition. There is no causality that would connect them with one another or, more precisely, their causality is inhibited or bound by no substantiveness. "Everything is possible": that is the worldview of the "cinema," and because its technique in every individual moment expresses the absolute (if only empirical) reality of this moment, the validity of the "possibility" as a category juxtaposed to "reality" is nullified; both categories are equated, they become an identity. "Everything is true and real, everything is equally true and equally real": the successions of images of the "cinema" teach this. Thus, a new, homogenous and harmonic, uniform [*einheitliche*] and varied world arises.[120]

Lukács identifies the fact that diegetic world building in film is misleading in its "reality" effects. Against the apparent relationship to a real from which images are taken, the sense produced from the succession of images, and therefore the mental states they induce, are not the result of a traditional causality, nor the content of the images. In this understanding, the continuity of the "uniform" world is created irrespective of the content of the images. In place of a spatiotemporal coherence or the syntactical unities of writing, Lukács contends that filmic narrative is founded on technical modalities in editing similar to Hans Vaihinger's positivistic visions of fictionality referenced by Richard Guttmann in chapter 2. Except in this case, the mechanics of the "as if" in which "reality" and "possibility" become interchangeable are the result of the discretized images of the cinematograph.

The viewer's interpellation of the narrative space of the film was an external, mechanical procedure that relied on the ability to break up individual moments and assemble them in a way that masked their discontinuities.

The internal opposition in the diagnosis of Wagner as both a well-formed, educated reader and a mass murderer unintentionally tested for two disparate logics of continuity. One was distinctly cinematic and the grounds for the outcry of the Kinoreformbewegung. The other was a tradition of literary education that critics saw as jeopardized. Kittler attributes this transformation around 1900 to the aggressive psychophysical discretization of medial techniques that were thought to be central to the development of a unitary literary subject.

> Following the heroic autoexperiments of Ebbinghaus, breaking down discourses into single and discrete functions became the task of an entire psychophysics of complex cultural practices. These functions have nothing to do with any unity imposed by consciousness; they are automatic and autonomous. . . . In 1900 speaking and hearing, writing and reading were put to the test in isolated functions, without any subject or thought as their shadowy supports. . . . Rather than the long genetic path to the word from its beginning in nature to its end in culture, what counts is the signifier's mechanism and how it runs under either normal or pathological circumstances.[121]

The fear among early critics of film who drew upon experimental psychology recognized in the psychophysical techniques of measurement and representation a threatening potential: that instruments like the tachistoscope intervened in the construction of inner life. Even Lukács's more sympathetic theorization of film reflects the turn described by Kittler away from a representational economy in which the sense of psychic completeness was generated by operations of reading. These were operations that produced a conceptual, linguistic universe that was one of "possibility." In this way, the sense of "reality" was just a function of endless possible permutations that created mental continuities from discrete frames presented in succession. It created a semiotically viable experience from discretized technics, despite the radically divergent qualitative character of Wagner's experience. This new methodology could affirm a patient like Wagner's simultaneous pathology and seeming coherence, as discontinuity in the machine-driven field of psychophysics had become the cornerstone of psychological continuity.

Coda

Where the Intervals End

> I am a little disoriented by the opposition between analogical and digital.
>
> —Gregory Bateson

Cinema has always been both a digital and an analog technology. This is what made it such a powerful and at times contentious tool for understanding the function of the psyche as an apparatus. For all the fleeting enchantments the screen offered, early cinema also created an enduring nexus between technical discretization and the continuities of what it meant to have a mind. It was both discrete and continuous, technical and semiotic. If the psyche had been rendered a machine, cinema rendered machines psychological. What a terrifying proposition.

Cinema would only seem to rejoin inquiry into questions of digital discretization on its putative deathbed. As celluloid has been increasingly digitized or displaced by born-digital films, the often elegiac response has been propelled by a sense that an old, modern, material medium has succumbed to a new, post-postmodern, virtual adversary. Jocelyn Szczepaniak-Gillece's introduction to the volume *Ends of Cinema* hilariously plays on the graven tone of such pronouncements when she begins by writing, "By the time you read this, cinema will have died."[1] Perhaps it did, and we are right to mourn. But perhaps its real legacy lives on in the medium believed to deal the fatal blow.

The forking path along which cinematic technologies continued to develop from their origins in psychophysiological instrumentation does not have as its exclusive destination infinitely replicable superhero franchises, cast and produced according to the business recommendations of artificial intelligence (AI) start-ups.[2] It also includes the AI used to make those decisions—reviving established anxieties that humans would cede the logic of inner life to machines. When looking to some of the foundations for where the artificiality of artificial intelligence emerged, one sees theoretical concerns familiar from the psychophysiological speculations about cinematic mechanisms.

At the 1950 Macy Conference on cybernetics, a charged exchange developed around many of the same issues that have been explored in this book. The neurophysiologist Ralph W. Gerard initiated a "discussion about the analogy between the human brain and the digital computer" by questioning "the digital representation of the brain as primarily a collection of on-and-off neurons and the nervous system as primarily controlled by on-and-off electrical impulses."[3] In the eruption of responses this provocation occasioned, a veritable who's-who list of twentieth-century intellectual titans, including John von Neumann, Warren McCulloch, Walter Pitts, Norbert Wiener, J. C. R. Licklider, and Gregory Bateson, sounded off, attempting to come to terms with not only whether the functional conception of the brain as a series of flip-flop mechanisms was sustainable but also the inseparability of discrete and continuous operations with respect to both minds and computational machines. Von Neumann summarized the issue as follows:

> In almost all parts of physics the underlying reality is analogical, that is, the true physical variables are in almost all cases continuous, or equivalent to continuous descriptions. The digital procedure is usually a human artifact for the sake of description. Digital models, digital descriptions arise by treating quantities, some of which or all of which are continuous, by combinations of quantities of which each has only a small number of stable (and hence discrete) state—usually two or three—and where one tries to avoid intermediate states.[4]

This was certainly not the final word among the parties involved. However, what von Neumann's comment gets to, just a short six years after he first visited the Electronic Numerical Integrator and Computer (ENIAC), is a vital challenge, apparent since the nineteenth century, that is inherent in attempts to understand human thought as a system of mechanical stops and starts.[5] The world, our experience of it, and the machines designed to approximate thought are not actually discrete. Computers themselves, as von Neumann notes, are not really discrete. An "electrical computing machine is based on an electric current, which is an analogical concept."[6] Thus, "both the man-made artifact as well as the natural organ" that we call "digital" are "in reality, continuous."[7] Discretization is a property of signification, a "description." Only signs can draw clean, absolute distinctions. At the same time, the ability to systematically signify for the gaps, stops, and breaks that form these distinctions is what makes representations of a continuous world themselves continuous. It is also what allows us to engineer and program the machines that make possible, shape, and constrain all the meaningful cultural content we transmit and store.

The discrete and the continuous are functionally inextricable. How their relationship to one another is operationalized forms the basis for contemporary notions of intelligence, all of which turn out to be artificial in nature. As Gerard noted in the address that kindled the dispute in 1950:

> The language, experience, and ways of thought, say, of communicating engineering seem to be admirably adapted to make us recognize explicitly that nerve impulse is not merely some physical-chemical event but a physical-chemical event carrying meaning. It is therefore a sign or a signal, as the case may be; and this is very important in physiological thinking.[8]

To recognize intelligence as artificial is already to acknowledge the ways that organic intelligence became comprehensible through technological systems that establish a connection between discrete sequences and the continuities of meaning. If after the revolution in psychophysics, the view of the brain and nervous system have largely been governed by their comparison with machines and circuitry, one could say that any answer to the question of meaning, human or otherwise, will be a technological one.

The cyberneticians were not the first to have this revelation. In 1877 Ernst Kapp remarked that the "comparison between the electrical telegraph and the *nervous system* is self-evident."[9] His prescient observation did not, however, suggest that the nature of the comparison was morphological. It was an operational technics, with the networked system of discrete switching mechanisms showing the way for how a tangled mess of nerves could emerge as a unity based on more than a given shape of the body. The dialectical movement between technical discretization and conceptual continuity that was itself a part of an ongoing dialectic between machines and the human body, and that Kapp extensively outlined, framed an informational insight amid a machine-age episteme. The hard, if contingent, age-defining epistemological distinctions that have driven forceful theories of technology from Michel Foucault to Donna Haraway to Friedrich Kittler (whose 1800/1900 distinction this book's title invokes) also admit of mixed lineages. No doubt, media archaeologists already know this. But it is not just the obscure, losing sides of progress narratives that need recovering from an imperious march of dominant technologies toward some telos of digital singularity. No one would argue that cinema failed to receive appropriate attention in the twentieth century. Yet the technics it instituted, particularly in its earliest period—achieving psychological continuities through mechanical intervals—are not commonly mentioned in histories of information that have made way for the hopes and fears about artificial intelligence. This is something that this book has, in small part, sought to remedy.

Anxieties about how technologies infringe on or destroy the territories of the uniquely human frequently demonstrate the degree to which our working models of the uniquely human are already entirely conditioned by those technologies. This was certainly true of early cinematic mechanisms, and it remains true of the advanced computational machines that regulate every aspect of human life—from the movies we watch to how we are defined as legally regulated subjects. The artificial intelligence of deep neural networks makes this case most explicitly: "a deep learning network is a mathematical model that is (loosely) inspired by the structure of the brain" that relies on many (hence deep) layers of weighted artificial neurons, many of which are "hidden."[10] From the large data sets passed through the neural network architectures as inputs, abstract patterns of higher and higher orders emerge from the nonlinear sequences of neurons that either do or do not fire. From these processes, neural networks can "learn" things like how to compose stylistically uniform sentences, visually recognize myriad potential hazards for autonomous vehicles, or profile people at an airport.[11] The applications are vast, and, as Kate Crawford writes, the "reproduction of harmful ideas is particularly dangerous now that AI has moved from being an experimental discipline used only in laboratories to being tested at scale on millions of people."[12]

But do these many layers of artificial neurons actually replicate the brain? Is neuromorphic computational hardware that looks to imitate the spiking functions in the brain really neuromorphic? Yes, so long as the brain is already imagined as a digital computer in the ways discussed at the Macy Conference in 1950. A series of on-off mechanisms can be imagined to reproduce the continuities we call thought, but only once we have the technics for understanding such a relationship—technics that were at work in the oft-drawn analogies between early cinematic machines and the human mind.

The splendid recursivity of these historical alternations between human and machine, continuity and discontinuity is beautifully underscored when one looks at endeavors within aesthetic science in neuro- and psychocinematics. These somewhat niche disciplines have attempted to "develop neuropsychological theories that describe the functional dynamics of brain activity" and to "identify the cognitive processes related to" the "illusions" and identifications created by movies.[13] The brain was rendered a machine by cinematic devices that were then used to produce illusions that are now studied using digital tools to detect the neuromechanical process originally modeled on cinema. This is a subtle irony that is not lost on the scholars pursuing work in this area, as they frequently point to the close mutual embeddedness of cinema and scientific psychology in their references to the work of psychophysicists and gestaltists like Wilhelm Wundt, Hugo Münsterberg, Rudolf Arnheim, and Wolfgang Köhler.

The perceived nefariousness of reappearing challenges by machines to the sovereignty of human thought stem from the very nature of semiotechnics at play in mechanical systems. Signifying continuities that depend on the intervals of machines—when they work properly—effectively *obscure* the underlying discretization we take to be the essence of machines. This is true of the hiddenness of "hidden" layers in deep neural networks and the designed opacity of other algorithmic "black box" processes that have gained an increasing invisibility since hypothetical "oracle machines" or "o-machines" received a brief description in Alan Turing's 1938 Princeton dissertation.[14] When machines run smoothly, we forget they are machines. All machines are liars. Kittler confirms as much as well when he refers to the "triumph of software" over hardware as a part of a "system of secrecy."[15]

Scholars of cinema know such charges well. The apparatus theory that graced the pages of *Cahiers du Cinéma* in the 1970s and 1980s with updated materialist critiques waged structurally similar arguments. To consolidate the many technical discontinuities "without which there would be no cinema" into the pure-seeming, transcendental subjectivity that undergirds "the ideology of the visible linked to Western logocentrism" required a "hidden part of technics."[16] Cinema was essentially a lie the audience both acknowledged and disavowed. This semiotechnical arrangement, or dispositif, that erased technological discontinuities in favor of symbolic continuities was what was called "ideology."

The positionality exhibited in both cinema and informational systems—whether spectators' subjective identification or second-order observation—is a function of an oscillation between discontinuity and continuity that characterizes all technics that work through discretization. One achieves a vantage point, and thus autonomy, by signifying for differences. This is Bateson's "difference that makes a difference" referenced in the introduction to this book.[17] Yet the technological regimes that institute such an arrangement account for a relatively circumscribed period of human history. It is thinkable now that the generative opposition between continuity and discontinuity that has driven a dialectic of semiotics and technics itself will be displaced. Although still framed in terms of digital versus analog, quantum computing's promise in the battle for computational supremacy challenges the very terms of machines that once seemed so threatening. For now, the freaky quantum aspects of superposition (that allows qubits to signify for multiple states of one or zero at the same time) or entanglement (in which two particles change states together instantly) are processed through classical digital instructions.[18] They have to be resolved as either analog or digital, reinserting the spooky instantaneity and simultaneously discrete and continuous nature of quantum properties into an older framework. However, this is an atavism of an episteme that started long ago and is not likely to continue. If the intervals end, and with them technics as we know it, we may have reason for nostalgia about a time when the worst machines could do was *replicate* the function of the human mind.

Acknowledgments

A great many stops and starts marked the intervals of work necessary for this book to appear. That these innumerable discontinuities were able to take shape as something continuous is creditable to a great many people who defined the periods of both activity and rest.

This book could not have happened without the generosity of Harpur College and Binghamton University, the Society for the Humanities at Cornell University, the Internationales Kolleg für Kulturtechnikforschung und Medienphilosophie (IKKM), and Princeton University. Thank you to my editor, Doug Armato, as well as Zenyse Miller at the University of Minnesota Press for guiding this project to completion.

My sincerest thanks are owed to my friends and colleagues at Binghamton University. Thank you to members of the Department of Art History—Pam Smart, Nancy Um, and Andrew Walkling—whose reliably sparkling intelligence, humor, and generosity made all the difference. It has been a rare gift to find myself in a department with Tom McDonough and John Tagg, whom I admired long before arriving, and whose guidance has remained inestimably important. I also owe a great debt to my colleagues, friends, and trivia partners, Kevin Hatch and Julia Walker, for their remarkable patience and supreme hilarity. Thank you to Carl Gelderloos for the marvelous conversations on the long journey from PhD students to professors in Upstate New York. I am also grateful to faculty and friends from across the university, which spans the length of Vestal Parkway, including John Havard, Brian Wall, Vincent Grenier, Matthew Wolf-Meyer, Alexandra Cuesta, Kenneth White, and Dan Thomas Davis. Thank you to Tina Chronopoulos, who put me up for years while I was commuting those hundreds of miles—and put up with me *wenn ich total die Nase voll hatte.*

This project was profoundly influenced by my multiple years as a fellow at the IKKM and the chance to share the company of some of the most formidable minds in the field, all of whom deserve a great deal of thanks. Foremost I am grateful to Bernhard Siegert, whose brilliance has shaped the entire arc of this project, and who has provided limitless intellectual and institutional support for more than a decade. I am grateful to everyone who was at the IKKM and created as close to an ideal intellectual environment as can exist. Thank you in no particular order to Lorenz Engell, Leander Scholz, Volker Pantenburg, Laura Frahm, Jimena Canales, Thomas Elsaesser, Christoph Engemann, Mary Ann Doane, Victor Mazin, and Christoph Eggersgluß. I am thankful to the faculty at Princeton University who supported my work in its earliest stages and who have continued to provide invaluable insight. Thank you to Tom Levin for his always effervescent input and to members of the Department of German: Mike Jennings, Nikolaus Wegmann, Joseph Vogl, Sally Poor, and Joel Lande. A special note of immense thanks to Devin Fore for many years of unwavering encouragement.

I am also grateful to the many people I worked with at Princeton who gave me essential feedback or helped me figure out what my work was even about, including Ed Eigen, Hal Foster, Zahid Chaudhary, Diana Fuss, and Hent de Vries. I am also thankful to the splendid peers I had during my time there, including Grant Wythoff, Hannes Mandel, John Benjamin, Megan Heuer, and Mareike Stoll. Thank you as well to John Hamilton at Harvard for a summer's worth of access to the fortress that is Widener Library.

The deepest possible thanks to my beloved Berlin fam, Harun Maye, Erika Thomalla, Cornelius Reiber, and Philipp Albers. Thank you to Christina Vagt for the tireless intellectual energy and to Philipp Felsch. Thanks to my friend and frequent intellectual copilot Leif Weatherby for reading hundreds of pages and spending an even greater number of hours riffing on ideas, and to my reliable friend and source of the smartest gchat cynicism, Chris Reitz. I am grateful to all my fellow members of the Digital Theory Lab for their generous inclusion in the group, and especially to Lisa Gitelman, Matthew Handelman, David Bering-Porter, and Joe Lemelin. I am grateful as well for the support of Paul Fleming and Annette Richards at the Cornell Society for the Humanities and the great weekly discussions with the other fellows during the dark time of the Covid-19 pandemic.

Since moving to Ithaca, I have also been thankful to have Sophie Pinkham, Nick Mulder, and Will Krieger as friends and neighbors. I am very much indebted to Orit Halpern for her marvelous suggestions on this project and so many others. To my dearest friends who had the wherewithal to stick around for periods of both work and rest, I am immensely grateful. Thank you to Beth Clevenger for twenty years of friendship, logic-defying optimism, and ruthless editing. To Daria Vaisman, thank you for lovingly negging me into finishing the book. Thank you also to enduring friends Gary Ferrini, Ian Thacker, and Ross Etherton, who represent both the long before and the long after to this project. Finally, to Lauren Oyler, who saved me from the abyss and a ton of dangling modifiers, this entire book is for you, although I would never expect you to read it again.

Notes

Introduction

1. Karl Marx, *Capital: A Critique of Political Economy,* vol. 1, trans. Ben Fowkes (New York: Penguin Books, 1982), 353; Friedrich Engels, *The Condition of the Working Class in England,* ed. David McLellan (Oxford: Oxford University Press, 1993); Bernard Stiegler, *The Age of Disruption: Technology and Madness in Computational Capitalism,* trans. Daniel Ross (Cambridge, UK: Polity Press, 2019).

2. Gottfried Wilhelm Leibniz, "De Progressione Dyadica, Pars I" (MS, March 15, 1679), published in Erich Hochstetter and Hermann-Josef Greve, eds., *Herrn von Leibniz' Rechnung mit Null und Eins* (Berlin: Siemens Aktiengesellschaft, 1966), 46–47.

3. Alonzo Church, "An Unsolvable Problem of Elementary Number Theory," *American Journal of Mathematics* 58, no. 2 (April 1936): 345–63; Alan Turing, "On Computable Numbers, with an Application to the Entscheidungsproblem," *Proceedings of the London Mathematical Society* s2–42, no. 1 (January 1937): 230–65; Claude Shannon, "A Symbolic Analysis of Relay and Switching Circuits" (master's thesis, MIT, 1940).

4. Alan Turing, "Lecture to the London Mathematical Society on 20 February 1947," in *Alan Turing: His Work and Impact,* ed. S. Barry Cooper and Jan van Leeuwen (Oxford: Elsevier, 2013), 486.

5. Alan Turing, "Computing Machinery and Intelligence," *Mind* 59 (October 1950): 436.

6. Norbert Wiener, *Cybernetics: Or Control and Communication in the Animal and the Machine,* 2nd ed. (Cambridge, Mass.: MIT Press, 1965); Donna Haraway, "A Cyborg Manifesto: Science, Technology, and Socialist-Feminism in the Late Twentieth Century," in *Manifestly Haraway* (Minneapolis: University of Minnesota Press, 2016), 3–90.

7. Friedrich Kittler, "There Is No Software," in *Literature, Media, Information Systems,* ed. John Johnston (Amsterdam: G+B Arts, 1997), 153.

8. Gregory Bateson, *Mind and Nature: A Necessary Unity* (New York: Dutton, 1979), 228.

9. Jean Epstein, *The Intelligence of a Machine,* trans. Christophe Wall-Romana (Minneapolis: Univocal, 2014), 13.

10. Epstein, 13.

11. W. H. Eccles and F. W. Jordan, "A Trigger Relay Utilising Three-Electrode Thermionic Vacuum Tubes," *The Electrician* 83 (September 19, 1919): 298. See also Morris Rubinoff, "Notes on the Design of Eccles-Jordan Flip-Flops," *Transactions of the American Institute of Electrical Engineers, Part I: Communication and Electronics* 71, no. 3 (July 1952): 215–20.

12. For an account of their relationship, beginning when Wittgenstein was a teenager working at a meteorological station outside Manchester, England, see Brian McGuinness, *Wittgenstein, a Life: Young Ludwig, 1889–1921* (Berkeley: University of California Press, 1988).

13. Robert Dennhardt, *The Flipflop-Legende und das Digitale: Eine Vorgeschichte des Digitalcomputers vom Unterbrecherkontakt zur Röhrenelektronik, 1837–1945* (Berlin: Kadmos, 2010), 14. All translations in this book are mine unless otherwise noted.

14. Bernhard Siegert, *Passage des Digitalen: Zeichenpraktiken der neuzeitlichen Wissenschaft, 1500–1900* (Berlin: Brinkmann & Bose, 2003), 406.

15. Tom Gunning, "The Cinema of Attractions: Early Film, Its Spectator and the Avant-Garde," *Wide Angle* 8, nos. 3/4 (Fall 1986): 63–70.

16. M. Beatrice Fazi convincingly takes up related questions in her theorization of "a computational aesthetics of discreteness" in "Digital Aesthetics: The Discrete and the Continuous," *Theory, Culture & Society* 36, no. 1 (2019): 3–26.

17. Edward L. Braun, *Digital Computer Design: Logic, Circuitry, and Synthesis* (New York: Academic Press, 1963), 73.

18. Eccles and Jordan, "A Trigger Relay," 298.

19. Charles Petzold provides a clear and detailed account of the Eccles-Jordan trigger circuit, noting, "A flip-flop circuit *retains information.* It '*remembers.*' . . . A flip-flop is very much like a seesaw. A seesaw has two stable states, never staying long in that precarious middle position. You can always tell from looking at the seesaw which side was pushed down most recently." Charles Petzold, *Code: The Hidden Language of Computer Hardware and Software* (Redmond, Wash.: Microsoft Press, 2000), 161. The function of common set-reset (SR) flip-flops is lucidly described (also using the seesaw metaphor) in Warren Sack, *The Software Arts* (Cambridge, Mass.: MIT Press, 2019).

20. Niklas Luhmann, "System as Difference," *Organization* 13, no. 1 (2006): 44.

21. N. Katherine Hayles, "Can Computers Create Meanings? A Cyber/Bio/Semiotic Perspective," *Critical Inquiry* 46 (Autumn 2019): 32–55. See also N. Katherine Hayles, *How We Became Posthuman: Virtual Bodies in Cybernetics, Literature, and Informatics* (Chicago: University of Chicago Press, 1999).

22. Hayles, "Can Computers Create Meanings?," 44.

23. Hayles, 44.

24. Hayles, 48. The phrase *absential phenomena* is derived from Terrence Deacon, *Incomplete Nature: How Mind Emerged from Matter* (New York: Norton, 2012).

25. Mike Davies et al., "Loihi: A Neuromorphic Manycore Processor with On-Chip Learning," *IEEE Micro* (January/February 2018): 82–99.

26. Schreyer was also a member of the Nazi party during the Holocaust and fled to Brazil after the war.

27. Paul Ceruzzi, "The Early Computers of Konrad Zuse, 1935 to 1945," *Annals of the History of Computing* 3, no. 3 (July 1981): 241–62. See also Hartmut Petzold, *Moderne Rechenkünstler: Die Industrialisierung der Rechentechnik in Deutschland* (Munich: C. H. Beck, 1992); and Lev Manovich, "Cinema and Digital Media," in *Perspectives of Media Art*, ed. Jeffrey Shaw and Hans Peter Schwarz (Ostfildern, Germany: Cantz, 1996).

28. Simon Lavington, *Early Computing in Britain: Ferranti Ltd. and Government Funding, 1948–1958* (Cham, Switzerland: Springer, 2019), 174.

29. Lavington, 172.

30. Alexander Galloway, *Laruelle: Against the Digital* (Minneapolis: University of Minnesota Press, 2014), 62.

31. Nelson Goodman, *Languages of Art: An Approach to a Theory of Symbols* (New York: Bobbs-Merrill, 1968), 161.

32. Umberto Eco, *A Theory of Semiotics* (Bloomington: University of Indiana Press, 1976), 8.

33. Kittler deployed the term *Semiotechnik* many times in his work, beginning with "Über die Sozialisation Wilhelm Meisters," in *Dichtung als Sozialisationsspiel: Studien zu Goethe und Gottfried Keller* (Göttingen: Vandenhoeck & Ruprecht, 1978). However, his use of the word concentrated primarily on purely semiotic techniques and practices as distinct from technical media. One sees this clearly where he writes, "When conditions of totalizing semiotechnics prevail, the only real question involves the media they implement." Friedrich A. Kittler, "Media and Drugs in Pynchon's Second World War," in *The Truth of the Technological World*, trans. Erik Butler (Stanford: Stanford University Press, 2013), 86.

34. Ernst Kapp, *Elements of a Philosophy of Technology: On the Evolutionary History of Culture*, ed. Jeffrey West Kirkwood and Leif Weatherby, trans. Lauren K. Wolfe (Minneapolis: University of Minnesota Press, 2018).

35. Kapp, 37.

36. Kapp, 37.

37. Peter Berz, *08/15: Ein Standard des 20. Jahrhunderts* (Munich: Wilhelm Fink, 2001), 98. For more on the relationship between Reuleaux, Kapp, and the nature of "Gestell," see Jeffrey West Kirkwood and Leif Weatherby, "Introduction: The Philosophy of Technology," in *Elements of a Philosophy of Technology*, ix–xliii; and Jeffrey West Kirkwood and Leif Weatherby, "Operations of Culture: Ernst Kapp's Philosophy of Technology," *Grey Room* 72 (Summer 2018): 6–15.

38. It is a question that has also been explored under the aegis of "biosemiotics," which looks at the centrality of semiosis in the evolution of organic life, including, or perhaps especially, among nonhuman organisms. See Jesper Hoffmann, *Biosemiotics: An Examination into the Signs of Life and the Life of Signs*, trans. Donald Favareau (Scranton, Penn.: University of Scranton Press); and Wendy Wheeler, *Expecting Earth: Life | Culture | Biosemiotics* (London: Lawrence & Wishart, 2016).

39. Geoffrey Winthrop-Young, "Cultural Techniques: Preliminary Remarks," *Theory, Culture & Society* 30, no. 6 (2013): 4–5.

40. Thomas Macho, "Second-Order Animals: Cultural Techniques of Identity and Identification," *Theory, Culture & Society* 30, no. 6 (2013): 31.

41. Bernhard Siegert, "Cultural Techniques: Or the End of the Intellectual Postwar Era in German Media Theory," *Theory, Culture & Society* 30, no. 6 (2013): 60.

42. Laura Mulvey, *Death 24x a Second: Stillness and the Moving Image* (London: Reaktion Books, 2007), 12.

43. Jacques Lacan, *The Seminar of Jacques Lacan, Book II: The Ego in Freud's Theory and in the Technique of Psychoanalysis, 1954–1955*, ed. Jacques-Alain Miller, trans. Sylvana Tomaselli (New York: Norton, 1991), 300.

44. Christian Metz, *Film Language: A Semiotics of the Cinema*, trans. Michael Taylor (Chicago: University of Chicago Press, 1991), 35–36.

45. Mary Ann Doane, *The Emergence of Cinematic Time: Modernity, Contingency, the Archive* (Cambridge, Mass.: Harvard University Press, 2002), 185.

46. Gilbert Simondon, *On the Mode of Existence of Technical Objects*, trans. Cecile Malaspina and John Rogove (Minneapolis: Univocal, 2017).

47. Klaus Kreimeier, *Traum und Exzess: Die Kulturgeschichte des frühen Kinos* (Vienna: Paul Zsolnay, 2011), 90.

48. André Bazin, "The Evolution of the Language of Cinema" (1953), in *What Is Cinema?*, trans. Hugh Gray (Berkeley: University of California Press, 2005), 30.

49. Ludwig Wittgenstein, *Philosophical Investigations*, trans. G. E. M. Anscombe (Oxford, UK: Basil Blackwell, 1986), 84e.

50. Simondon, *On the Mode of Existence of Technical Objects*, 81.

51. Simondon, 157.

52. Viktor Tausk, "Über die Entstehung des 'Beeinflussungsapparates' in der Schizophrenie," *Internationale Zeitschrift für Ärtzliche Psychoanalyse* 5 (1919): 1–33.

1. Engineering the Interval

1. Gilbert Simondon, *On the Mode of Existence of Technical Objects*, trans. Cecile Malaspina and John Rogove (Minneapolis: Univocal, 2017), 150.

2. Simondon, 150.

3. Anson Rabinbach, *The Human Motor: Energy, Fatigue, and the Origins of Modernity* (New York: Basic Books, 1990), 55.

4. Norbert Wiener, *The Human Use of Human Beings: Cybernetics and Society* (1950; repr., London: Free Association Books, 1989), 16.

5. Simondon, *On the Mode of Existence of Technical Objects,* 150.

6. Simondon, 150.

7. Karl Marbe, *Experimentell-psychologische Untersuchungen über das Urteil* (Leipzig: Wilhelm Engelmann, 1901); George Mandler, *Modern Experimental Psychology: From James and Wundt to Cognitive Science* (Cambridge, Mass.: MIT Press, 2007), 80.

8. Erica Fretwell, *Sensory Experiments: Psychophysics, Race, and the Aesthetics of Feeling* (Durham, N.C.: Duke University Press, 2020), 1, 2.

9. Fechner did so by modifying Ernst Heinrich Weber's earlier observations, and the resulting hypothesis was referred to as the Weber-Fechner Law.

10. Gustav Fechner, *Elemente der Psychophysik,* vol. 1 (Leipzig: Breitkopf & Härtel, 1907), 247. Fechner also accounts for the complexity of a mental image—which can only be resolved by passing through the mental apparatus—by describing the effect of a prism, which indicates parts of the electromagnetic spectrum that are otherwise invisible. With the use of the prism, the presence of ultraviolet light is represented, though not revealed, as its frequency is decreased. The example becomes profoundly useful for later thinking about the relationship between conscious material and unconscious material as a function of the mental apparatus rather than the material itself. Fechner, *Elemente der Psychophysik,* 1:239.

11. Karl Marbe, "Die stroboskopischen Erscheinungen," *Philosophische Studien* 14 (1898): 376–401.

12. Simon von Stampfer, *Die stroboskopischen Scheiben oder optischen Zauberscheiben: Deren Theorie und wissenschaftliche Anwendung* (Vienna: Trentsenky & Vieweg, 1833). This became a part of the nineteenth-century scientific vocabulary, and Stampfer was credited with inventing the Stampfer Disc independent of Joseph Plateau and his Phenakistoscope. These early optical "toys" were critical to the development of scientific psychology during the nineteenth century.

13. Sigmund Freud, *Die Traumdeutung,* Studienausgabe 2 (Frankfurt am Main: S. Fischer, 1989). Freud uses the heuristic model of optical devices like the telescope as a well-known departure from his earliest mechanistic model of the psyche posthumously published in his *Entwurf einer Psychologie* (1895), in *Gesammelte Werke, Nachtragsband: Texte aus den Jahren 1885 bis 1938,* ed. Angela Richards (Frankfurt am Main: S. Fischer, 1987), 375–486. Many aspects of his original model remain intact and reflect a persisting interest in maintaining a vision of an energetic economy in the "mental instrument" that allows him to continue speaking of his observations, and psychoanalysis in general, as scientific. The work was originally written in notebooks that were a part of Freud's correspondence with Wilhelm Fliess and were published only posthumously.

14. Jacques Lacan, *The Seminar of Jacques Lacan, Book II: The Ego in Freud's Theory and in the Technique of Psychoanalysis, 1954–55*, ed. Jacques-Alain Miller, trans. Sylvana Tomaselli (New York: Norton, 1991), 61.

15. Philipp Sarasin, *Reizbare Maschinen: Eine Geschichte des Körpers, 1765–1914* (Frankfurt am Main: Suhrkamp, 2001), 352.

16. Freud's use of optical heuristics, particularly in *The Interpretation of Dreams*, trans. James Strachey (New York: Basic Books, 2010), is considered more directly in chapter 3.

17. Marbe, "Die stroboskopischen Erscheinungen," 398–99 (emphasis mine).

18. Hans Lehmann, *Die Kinematographie: Ihre Grundlagen und ihre Anwendungen* (Leipzig: B. G. Teubner, 1911), 19. Paul Linke published his results and theory on the illusion of movement in *Die stroboskopischen Erscheinungen als Täuschungen des Identitätsbewusstseins und das Problem des Sehens von Bewegungen* (Leipzig: Wilhelm Engelmann, 1907).

19. Wolfgang Jacobsen, "Frühgeschichte des deutschen Films: Licht am Ende des Tunnels," in *Geschichte des deutschen Films*, ed. Wolfgang Jacobsen, Anton Kaes, and Hans Helmut Prinzler (Stuttgart: J. B. Metzler, 1993), 16. Given that there are entire sections in Lehmann's book devoted to genres such as trick films that used filmic techniques of diegetic space construction that did not merely "reproduce" theatrical space, one might argue that Lehmann's interest in technical effects was related to the filmic means of narrativity and was not merely a result of the varieté format.

20. Karl Marbe, *Theorie der kinematographischen Projektionen* (Leipzig: Johann Ambrosius Barth, 1910), 3.

21. Marbe, 7.

22. Naldo Felke, "Cinema's Damaging Effects on Health" (1913), originally published as "Die Gesundheitsschädlichkeit des Kinos," *Die Umschau: Wochenschrift über die Fortschritte in Wissenschaft und Technik* 17, no. 13 (March 22, 1913): 254–55, and reprinted in *The Promise of Cinema: German Film Theory, 1907–1933*, ed. Anton Kaes, Nicholas Baer, and Michael Cowan (Berkeley: University of California Press, 2016), 235.

23. Robert Tigerstedt, *Lehrbuch der Physiologie des Menschen* (Leipzig: S. Hirzel, 1898), 229. In *The Human Motor*, Rabinbach famously discusses the late nineteenth-century scientific conceptions of mental and physiological "fatigue" (*Ermüdung*) as a part of mechanical theories of thermodynamics.

24. Carl Forch, *Der Kinematograph und das sich bewegende Bild: Geschichte und technische Entwicklung der Kinematographie bis zur Gegenwart* (Leipzig: A. Hartleben, 1913), 51. There were various schools of thought about the best design for shutters and the intermittent mechanisms for advancing the filmstrip. Rouleau shutters or roll-blind shutters slid in front of the aperture from the sides during the advancement of the filmstrip, while rotating shutters were bladed,

continuously turning and synchronized to cover the light source while the pawl or *Klaue* pulled the filmstrip forward intermittently with each quarter rotation of the Geneva drive. There were also slit shudders and a number of other mechanisms for blocking the light source during the movement of film, ensuring that the apparent movement of the image did not result from the movement of the image itself but instead from the succession of multiple static images. There were a number of manuals and histories of cinematographic devices available at the time, one of which was Karl Wilhelm Wolf-Czapek's *Die Kinematographie: Wesen, Entstehung und Ziele des lebenden Bildes* (Dresden: Union Deutsche Verlagsgesellschaft, 1908).

25. Ludwig Vogl-Bieneck, "Die historische Projektionskunst: Eine offene geschichtliche Perspektive auf den Film als Aufführungsereignis," in *KINtop: Jahrbuch zur Erforschung des frühen Films,* vol. 3, ed. Frank Kessler, Sabine Lenk, and Martin Loiperdinger (Frankfurt am Main: Stroemfeld, 1994), 13.

26. Siegfried Kracauer, "Cult of Distraction," in *The Mass Ornament: Weimar Essays,* trans. Thomas Y. Levin (Cambridge, Mass.: Harvard University Press, 1995), 324.

27. Siegfried Zielinski, *Audiovisions: Cinema and Television as Entr'actes in History,* trans. Gloria Custance (Amsterdam: Amsterdam University Press, 1999), 99.

28. Lehmann, *Die Kinematographie,* 5.

29. Lehmann, 5.

30. This point about the dialectic between technologies and organs had already been made more generally in 1877 by Ernst Kapp.

31. Walter Benjamin, "On Some Motifs in Baudelaire," in *The Writer of Modern Life: Essays on Charles Baudelaire,* ed. Michael Jennings (Cambridge, Mass.: Belknap Press of Harvard University Press, 2006), 191.

32. Lehmann, *Die Kinematographie,* 16, emphasis mine. The historical significance of and exchange between Marbe and Linke, Linke's criticism of Marbe, and the cultural reception of their work by figures like Arnheim and Münsterberg, along with a longer history of stroboscopic experimental design, can be found in Christoph Hoffmann, *Unter Beobachtung: Naturforschung in der Zeit der Sinnesapparate* (Göttingen: Wallstein, 2006).

33. Linke, *Die stroboskopischen Täuschungen,* 461.

34. Linke, 463.

35. Wilhelm Wundt, "Ueber die Messung psychischer Vorgänge," *Philosophische Studien* 1 (1883): 251, 252.

36. Wundt, 253.

37. Wundt, 254.

38. Franz Reuleaux, *Kinematik: Grundzüge einer Theorie des Maschinenwesens* (Braunschweig: Friedrich Vieweg und Sohn, 1875). An early English translation of the work was published as Franz Reuleaux, *The Kinematics of Machinery: Outlines*

of a Theory of Machines, trans. Alexander B. W. Kennedy (1876; repr., Mineola, N.Y.: Dover, 2012).

39. Reuleaux, *The Kinematics of Machinery,* 42.

40. On kinematics, see Lisa Gitelman, "Popular Kinematics: Technical Knowing in the Age of Machines," *History & Theory* 59, no. 4 (December 2020): 67–85.

41. Martin Heidegger, "Der Ursprung des Kunstwerkes (1935/36)," in *Gesamtausgabe 5: Holzwege* (Frankfurt am Main: Vittorio Klostermann, 1977). In *The Cyclinder: Kinematics of the Nineteenth Century* (Berkeley: University of California Press, 2012), Helmut Müller-Sievers claims that Heidegger's understanding of Gestell was derived, at least in part, from his reading of Reuleaux, for whom the term also figures prominently. In a footnote, he mentions that in Heidegger's preparatory notes for "The Question Concerning Technology," there is likely a direct citation about "*Drehbewegung*" from Reuleaux (174). There is also a strong case to be made that the notion of Gestell is closely related to gestalt as found in gestalt psychology, which was perhaps a product of Heidegger's relationship with Theodor Husserl but also bears a strong conceptual resemblance to work by gestalt psychologists such as Kurt Lewin, who was also cited by Rudolf Arnheim, who himself had repeatedly identified Heidegger as a thinker important for his work. This creates a kind of lineage from Reuleaux through gestalt psychology, in which the conditions for perception and ideation are rooted in theories of mechanics, particularly in the case of art. This relationship between Gestell and gestalt in Heidegger and in modern discourses on vision more broadly is explored in David Kleinberg-Levin, *The Philosopher's Gaze: Modernity in the Shadows of Enlightenment* (Berkeley: University of California Press, 1999).

42. Reuleaux, *Kinematik,* 87–88 (emphasis mine). It is important to mention that the term *Phoronomy,* used by Reuleaux, was already a part of Immanuel Kant's theory of motion in a work in which he expressly denied the possibility of a scientific psychology. Immanuel Kant, *Metaphysische Anfangsgründe der Naturwissenschaft, Werkausgabe,* vol. 9, ed. Wilhelm Weischedel (Frankfurt am Main: Suhrkamp, 1977).

43. Parmenides's fragment 8 has been interpreted as an argument for the illusory nature of change. Change would require creation ex nihilo and thus must be illusory. John Palmer, *Parmenides and Presocratic Philosophy* (Oxford: Oxford University Press, 2009), 30–31.

44. Peter Berz, *08/15: Ein Standard des 20. Jahrhunderts* (Munich: Wilhelm Fink, 2001), 98, 138.

45. Wolfgang Schäffner, "Bildmaschinen," *Kaleidoskopien: Theatricalität—Performance—Medialität,* no. 1 (1996): 25.

46. Edmund Burke Delabarre, *Über Bewegungsempfindungen* (Freiburg: Buchdruckerei Hch. Epsein, 1891), 1–2.

47. Delabarre, 2.

48. Kurt Danziger, "The Unknown Wundt: Drive, Apperception, and Volition," in *Wilhelm Wundt in History: The Making of Scientific Psychology,* ed. Robert W. Reiber and David Keith Robinson (New York: Plenum, 2001), 114.

49. Wolfgang Köhler, *Gestalt Psychology: An Introduction to New Concepts in Modern Psychology* (New York: Norton, 1992), 122. His mention of "psychical causality" is a reference to Wilhelm Wundt's *Grundriss der Psychologie* (1896; repr., Leipzig: Engelmann, 1907), 18–19.

50. Köhler, *Gestalt Psychology,* 122.

51. Rudolf Arnheim, *Film als Kunst* (1932; repr., Berlin: Suhrkamp, 2002), 104.

52. Wertheimer borrowed the tachistoscope from the experimental psychologist Friedrich Schumann and modified it for his 1912 experiments. Schumann's experiments with the tachistoscope, as discussed in chapter 3, were used to refute the letter-by-letter spelling theory of reading.

53. Arnheim, *Film als Kunst,* 104. Max Wertheimer's historically groundbreaking work on the perception of movement was originally published as "Experimentelle Studien über das Sehen von Bewegung," *Zeitschrift für Psychologie* 61 (1912): 161–265. For a detailed account of Wertheimer's work and its role in the development of gestalt psychology, see D. Brett King and Michael Wertheimer, *Max Wertheimer and Gestalt Theory* (New Brunswick, N.J.: Transaction, 2009).

54. Arnheim, *Film als Kunst,* 98.

55. Jean-Louis Comolli, "Machines of the Visible," in *The Cinematic Apparatus,* ed. Teresa de Lauretis and Stephen Heath (New York: St. Martin's, 1980), 130.

56. This history is detailed in Laurent Mannoni's magnificent archaeology of cinematographic apparatuses, *The Great Art of Light and Shadow: Archaeology of the Cinema,* trans. Richard Crangle (Exeter, UK: University of Exeter Press, 2000).

57. Tom Gunning, "In Your Face: Physiognomy, Photography, and the Gnostic Mission of Early Film," in *The Mind of Modernism: Medicine, Psychology, and the Cultural Arts in Europe and America, 1880–1940,* ed. Mark S. Micale (Stanford: Stanford University Press, 2004), 164.

58. This point is made by both Gunning and Jimena Canales in their identification of an essential conflict between the scientific dissection of movement into stills and their phantasmagoric reassembly to produce the appearance of motion in the history of the development of the cinematograph.

59. Jimena Canales, "Desired Machines: Cinema and the World in Its Own Image," *Science in Context* 24, no. 3 (2011): 348.

60. Henri Bergson, *Creative Evolution,* trans. Arthur Mitchell (New York: Modern Library, 2005), 332–33 (emphasis mine in the first sentence). This translation was authorized by Bergson himself and as the translator notes, he was helped by the "friendly interest of Professor William James" (v).

61. Wolfgang Ernst, *Chronopoetics: The Temporal Being and Operativity of Technological Media,* trans. Anthony Enns (New York: Rowman & Littlefield, 2016), 47.

62. Georg Lukács, "Gedanken zu einer Aesthetik des 'Kino'" (1911), ed. Thomas Y. Levin, reprinted in *Kino-Schriften 3: Jahrbuch der Gesellschaft für Filmtheorie* (Vienna: Verlag der wissenschaftlichen Gesellschaften Österreichs, 1992), 237 (emphasis mine). The reprint of the text includes revisions and additions in the footnotes that Lukács made to the later 1913 version.

63. Sigmund Freud, "Zur Einführung des Narzissmus" (1924), in *Gesammelte Werke,* Band 10 (Frankfurt am Main: S. Fischer, 1967), 138–70; Sigmund Freud, "Das Unheimliche" (1919), in *Gesammelte Werke,* Band 12 (Frankfurt am Main: S. Fischer, 1967), 229–68.

64. Lukács, "Gedanken zu einer Aesthetik des 'Kino,'" 240. This passage was added in the 1913 version.

65. Lukács, 237.

66. *Der Müller und sein Kind* is the oldest surviving complete Austrian narrative film in the archives. *Die Verräterin* is the fifth Asta Nielsen feature, directed by Urban Gad and released less than a year after Lukács's essay. It includes a number of more sophisticated filming and staging techniques in support of narrative continuity, such as parallel editing. David Bordwell notes about the film in *The Poetics of Cinema* (New York: Routledge, 2008): "The drama could hardly be more rudimentary, but Gad stages it elegantly" (264).

2. The Semiotechnical Subject

1. An introduction to the history and economics of early cinemas in Germany and Austria can be found in Corinna Müller, *Frühe deutsche Kinematographie: Formale, wirtschaftliche und kulturelle Entwicklungen, 1907–1912* (Stuttgart: Metzler, 1994); Corinna Müller and Harro Segeberg, eds., *Kinoöffentlichkeit (1895–1920): Entstehung—Etablierung—Differenzierung* (Marburg: Schüren, 2008); Thomas Schorr, "Die Film- und Kinoreformbewegung und die deutsche Filmwirtschaft: Eine Analyse des Fachblatts 'Der Kinematograph' (1907–1935) unter pädagogischen und publizistischen Aspekten" (PhD diss., Universität der Bundeswehr München, Institut für Medienpädagogik, 1990); Janet Bergstrom, "Asta Nielsen's Early German Films," in *Before Caligari: German Cinema, 1895–1920,* ed. Paolo Cherchi Usai and Lorenzo Codelli (Pordenone: Edizioni Biblioteca dell'Immagine, 1990), 162–84; and Thomas Elsaesser and Michael Wedel, "Distribution," in *Encyclopedia of Early Cinema,* ed. Richard Abel (New York: Routledge, 2006), 390–92.

2. An international market for instructional books like Bernard E. Jones's *The Cinematograph Book: A Complete Practical Guide to the Taking and Projecting of Cinematographic Pictures* (New York: Cassell, 1915) developed around this time, indicating an increasing normalization of technical equipment and techniques. The formulation of a repertoire of more standard editing and narrative practices that accompanied this trend—fueled particularly by monopolization—is explored

in Thomas Elsaesser, "Wie der frühe Film zum Erzählkino wurde: Vom kollektiven Publikum zum individuellen Zuschauer," in *Erlebnisort Kino*, ed. Irmbert Schenk (Marburg: Schüren 2000), 34–54; and Peter Lähn, "*Afgrunden* und die deutsche Filmindustrie: Zur Entstehung des Monopolfilms," in *Schwarzer Traum und weisse Sklavin: Deutsch-dänische Filmbeziehungen, 1910–1930*, ed. Manfred Behn (Munich: Edition Text + Kritik), 15–22.

3. Whether or not these cultural responses to the effects of cinema can be legitimately characterized as a part of a monolithic reform movement, they are nevertheless foundational to film history and historiography. For sourcebooks and historical overviews that include the writings and context for the cinema reform movement in Germany, see Jörg Schweinitz, ed., *Prolog vor dem Film: Nachdenken über ein neues Medium, 1909–1914* (Leipzig: Reclam, 1992); Fritz Güttinger, *Stummfilm im Zitat der Zeit* (Frankfurt: Deutsches Filmmuseum, 1984); Fritz Güttinger, ed., *Kein Tag ohne Kino: Schriftsteller über den Stummfilm* (Frankfurt: Deutsches Filmmuseum, 1984); Herbert Birett, *Lichtspiele: Der Kino in Deutschland bis 1914* (Munich: Q-Verlag, 1994); Helmut H. Diederichs, *Anfänge deutscher Filmkritik* (Stuttgart: R. Fischer + U. Wielerroither, 1986); Thomas Elsaesser, *Filmgeschichte und frühes Kino: Archäologie eines Medienwandels* (Munich: Edition Text + Kritik, 2002); Thomas Elsaesser, ed., *A Second Life: German Cinema's First Decades* (Amsterdam: Amsterdam University Press, 1996); and Anton Kaes, *Kino-Debatte: Texte zum Verhältnis von Literatur und Film, 1909–1929* (Tübingen: Niemeyer, 1978). Collectively, these texts demonstrate the degree to which the objectives and intellectual commitments of the reform movement were not singular but ran the gamut, from a total opposition to film to calls for the production of artistically worthy films that might fully realize the potential of the medium and produce viewers who were no longer interested in pulp films (*Schundfilme*).

4. This complaint about the sexualized setting of cinemas and the scintillating content of films was nearly ubiquitous in early appeals to reform the production and regulation of film. There was a common call from myriad regional organizations and moral societies (*Sittlichkeitsvereine*) with names like Verein zur Hebung des Kinematographenwesens (Association for the Elevation of the Character of Cinema) in Leipzig as well as articles in journals like *Bild und Film* to limit the content of films to educational topics, control the age and gender of the audiences, and control the importation of foreign films, which were thought to undermine efforts to educate children and citizens to a German cultural and literary tradition as part of an educational program. See also Sabine Hake, *The Cinema's Third Machine: Writing on Film in Germany, 1907–1933* (Lincoln: University of Nebraska Press, 1993), 27–42.

5. As but one instance, the 1910 Mann Act in the United States was introduced to regulate the interstate transport of "white slaves," a moralistic public obsession that had been stoked by films like George Loane Tucker's *Traffic in Souls.*

The real impact of such laws was exacted upon figures like the Black boxer, Jack Johnson, who had defeated the "great white hope," Jim Jeffries, in 1910. Cinematic depictions of the match caused a national convulsion of violence, with marauding white people attacking and killing Black people from New York City to Pueblo, Colorado; Shreveport, Louisiana; and Los Angeles, California. In a racially opportunistic response to white rioting, Congress passed the Sims Act in 1912, barring pictorial representations of prize fights (primarily boxing matches) from being transported across state lines. These histories are detailed in Geoffrey C. Ward, *Unforgivable Blackness: The Rise and Fall of Jack Johnson* (New York: Vintage, 2004); Dan Streible, *Fight Pictures: A History of Boxing in Early Cinema* (Berkeley: University of California Press, 2008); and Lee Grieveson, *Policing Cinema: Movies and Censorship in Early-Twentieth-Century America* (Berkeley: University of California Press, 2004).

6. Sabine Lenk situates the heterogeneous motives of the Kinoreformbewegung as part of a climate of morality movements concentrated on youth and popular education and the rhetorics of nationalistic moral preservation. Sabine Lenk, "Völkisches Gedankengut im Umfeld der Kinoreformbewegung," in *Handbuch zur "Völkische Bewegung," 1871–1918,* ed. Frank Almai, Johann S. Koch, and Uwe Schneider (Munich: K.G. Saur, 1996), 797–805. While the nomenclature and announced objectives of opponents of Schundfilme and Schundliteratur were very similar—having a shared cultural and institutional lineage—Kaspar Maase notes: "Trash literature denoted a sector of narrative literature was generally recognized as an art form." Kaspar Maase, *Die Kinder der Massenkultur: Kontroversen um Schmutz und Schund seit dem Kaiserreich* (Frankfurt am Main: Campus, 2012), 122.

7. Maase, *Die Kinder der Massenkultur,* 35.

8. Otto von Leixner, *Zum Kampfe gegen den Schmutz in Wort und Bild* (Leipzig: Dietrich, 1904). For more on von Leixner and other figures in the anti-Schund movement around 1900, see Andrew Lees, *Cities, Sin, and Social Reform in Imperial Germany* (Ann Arbor: University of Michigan Press, 2002); and Kara L. Ritzheimer, "Protecting Youth from 'Trash': Anti-*Schund* Campaigns in Baden, 1900–1933" (PhD diss., SUNY Binghamton, 2007).

9. Ritzheimer, "Protecting Youth from 'Trash,'" 50–51. Brunner was a professor and powerful advisor to the Berliner Polizeipräsidiums and worked in tandem with the Verein der Verleger für Volksliteratur (Association of Publishers of People's Literature) to censor literature and shut down publications.

10. Victor Noack, *Der Kino: Etwas über sein Wesen und Seine Bedeutung* (Leipzig: Felix Dietrich, 1913).

11. Robert Gaupp, "Die Gefahren des Kinos," *Süddeutsche Monatshefte* 9, no. 2 (July 1912): 365.

12. Anton Kaes, Nicholas Baer, and Michael Cowan, eds., *The Promise of Cinema: German Film Theory 1907–1933* (Oakland: University of California Press,

2016), is a large sourcebook of previously untranslated early German film criticism that takes a significant step toward considering seriously the theoretical work done by these early critics.

13. Klaus Kreimeier, *Traum und Exzess: Die Kulturgeschichte des frühen Kinos* (Vienna: Paul Zsolnay, 2011), 90. There is a wealth of literature on discourses of nerves and nervousness in Germany around the turn of the twentieth century, suggesting that literary, scientific, and philosophical conceptions of human perception and consciousness were transformed by electrification and new technological conditions. On this topic, see Joachim Radkau, *Das Zeitalter der Nervosität: Deutschland zwischen Bismarck und Hitler* (Munich: Hanser, 1998); Andreas Killen, *Berlin Electropolis: Shock, Nerves, and German Modernity* (Berkeley: University of California Press, 2006); and Michael Cowan, *Cult of the Will: Nervousness and German Modernity* (University Park: Pennsylvania State University Press, 2008).

14. In her analysis of the Dada montage, for instance, Brigid Doherty argues that "the shocks of the trenches are simulated by the shocks of the metropolis." She goes on to claim that George Grosz's artistic practice gives expression to a distinctly modern "pathology of the machine" in which the "pressure gauge has blown." Brigid Doherty, "'See: *We Are All Neurasthenics!*' or, The Trauma of Dada Montage," *Critical Inquiry* 24, no. 1 (Autumn 1997): 95, 97.

15. Oswald Spengler, *Der Untergang des Abendlandes: Umrisse einer Morphologie der Weltgeschichte* (1923; repr., Munich: C. H. Beck, 1998), 1191.

16. Jonathan Crary, *Techniques of the Observer: On Vision and Modernity in the Nineteenth Century* (Cambridge, Mass.: MIT Press, 1992), 17.

17. Crary, 96.

18. Gaupp, "Die Gefahren des Kinos," 364.

19. Gaupp, 364, 365.

20. This term receives more attention in the following chapters.

21. With the rise of commercial computing in the middle of the twentieth century, this would become a central question of cybernetics and systems theory and a preoccupation of everyone from Marvin Minsky to Heinz von Foerster to Niklas Luhmann.

22. On the specific worry about the state of hypersuggestibility and influence induced by films of the later Weimar period in Germany, see Stefan Andriopoulos, *Possessed: Hypnotic Crimes, Corporate Fiction, and the Invention of Cinema,* trans. Peter Jansen and Stefan Andriopoulos (Chicago: University of Chicago Press, 2008). Jeffrey Sconce, *Haunted Media: Electronic Presence from Telegraphy to Television* (Durham, N.C.: Duke University Press, 2000), deals with a broader history of technophobic and spiritual discourses that accompanied new media.

23. Max Nordau, *Entartung,* vol. 2 (Berlin: Carl Dunder, 1893), 524. William James ridiculed Nordau's appropriation of scientific language to lend authority to his decidedly unscientific reflections on social and aesthetic degeneration and

referred to the work as his "bulky book" in *The Varieties of Religious Experience*, vol. 13 (Cambridge, Mass.: Harvard University Press, 1985), 23. Perhaps the most important works recovering the nineteenth-century discourses on "Aufmerksamkeit" connected to new visual technologies and psychophysical experimentation are Jonathan Crary's books *Techniques of the Observer* and *Suspensions of Perception: Attention, Spectacle, and Modern Culture* (Cambridge, Mass.: MIT Press, 2001).

24. Journals of empirical psychology from the late 1890s through the early 1900s were topically dominated by problems of optical illusions (*optische Täuschungen*), and particularly the perceptual effect of *Verschmelzung.* The journals *Philosophische Studien,* edited by Wilhelm Wundt, and *Zeitschrift für Psychologie und Physiologie der Sinnesorgane,* founded by Hermann Ebbinghaus and Arthur König, were filled with articles and reviews about apparent movement experiments by Wilhelm Wundt, Theodor Ziehen, Carl Stumpf, Ernst Dürr, Oswald Külpe, and Paul Linke, to name only a few major figures in the field.

25. Martin Heidegger, *Sein und Zeit* (Tübingen: Max Niemeyer, 2002), 66–72.

26. Adolf Sellmann, *Der Kinematograph als Volkserzieher?* (Langensalza: Beyer & Mann, 1912), 26. Sellmann supports this claim by referencing an experiment by an unnamed scientist in Stockholm, who was likely Robert Tigerstedt.

27. Karl Marbe, *Theorie der kinematographischen Projektionen* (Leipzig: Johann Ambrosius Barth, 1910), 74.

28. R. Stigler, "Über das Flimmern der Kinematographen," *Archiv für die gesamte Physiologie des Menschen und der Tiere* 123, no. 4 (June 2, 1908): 224. Marbe frequently cites Paul Liesegang's *Handbuch der praktischen Kinematographie* (Leipzig: Liesegang, 1908). Liesegang also later wrote and edited a large and encyclopedic book on the cinematograph, its construction, and its applications for medicine, science, and education, *Wissenschaftliche Kinematographie* (Leipzig: Liesegang, 1920).

29. H. Sch., "Über das Flimmern der Kinematographen," *Der Mechaniker: Zeitschrift zur Förderung der Präzisions-Mechanik und Optik* 16, no. 18 (September 20, 1908): 209.

30. Carl Forch, *Der Kinematograph und das sich bewegende Bild: Geschichte und technische Entwicklung der Kinematographie bis zur Gegenwart* (Leipzig: A. Hartleben, 1913), 58.

31. Ramon Reichert, "Kinematographie der Objektivität: Zur Medienästhetik des Wissens um 1900," in *Aisthesis: Wahrnehmungsprozesse und Visualisierungsformen in Kunst und Technik,* ed. Bernhard Dotzler and Christoph Wagner (Munich: Schnell und Steiner, 2009), 105.

32. Henning Schmidgen, "Das Experimentelle und das Pathologische: Zur Geschichte psychophysiologischer Zeitmessungen, 1880–1900," in *Maß und Eigensinn: Studien im Anschluß an Georges Canguilhem,* ed. Cornelius Borck, Volker Hess, and Henning Schmidgen (Munich: Wilhelm Fink, 2005), 215.

33. Lorrain Daston and Peter Galison, *Objectivity* (New York: Zone Books, 2007), 259. The discussion specifically regards the famous experimental psychologist Wilhelm Wundt's book *Grundzüge der physiologischen Psychologie,* vol. 1 (Leipzig: Verlag von Wilhelm Engelmann, 1874).

34. Barry Salt's use of ASL as a quantitative measure for gauging the progressive development toward ever-more sophisticated narrative continuity through editing is a good, if much criticized, example of how temporal and spatial discontinuity in film is thought to produce diegetic continuity. As Salt noticed, the ASL decreased over time as the narrative coherence increased. Barry Salt, *Film Style and Technology: History and Analysis* (London: Starword, 1992). He also gives an account of the repertoire of visual devices that arise with the "evolution" of narrative film and shorter ASL, which he locates around 1903–4. Barry Salt, "Film Form: 1900–1906," *Sight and Sound* 47, no. 3 (Summer 1978): 148–62. Gunning has suggested a four-part schematization of early cinema relying on exactly this opposition between filmic and narrative continuities and discontinuities. Tom Gunning, "Non-Continuity, Continuity, Discontinuity: A Theory of Genres in Early Films," *Iris* 2, no. 1 (1984): 101–12.

35. Corinna Müller, "Variationen des Kinoprogramms: Filmform und Filmgeschichte," in *Die Modellierung des Kinofilms: Zur Geschichte des Kinoprogramms zwischen Kurzfilm und Langfilm, 1905/06–1918,* vol. 2, ed. Corinna Müller and Harro Segeberg (Munich: Wilhelm Fink, 1998), 43–76.

36. The first issue of *Bild und Film* was released in 1912 and continued publishing reformist contributions until 1915, while *Der Kinematograph,* which began as a short, critical newspaper, started in 1907 and served as an outlet for cinema reformists until the editor Emil Perlmann was replaced by Alfred Rosenthal, who was more concerned with a conservative view of film production as an industry. The objectives of *Bild und Film* were not to eliminate cinema but to critique trashy films and to speculate about how to elevate cinematic standards in accordance with bourgeois values. The bulk of cinema reform conferences, such as the ones in Dortmund, Hagen, and Eickel, occurred between 1912 and 1915, as did the publication of longer book-length works by renowned critics of cinema and mouthpieces for the reform movement, such as Adolf Sellmann and Hermann Häfker. It is also important to note that reformist responses to film were varied and often included, as the moniker "reform movement" suggests, programs and calls for changes to cinema that they thought would maximize the educational and scientific potential of the medium. As an instance of this, Häfker argued that given the proper conditions and sensitivity to the pitfalls and strengths of the medium, film could serve as a useful accompaniment to lessons about geography, bridging from the abstraction of description to representations of actual travel. However, he was adamant that to praise film for its reality effects was to misapprehend its essential function, as its success depicting movement was the result of a fundamental

deception. See Hermann Häfker, *Kino und Erdkunde* (Gladbach: Volksvereins-Verlag, 1914).

37. Tom Gunning, "The Cinema of Attractions: Early Film, Its Spectator and the Avant-Garde," *Wide Angle* 8, no. 3/4 (Fall 1986): 63–70.

38. Maxim Gorki, "Der Kinematograph von Lumière," in *KINtop: Jahrbuch zur Erforschung des frühen Films,* vol. 4, ed. Frank Kessler, Sabine Lenk, and Martin Loiperdinger (Basel: Stroemfeld / Roter Stern, 1995), 16–20.

39. Pasi Väliaho, *Mapping the Moving Image: Gesture, Thought and Cinema circa 1900* (Amsterdam: Amsterdam University Press, 2010), 43.

40. André Gaudreault, *Cinéma et attraction: Pour une nouvelle histoire du cinématographe* (Paris: CRNS Editions, 2008); André Gaudreault, *Film and Attraction: From Kinematography to Cinema,* trans. Timothy Barnard (Urbana: University of Illinois Press, 2011), 50.

41. Georg Simmel, "Die Großstädte und das Geistesleben," in *Gesamtausgabe,* vol. 1, ed. Rüdiger Kramme, Angela Rammstedt, and Otthein Rammstedt (Frankfurt am Main: Suhrkamp, 1995), 122.

42. By examining a wealth of historical documentation, from police reports to advertisements, Martin Loiperdinger goes to great lengths to demonstrate the dubious, if historically important, origins of this apocryphal story. Martin Loiperdinger, "Lumiere's Arrival of the Train: Cinema's Founding Myth," *Moving Image* 4, no. 1 (Spring 2004): 89–118. The function of such a myth has also been tied to the ideological operations of film and the category of "Uncle Josh" films, where an uninitiated, uneducated rube is depicted foolishly interacting with the screen as if it were real. Stephen Heath discusses Edwin S. Porter's 1902 film *Uncle Josh at the Moving Picture Show,* writing that such a film already stakes out an ideologically determined space of proper viewership in which "the initial question is not 'where is reality?' but 'how does this function?,' 'where is the reality *in that*?'" Stephen Heath, *Questions of Cinema* (London: Macmillan, 1981), 5.

43. A. Günsberg, "Künstlerische Regie bei kinematographischen Aufnahmen und Vorführungen," *Der Kinematograph,* no. 1 (January 6, 1907), reprinted in *Geschichte der Filmtheorie: Kunsttheoretische Texte von Melies bis Arnheim,* ed. Helmut H. Diederichs (Frankfurt am Main: Suhrkamp, 2004), 45.

44. Hugo Münsterberg, *The Photoplay: A Psychological Study* (New York: D. Appleton, 1916); Richard Guttmann, *Die Kinomenschheit: Versuch einer prinzipiellen Analyse* (Vienna: Anzengruber, 1916). Beyond his exchanges with Karl Kraus in Viennese newspapers, Guttmann was known as the biographer for the physician and popular philosopher Ernst von Feuchtersleben, whose 1838 *Diätetik der Seele* was, according to Guttmann, the most widely read book between "the publication of Goethe's *Werther*" and 1850, and, interestingly, whose legacy included the introduction of the term *psychosis.* More on this is available in the introduction to Gustav Pollak's *The Hygiene of the Soul: Memoir of a Physician and Philosopher*

(New York: Dodd, Mead, 1910). A very short segment of Guttmann's text is translated in Kaes, Baer, and Cowan, *The Promise of Cinema,* 238–40.

45. Noël Carroll has remarked on the fact that Münsterberg "presaged" the frequent theoretical invocation of an analogy between the operations of thought and those of film in the work of Jean-Louis Baudry and Christian Metz, though he rightfully notes that "Munsterberg's analogies were to, what might be thought of as, rational mental processes, whereas contemporary film theorists prefer analogs with irrational processes." Noël Carroll, "Film/Mind Analogies: The Case of Hugo Munsterberg," *Journal of Aesthetics and Art Criticism* 46, no. 4 (Summer 1988): 490. When Münsterberg outlined the similarities between psychic and filmic operations, he was clearly relying on some notion of a standard, healthy psyche, though he does little in the work to elucidate such a postulate.

46. Guttmann, *Die Kinomenschheit,* 22.

47. Guttmann, 7

48. Guttmann, 8.

49. Guttmann, 8.

50. Wundt attempted in various works to outline the principles of what he termed "psychical causality." One of the more direct formulations is present in his article "Über psychische Kausalität und das Prinzip des psychologischen Parallelismus," *Philosophische Studien* 10, no. 1 (1894): 1–124. His reckoning with the idea of a causal order in mental operations has been discussed by Kurt Danziger in *Constructing the Subject: Historical Origins of Psychological Research* (Cambridge: Cambridge University Press, 1998). It is also discussed in Mitchell G. Ash's comprehensive historical analysis of gestalt psychology, *Gestalt Psychology in German Culture, 1890–1967: Holism and the Quest for Objectivity* (Cambridge: Cambridge University Press, 1998).

51. Hans Vaihinger, *Die Philosophie des Als Ob: System der theoretischen, praktischen und religiösen Fiktionen der Menschheit auf Grund eines idealistischen Positivismus* (1911; repr., Leipzig: Felix Meiner, 1922). As the editor of the famous journal *Kant-Studien,* Vaihinger published articles by Georg Simmel and Wilhelm Dilthey, the latter having also contacted him about editing unpublished notes and fragments from Kant's *Nachlass.* Vaihinger's connection to Dilthey is especially interesting in that Dilthey is credited with developing a concept of Bildung that unified the work of *Wissenschaft* (science) as a mode of acculturation. What reading, study, fiction, and science meant and how they functioned were thus implicated in a model of the ideal educated subject.

52. Guttmann, *Die Kinomenschheit,* 28.

53. Guttmann, 29.

54. Vaihinger, *Die Philosophie des als ob,* ix.

55. Vaihinger, 557.

56. Vaihinger, 1.

57. Vaihinger, 3.

58. Vaihinger, 7.

59. Will Scheller, "Die neue Illusion," *Bild und Film*, nos. 9/10 (1913/14): 228. Diederichs briefly mentions this passage when considering cinema's reception as a part of life in the big city in *Anfänge Deutscher Filmkritik*, 161.

60. Scheller, "Die neue Illusion," 228.

61. Scheller, 228.

62. Sigmund Freud, *The Interpretation of Dreams*, trans. James Strachey (New York: Basic Books, 2010).

63. Sigmund Freud, *Entwurf einer Psychology* (1895), in *Gesammelte Werke, Nachtragsband: Texte aus den Jahren 1885 bis 1938* (Frankfurt am Main: S. Fischer, 1987), 387–477. See also Jacques Lacan, *The Seminar of Jacques Lacan, Book II: The Ego in Freud's Theory and in the Technique of Psychoanalysis, 1954–1955*, ed. Jacques-Alain Miller, trans. Sylvana Tomaselli (New York: Norton, 1991); Friedrich Kittler, *Gramophone, Film, Typewriter*, trans. Geoffrey Winthrop-Young and Michael Wutz (Stanford: Stanford University Press, 1999); Anson Rabinbach, *The Human Motor: Energy, Fatigue, and the Origins of Modernity* (New York: Basic Books, 1990); Frank J. Sulloway, *Freud, Biologist of the Mind: Beyond the Psychoanalytic Legend* (Cambridge, Mass.: Harvard University Press, 1992).

64. Jacques Lacan, "Science and Truth" (1966), in *Écrits*, trans. Bruce Fink (New York: Norton, 2006), 728.

65. Sigmund Freud, *Die Traumdeutung* (1905), in *Studienausgabe*, Band 2 (Frankfurt am Main: S. Fischer, 1989), 464.

66. Freud, 464.

67. Sigmund Freud, "Das Unbewusste," (1915), in *Gesammelte Werke*, Band 10 (Frankfurt am Main: S. Fischer, 1967), 286.

68. Jacques Derrida and Jeffrey Mehlman, "Freud and the Scene of Writing," *Yale French Studies*, no. 48 (1972): 85, 89.

69. Max Brethfeld, "Kinematograph im Dienste der Volks-und Jugendbildung," in *Neue Bahnen: Illustrierte Zeitschrift für Erziehung und Unterricht, 1908–1909*, ed. Ewald Niemann, Feodor Lindemann, and Rudolf Schulze (Leipzig: R. Voigtländer, 1909), 501.

70. Brethfeld's comments came in the wake of the Gesellschaft der Freunde des vaterländischen Schul- und Erziehungswesens zu Hamburg (Hamburg Society of Friends of Patriotic School and Educational Systems) or the "Hamburg movement," which had instituted a commission of pedagogues and teachers to make suggestions about the oversight and regulation of film and movie houses that were beginning to proliferate. This resulted in the ban on children at the cinema without an accompanying adult, which was later modified, and a series of new official regulations informed by the input of pedagogues. Although films were already routinely subject to censorship by state and city authorities, the intensification of

oversight and regulation by the Berlin police in 1906 created a precedent for other cities and states that continued to develop their own local rules and practices of censorship, increasing the percentage of films censored through World War I.

71. Brethfeld, "Kinematograph im Dienste der Volks-und Jugendbildung," 503.

72. Brethfeld, 502.

73. Brethfeld, 502.

74. More recent commentaries on the film limit their analysis to its reflexivity and general polemics against censors and reformers. Film scholarship on early German cinema has rightly focused on the ways in which the new medium made the conditions of its own production evident in the early years of its development, especially in narrative film. *How Cinema Got Its Revenge* is used to adduce this line of argument in Sabine Hake, "Self-Referentiality in Early German Cinema," *Cinema Journal* 31, no. 3 (Spring 1992): 37–55; Sabine Hake, *German National Cinema* (New York: Routledge, 2002); and Thomas Brandlmeier, "Early German Film Comedy, 1895–1917," in *A Second Life: German Cinema's First Decades*, ed. Thomas Elsaesser (Amsterdam: Amsterdam University Press, 1996), 103–13.

75. Heide Schlüpmann, *Unheimlichkeit des Blicks: Das Drama des frühen deutschen Kinos* (Frankfurt am Main: Stroemfeld / Roter Stern, 1990), 59.

76. *Uncle Josh at the Moving Picture Show*, from which the genre takes its name, was a remake of Robert Paul's film *The Countryman's First Sight of the Animated Pictures* (1901). For more on the larger genre of the "Rube film," see Thomas Elsaesser, "Discipline through Diegesis: The Rube Film between 'Attractions' and 'Narrative Integration,'" in *The Cinema of Attractions Reloaded*, ed. Wanda Strauven (Amsterdam: Amsterdam University Press, 2006), 205–26. Here he considers the rube film as an internalized form of training of cinematic spectatorship.

77. Cornelius Borck, *Hirnströme: Eine Kulturgeschichte der Elektroenzephalographie* (Göttingen: Wallstein, 2005), 17. Borck is primarily concerned with the graphical means for representing the psyche that accompanied Hans Berger's work with the electroencephalograph beginning in the 1920s.

78. Fraktur was itself the fulcrum for a debate about the essential properties of a specifically German moral character as bound to its literary tradition beginning in the seventeenth century and reaching an apex in the 1910s. Some pedagogical theorists, such as Joachim Heinrich Campe, linked the "typographical medium of composition" of texts to the uncorrupted expression of characteristically German ideas as well as a reduction of physiological strain in reading. In short, the disputes about the materialities of printed texts had long been involved in larger pedagogical and moral arguments about training readers and were extended into a radicalized debate about the educational practices implied by films that drew from a media-pedagogical vocabulary developed in literary debates. For a comprehensive overview of these debates, see Christina Killius's dissertation, published as *Die Antiqua-Fraktur Debatte um 1800 und ihre historische Herleitung* (Wiesbaden:

Harrassowitz, 1999). As is well known, the metastacization of these ideas about the media-typographical implications of text for national and moral character eventuated themselves in the banning of Fraktur by the Nazi party. The media-technological elements of these debates were quite apparent and foregrounded in publications contemporary with cinema reform literature, explicitly making the connection between the cultivation of subjectivity and the technics of reading. This was reflected in the contentions of the experimental psychologist August Kirschmann, who began his book *Antiqua oder Fraktur? (Lateinische oder deutsche Schrift)* (Leipzig: Deutschen Buchgewerbevereins, 1907) with a suggestion that the print's physical properties and how it was systematized influenced the kinds of readers and writers it produced.

79. There were still many reformist charges whose central claim was mostly confined to a xenophobic suspicion about the infiltration of foreign influence over audiences prompted by the highly international nature of the early film industry. One of the most often cited examples of this critique is Karl Brunner's *Der Kinematograph von Heute: Eine Volksgefahr* (Berlin: Vaterländischer Schriftenverband, 1913). Fittingly, Brunner was also the most powerful advisor to the Berlin police censors responsible for controlling literature and film. As Andrew Lees remarks, Brunner attacked the "selfish, unscrupulous businessmen, many of them foreigners," whose films undermined the strong German national moral fiber. Lees, *Cities, Sin, and Social Reform in Imperial Germany,* 129. See also Corey Ross, *Media and the Making of Modern Germany: Mass Communications, Society, and Politics from the Empire to the Third Reich* (Oxford: Oxford University Press, 2008).

80. Heide Schlüpmann, *Ungeheure Einbildungskraft: Die dunkle Moralität des Kinos* (Frankfurt am Main: Stroemfeld, 2007), 250.

81. Schlüpmann, 254, 257.

82. Schlüpmann, 258

83. Schlüpmann, 277.

84. Immanuel Kant, "Über ein vermeintes Recht aus Menschenliebe zu lügen," (1797), in *Kants Werke,* vol. 8 (Berlin: de Gruyter, 1968), 423–30.

85. Noël Carroll, "The Wheel of Virtue: Art, Literature, and Moral Knowledge," *Journal of Aesthetics and Art Criticism* 60, no. 1 (Winter 2002): 19. Carroll is actually wagering a defense here of the philosophical value of arts and literature against detractors who find the medium incapable of formulating philosophical arguments.

86. This is considered at length in chapter 4.

87. Béla Balázs, "Kurbelndes Bewußtsein," *Der Tag,* no. 829 (March 22, 1925): 3–4, reprinted as "Reel Consciousness," trans. Christopher M. Geissler, in Kaes, Baer, and Cowan, *The Promise of Cinema,* 59. Both Guttmann's book and Balázs's book *Das Sichtbare Mensch oder die Kultur des Films* (1924; repr., Frankfurt am Main: Suhrkamp, 2001) were favorably reviewed together by Fritz Rosenfeld in the

Vienna socialist newspaper *Arbeiter-Zeitung* (June 19, 1927): 15. In addition to praising the novel conceptual framework introduced by Guttmann, Rosenfeld argued that *Die Kinomenschheit* prepared the way for important later analysis.

88. Guttmann., *Die Kinomenschheit,* 30, emphasis mine.

89. Guttmann, 13.

90. Guttmann, 6.

3. Discrete Reading

1. Bernhard Siegert, *Cultural Techniques: Grids, Filters, Doors, and Other Articulations of the Real,* trans. Geoffrey Winthrop-Young (New York: Fordham University Press, 2015), 10.

2. See Franco Moretti, *Distant Reading* (New York: Verso, 2013); and Ted Underwood, *Distant Horizons: Digital Evidence and Literary Change* (Chicago: University of Chicago Press, 2019).

3. See Nan Z. Da, "The Computational Case against Computational Literary Studies," *Critical Inquiry* 45 (Spring 2019): 601–39. This article sparked a debate and a number of responses from proponents of computational literary studies, such as Ted Underwood, which were also published in *Critical Inquiry.*

4. Zeynep Çelik Alexander, "Scanning: A Technical History of Form," in *Design Technics: Archaeologies of Architectural Practice,* ed. Zeynep Çelik Alexander and John May (Minneapolis: University of Minnesota Press, 2019), 74.

5. Wilhelm Wundt, "Über reine und angewandte Psychologie," *Psychologische Studien* 5 (1910): 1–47.

6. Martin Kusch goes into more depth on Wundt's attitude toward pedagogy and the Würzburg school, and also describes the evolution of his political commitments, particularly with respect to Bildung and his involvement in *Bildungsvereine* until 1865. Martin Kusch, *Psychological Knowledge: A Social History and Philosophy* (New York: Routledge, 1999).

7. Johann Gottfried Herder, *Abhandlung über den Ursprung der Sprache,* reprinted in *Herders Sämtliche Werke,* vol. 5 (Berlin: Weidmannsche Buchhandlung, 1891), 5.

8. Herder, 21. With his characteristic flair for polemics, he goes on in this section to identify what he saw as the errors in earlier French theories of language and education developed by Jean-Jacques Rousseau and Étienne Bonnot de Condillac. Herder's affinities and—more often than not—objections to Rousseau and Condillac's philosophies of the origins of language education are discussed at length in Astrid Gesche, *Johann Gottfried Herder: Sprache und die Natur des Menschen* (Würzburg: Könnigshausen und Neumann, 1993). The cited passages are also well known in part owing to Heidegger's notes for their close reading in *Vom Wesen der Sprache: Zu Herders Abhandlung "Über den Ursprung der Sprache," Gesamtausgabe,*

vol. 85 (Frankfurt am Main: Vittorio Klostermann, 1999). What Heidegger faulted Herder for, namely "remaining within the tradition of metaphysics, characterized by subjectivism and a reification of the human," is precisely the relationship that language was thought to bear to the continuity of mind that was the goal in the education of the reading subject. Sonia Sikka, *Herder on Humanity and Cultural Difference: Enlightened Relativism* (Cambridge: Cambridge University Press, 2011), 184.

9. Herder, *Abhandlung über den Ursprung der Sprache,* 6.

10. Gesche, *Johann Gottfried Herder,* 139.

11. John William Adamson, *The Practice of Instruction: A Manual of Method General and Special* (London: National Society's Depository, 1907), 63.

12. Johann Gottfried Herder, *Herders Sämmtliche Werke,* vol. 1 (Berlin: Weidmannsche Buchhandlung, 1877), 386.

13. Herder, 395. Matthias Rothe comments about this passage that although written language was dead and only approximated the unity of the soul, according to Herder, it nonetheless was key to both the articulation and the development of internal and expressive unities. Matthias Rothe, *Lesen und Zuschauen im 18. Jahrhundert: Die Erzeugung und Aufhebung von Abwesenheit* (Würzburg: Königshausen & Neumann, 2005), 60.

14. Bernhard Dotzler notes that Herder was an early proponent of self-education, but chance (*Fortuna*) had much to do with the production of the person. Bernhard Dotzler, *Papiermaschinen: Versuch über Communication & Control in Literature und Technik* (Berlin: Akademie, 1996). One might argue, however, that such fortune and chance only become meaningful when integrated into a coherent diegetic structure.

15. Ulrich Herrmann, "Pädagogisches Denken und Anfänge der Reformpädagogik," in *Handbuch der deutschen Bildungsgeschichte, 1870–1918: Von der Reichsgründung bis zum Ende des Ersten Weltkriegs,* vol. 4, ed. Christa Berg (Munich: C. H. Beck, 1991), 153.

16. Frederick Beiser, *The Fate of Reason: German Philosophy from Kant to Fichte* (Cambridge, Mass.: Harvard University Press, 1987), 135, 136; Dietrich Tiedemann, *Versuch einer Erklärung des Ursprunges der Sprache* (Riga: Johann Friedrich Hartknoch, 1772). Beiser pursues the lines of argument between the three figures, which involved significant overlap regarding the origins and nature of language and thought, despite the searing invectives, which Hamann also directed at Herder, who had been his student. Hamann's scathing review is reprinted in Johann Georg Hamann, *Sämtliche Werke,* vol. 3, ed. Josef Nadler (Wuppertal: Brockhaus, 1999), 13–24.

17. It is important to note here that Tiedemann kept a diary between 1781 and 1784, which included a forty-page observational record of the development of his son in the first thirty months of his life, detailing the development of his speech.

This is often associated with the philanthropic pedagogue Joachim Heinrich Campe's publication of a sixteen-volume revision of education, the preface of which suggested that there be a competition for such diary writing as a part of pedagogical reform. In short, an attenuated account of philosophies of language, psychology, and pedagogy shows the degree to which the methods of studying language were closely affiliated with questions of education and subject formation from the eighteenth century onward. This is discussed in Willem J. M. Levelt's incredible resource *A History of Psycholinguistics: The Pre-Chomskyan Era* (Oxford: Oxford University Press, 2013). Campe's reformist educational tract can be found in Joachim Heinrich Campe, *Allgemeine Revision des gesammten Schul- und Erziehungswesens von einer Gesellschaft praktischer Erzieher* (Hamburg: Carl Ernst Bohn, 1785–92). He also, importantly, wrote an instructional manual for educating children to read. Eckhardt Fuchs describes Campe's pedagogical reform program as "the most complete pedagogical handbook of the Enlightenment," which sought to "systematically" observe infants and "study the physical and mental development of the child and to apply the knowledge to educational theory." Eckhardt Fuch, "Nature and *Bildung*: Pedagogical Naturalism in Nineteenth-Century Germany," in *The Moral Authority of Nature,* ed. Lorraine Daston and Fernando Vidal (Chicago: University of Chicago Press, 2004), 158.

18. Fuch, "Nature and *Bildung,*" 165. See also Ernst Christian Trapp, *Versuch einer Pädagogik* (Berlin: Friedrich Nicolai, 1780).

19. Dotzler, *Papiermaschinen,* 480.

20. Trapp, *Versuch einer Pädagogik,* 358. Later in the passage, he mentions Campe and Basedow by name.

21. Joseph Theodor Abs, *Bericht über eine vaterländische Erziehungs- und Unterrichtsanstalt zu Halberstadt; nebst einer Übersicht der Übungen an und in der Sprachzeichenlehre* (Berlin: Mittler, 1818), 28.

22. Heinrich Bosse, "'Wie schreibt man Madam'? Lenz, *Die Soldaten* I/1," in *Mir ekelt vor diesem tintenklecksenden Säkulum,* ed. Martin Stingelin (Munich: Wilhelm Fink, 2004), 71.

23. Dotzler, *Papiermaschinen,* 481.

24. Dotzler, 472.

25. Dotzler, 473.

26. Karl Philipp Moritz, *Neues ABC-Buch mit Kupfern von Peter Haas,* 2nd ed. (Berlin: Christian Gottfried Schöne, 1794), n.p.

27. Annette Keck, *Buchstäbliche Anatomien: Vom Lesen und Schreiben des Menschen—Litieratugeschichten der Moderne* (Würzburg: Königshausen & Neumann, 2007), 173–74, supports this interpretation of Moritz's ABC book. In contrast with Keck, however, it is my argument that although Moritz identified the relationship of reading to the cultivation of the subject, his method was not instituted in the nineteenth century but was overturned.

28. Karl Philipp Moritz, *Anton Reiser: Ein psychologischer Roman* (Berlin: Friedrich Maurer, 1785), 15.

29. Moritz, 16. Moritz was disappointed when he met Basedow, who had originally been a source of inspiration for his beliefs about teaching. Nonetheless, Moritz echoes the pedagogical positions of Basedow in this passage, emphasizing that without first "stimulating children's sense perception and activating their powers of analytic reasoning," verbal cognition "remained empty" and constituted "the rote memorization of words." Elliott Schreiber, *The Topology of Modernity: Karl Philipp Moritz and the Space of Autonomy* (Ithaca, N.Y.: Cornell University Press, 2012), 63.

30. Friedrich Kittler, *Discourse Networks 1800/1900,* trans. Michael Metteer and Chris Cullens (Stanford: Stanford University Press, 1990), 74.

31. Kittler, 74.

32. Kittler, 74.

33. Kant's rejection of the possibility of scientific psychology (as well as other sciences) was outlined in part in Immanuel Kant, *Metaphysische Anfangsgründe der Naturwissenschaft, Werkausgabe,* vol. 9, ed. Wilhelm Weischedel (Frankfurt am Main: Suhrkamp, 1977). Among other reasons, this work is significant for the study of psychology and image technologies because a majority of the treatise is dedicated to analyzing motion as a property of observable and abstract space. Herbart's rejection of the Kantian prohibition can be found in Johann Friedrich Herbart, *Psychologie als Wissenschaft: Neu gegründet auf Erfahrung, Metaphysik und Mathematik,* 2 vols. (Amsterdam: Bonset, 1968). It is also notable that Herbart's endeavor to found a field of scientific psychology was connected to his work as a pedagogue. Of scientific pedagogical study, he wrote, "Science may be glasses to others; to me it is an eye, and truly the best eye humans have to observe their affairs." Johann Friedrich Herbart, *Allgemeine Pädagogik aus dem Zweck der Erziehung abgeleitet* (Leipzig: Siegesmund & Volkening, 1894), 6.

34. Henning Schmidgen, "Das Experimentelle und das Pathologische zur Geschichte psychophysiologischer Zeitmessungen, 1880–1900," in *Maß und Eigensinn: Studien im Anschluß an Georges Canguilhem,* ed. Cornelius Borck, Volker Hess, and Henning Schmidgen (Munich: Wilhelm Fink, 2005), 199.

35. A more detailed history of the chronoscope and experimental mechanisms for measuring reaction times is available in Henning Schmidgen, "Physics, Ballistics, and Psychology: A History of the Chronoscope in/as Context, 1845–1890," *History of Psychology* 8, no. 1 (2005): 46–78; and Jimena Canales, *A Tenth of a Second: A History* (Chicago: University of Chicago Press, 2010). The chronoscope went through a number of permutations during the nineteenth century. The first chronoscope was designed in the 1830s by Claude Pouilllet and is often referred to as a ballistic galvanometer. Later versions—following Wheatstone and the Swabian clockmaker and engineer Matthäus Hipp's modifications—used a clockwork mechanism that measured the period between when an electromagnet was engaged and

disengaged following test subjects' reactions. Later versions included direct- and indirect-reading pendulum chronoscopes in the 1890s. A brief overview of these instruments is available in Robert Bud and Deborah Jean Warner, eds., *Instruments of Science: An Historical Encyclopedia* (Washington, D.C.: Smithsonian Institution Press, 1998).

36. In *A Tenth of a Second*, Canales writes at length about the "personal equation." The Swiss astronomer Adolph Hirsch noticed that the time required to physically transmit signals within the body influenced the accuracy of records made of astronomical measurement. See Adolph Hirsch, "Chronoskopische Versuche über die Geschwindigkeit der verschiedenen Sinneseindrücke und der Nerven-Leitung," *Untersuchungen zur Naturlehre des Menschen und der Thiere* 9 (1865): 183–99.

37. Schmidgen provides a short history of the chronoscope's use in experimental psychology and the major figures involved in its development and application. See Henning Schmidgen, "Zur Genealogie der Reaktionsversuche in der experimentellen Psychologie," in *Instrument—Experiment: Historische Studien*, ed. Christoph Meinel (Berlin: Diepholz, 2000), 168–79. See also Henning Schmidgen, "Repetitions and Differences: Psychophysiological Time Machines, 1850–1865," in *On Deep Time Relations of Arts, Sciences and Technologies*, ed. Siegfried Zielinski and Silvia M. Wagnermaier (Cologne: Walther König, 2005), 145–58, for a history of errors and reaction-time experimental design. Additionally, he has written about the impacts in psychology of Hirsch's work. See Henning Schmidgen, "Time and Noise: The Stable Surroundings of Reaction Experiments, 1860–1890," *Studies in History and Philosophy of Biological and Biomedical Sciences* 34 (2003): 237–75.

38. Hugo Münsterberg, "Zeitausfüllung," in *Beiträge zur experimentellen Psychologie*, vol. 4, ed. Hugo Münsterberg (Freiburg: Mohr, 1892), 89–120. His divergence with Wundt is evident in this study, in which he claims that the "perceptual complexes" reside in "peripheral body processes" rather than generating new, central psychic processes (120).

39. Hugo Münsterberg, "Zeitsinn," in *Beiträge zur experimentellen Psychologie*, vol. 2, ed. Hugo Münsterberg (Freiburg: Mohr, 1889), 1–2.

40. Münsterberg, 49.

41. Friedrich Kittler, *Gramophone, Film, Typewriter*, trans. Geoffrey Winthrop-Young and Michael Wutz (Stanford: Stanford University Press, 1999), 16.

42. Kittler, 16.

43. Münsterberg, "Zeitsinn," 1–2.

44. André Bazin, "The Evolution of the Language of Cinema" (1953), in *What Is Cinema?*, trans. Hugh Gray (Berkeley: University of California Press, 2005), 30.

45. The combination of the two devices ultimately came to be called simply the "tachistoscope."

46. Volkmann describes his invention, which he claimed he had been using for some time, as "the tachistoscope, an instrument that uses an electrical spark to

investigate momentary vision." A. W. Volkmann, "Das Tachistoskop, ein Instrument, welches bei Untersuchung des momentanen Sehens den Gebrauch des elektrischen Funkens ersetzt," *Bericht über die Verhandlungen der Königlich Sächsischen Gesellschaft der Wissenschaft zu Leipzig: Mathematisch-physische Classe* 11 (1859): 90–98. Ruth Benschop has written the definitive, if short, history of the tachistoscope. See Ruth Benschop, "What Is a Tachistoscope? Historical Explorations of an Instrument," *Science in Context* 11, no. 1 (March 1998): 23–50.

47. Benschop, "What Is a Tachistoscope?," 25. See also Werner Traxel, Rolf Grundlach, and Ulrich Zschuppe, "Zur Geschichte der apparativen Hilfsmittel der Psychologie," in *Handbuch der apparativen Verfahren der Psychologie,* ed. Rolf Brickenkamp (Göttingen: Hogrefe, 1986), 1–22. James McKeen Cattell details this drum-based device in "Ueber die Zeit der Erkennung und Benennung von Schriftzeichen, Bildern und Farben," *Philosophische Studien* 2 (1885): 635–50.

48. Benschop, "What Is a Tachistoscope?," 33. The first mention of this mechanism, called the "gravity chronoscope," is presumably made by Cattell in 1883, when he mentions awaiting an "apparatus" in Baltimore. James McKeen Cattell, *An Education in Psychology: James McKeen Cattell's Journal and Letters from Germany and England, 1880–1888* (Cambridge, Mass.: MIT Press, 1981), 87. Cattell and Wundt, who was known as an irascible opponent, ultimately parted ways in the 1890s over a disagreement about whether the fall mechanism could calibrate the chronoscope. Wundt criticized early experiments for, among other things, failing to control the light conditions in which stimuli were presented. Wilhelm Wundt, "Zur Kritik tachistoskopischer Versuche," *Philosophische Studien* 15 (1900): 287–317.

49. Jonathan Crary, *Suspensions of Perception: Attention, Spectacle, and Modern Culture* (Cambridge, Mass.: MIT Press, 2001), 305, 309.

50. Crary, 306.

51. Hubert von Grashey, "Ueber Aphasie und ihre Beziehung zur Wahrnehmung," *Archiv für Psychiatrie und Nervenkrankenheiten* 16 (1885): 654–88. On this point, see Levelt, *A History of Psycholinguistics.*

52. Carl Wernicke, *Der aphasische Symptomencomplex: Eine psychologische Studie auf anatomischer Basis* (Breslau: Max Cohn & Weigert, 1874); Ludwig Lichtheim, "Über Aphasie," *Deutsches Archiv für klinische Medizin* 36 (1885): 433–84. Wernicke praised the importance of Grashey's work directly following its publication. Carl Wernicke, "Einige neue Arbeiten über Aphasie" (1885/86), in *Gesammelte Aufsätze und kritische Referate zur Pathologie des Nervensystems* (Saarbrücken: VDM Verlag, 2006), 92–192.

53. Sigmund Exner, *Untersuchungen über die Localisation der Functionen in der Grosshirnde des Menschen* (Vienna: Baumüller, 1881).

54. Cattell, "Ueber die Zeit der Erkennung und Benennung von Schriftzeichen, Bildern und Farben," 648.

55. Wundt, "Zur Kritik tachistoskopischer Versuche," 288.

56. Kurt Danziger details the circumstances surrounding Wundt and the emergence of "introspectionism." Kurt Danziger, *Constructing the Subject: Historical Origins of Psychological Research* (Cambridge: Cambridge University Press, 1998).

57. Danziger, 43. This point was underscored by Guy Montrose Whipple while commenting on Cattell's reading experiments and design of the tachistoscope: "in no other experiment are the results more evidently conditioned by the *form of apparatus* and type of procedure employed." Guy Montrose Whipple, *Manual of Mental and Physical Tests: Complex Processes* (Baltimore: Warwick & York, 1914), 264.

58. Dodge is known for redesigning the tachistoscope according to the demands outlined by Wundt.

59. Benno Erdmann and Raymond Dodge, *Psychologische Untersuchungen über das Lesen auf experimenteller Grundlage* (Halle: Max Niemeyer, 1898). This is not to contend that Erdmann and Dodge had the final word in these disputes. Others, such as Julius Zeitler, continued to maintain various permutations of the succession thesis, in which letter position, order, and recognition were seen as more important than total "word image" (*Wortbild*) recognition. Zeitler claimed that word recognition could only be divided into two groups, "known" and "unknown." In both cases, however, the recognition was distinct from the meaning, which he reiterates multiple times in the study. It was a mechanical rather than a hermeneutic operation. Unfamiliar words were spelled and familiar words were "assimilated" according to a visual structure dominated by certain prominent letters, from which one proceeded to the meaning of the word. Julius Zeitler, *Tachistoskopische Untersuchungen über das Lesen* (Leipzig: Wilhelm Engelmann, 1900).

60. Erdmann and Dodge, *Psychologische Untersuchungen über das Lesen auf experimenteller Grundlage*, 63.

61. Erdmann and Dodge, 3.

62. Erdmann and Dodge, 2.

63. Erdmann and Dodge, 3.

64. Hermann Ebbinghaus, *Über das Gedächtnis: Untersuchungen zur experimentellen Psychologie* (Leipzig: Duncker & Humber, 1885).

65. Kittler, *Gramophone, Film, Typewriter*, 246.

66. An early description of this device was given in a report from the Psychologischer Verein zu Berlin in December 1898 in which Schumann demonstrated his new apparatus. Ferdinand Kemsier and Leo Hirschlaff, eds., *Zeitschrift für Pädagogische Psychologie und Pathologie* (Leipzig: Quelle & Meyer, 1899).

67. Friedrich Schumann, "Die Erkennung von Buchstaben und Worten bei momentaner Beleuchtung," in *Bericht über den I. Kongreß für experimentelle Psychologie in Gießen, vom 18. bis 21. April, 1904* (Leipzig: Johann Ambrosius Barth, 1904), 35.

68. As noted in chapter 1, Wertheimer's description of the experiments is available in "Experimentelle Studien über das Sehen von Bewegung," *Zeitschrift für*

Psychologie 61 (1912): 161–265. It was also cited by his student and famous film theorist Rudolf Arnheim in *Film als Kunst* (1932; repr., Berlin: Suhrkamp, 2002), 104.

69. The forms of pathological autonomy associated with film are discussed at length in chapter 5.

70. Adolf Sellmann, *Der Kinematograph als Volkserzieher?* (Langensalza: Beyer & Mann, 1912), 26–27. Nachdenken has been a perpetual part of the Bildungs discourse since Goethe. This is discussed in greater detail in chapter 4. See also Robert Gaupp, "Die Gefahren des Kinos," *Süddeutsche Monatshefte* 9, no. 2 (July 1912): 363–66; and Friedrich Paulsen, *Pädagogik* (1911; repr., Paderborn: Salzwasser, 2013). In the latter, Paulsen claims, for instance, that, unlike in scientific and mathematical pedagogy, in which the student is confined to the passive reception of laws and forms, literary and aesthetic training requires active "Nachdenken" and the translation of sentences from mere forms to larger meanings (383).

71. Kittler, *Discourse Networks,* 48.

72. Sellmann, *Der Kinematograph als Volkserzieher?,* 33.

4. The Technics of *Bildung*

1. Charles Sanders Peirce, *The Collected Papers of Charles Sanders Peirce,* vols. 5 and 6 in one vol., ed. Charles Hartshorne and Paul Weiss (Cambridge, Mass.: Belknap Press of Harvard University Press, 1974), 68.

2. Peirce, 68.

3. Peirce, 170.

4. Heinz von Foerster, "Thoughts and Notes on Cognition," in *Understanding Understanding: Essays on Cybernetics and Cognition* (New York: Springer, 2003), 189.

5. Marvin Minsky and Seymour Papert, *Perceptrons: An Introduction to Computational Geometry* (Cambridge, Mass.: MIT Press, 1988), 150.

6. Orit Halpern, "Repeating: Cybernetic Intelligence," in *Design Technics: Archaeologies of Architectural Practice,* ed. Zeynep Çelik Alexander and John May (Minneapolis: University of Minnesota Press, 2019), 193.

7. The term GOFAI was coined by John Haugeland in *Artificial Intelligence: The Very Idea* (Cambridge, Mass.: MIT Press, 1985).

8. N. Katherine Hayles, "Can Computers Create Meanings? A Cyber/Bio/Semiotic Perspective," *Critical Inquiry* 46 (Autumn 2019): 44.

9. "Instruktion für Schulmeister in der Hochgräflich Oetting-Wallersteinischen Stadt," *Magazin für Schulen und die Erziehung überhaupt* 4 (1769): 144.

10. Heinrich Bosse, "Die moderne Bildungsrevolution," in *Bildungsrevolution, 1770–1830,* ed. Nacim Ghanbary (Heidelberg: Universitätsverlag, 2012), 61.

11. Johann Gottfried Herder, "Vom Dinge an sich, neben und hinter aller Erscheinung," in *Sämtliche Werke,* vol. 21 (Berlin: Weidmannsche Buchhandlung, 1881), 173.

12. Robert S. Leventhal, *The Disciplines of Interpretation: Lessing, Herder, Schlegel* (Berlin: de Gruyter, 1994), 200.

13. Bosse, "Die moderne Bildungsrevolution," 74.

14. Humberto Maturana and Francisco Varela, *Autopoiesis and Cognition: The Realization of the Living* (Boston: D. Reidel, 1980), xx. For a decisive outline of Maturana and Varela's role in the movement from first-order to second-order cybernetics and a concern with recursivity, see Cary Wolfe, "In Search of Posthumanist Theory: The Second-Order Cybernetics of Maturana and Varela," *Cultural Critique,* no. 30 (Spring 1995): 33–70.

15. Maturana and Varela, *Autopoiesis and Cognition,* 81.

16. Friedrich Kittler, "Über die Sozialisation Wilhelm Meisters," in *Dichtung als Sozialisationsspiel: Studien zu Goethe und Gottfried Keller* (Göttingen: Vandenhoeck & Ruprecht, 1978), 106. As the passage makes clear, the analysis in this text would serve as one of the foundations for his later book *Discourse Networks.*

17. Kittler, "Über die Sozialisation Wilhelm Meisters," 104.

18. Kittler, 55.

19. Ernst Schultze, *Kulturfragen der Gegenwart: Beiträge zur geistig-sittlichen Kenntnis unserer Zeit* (Berlin: W. Kohlhammer, 1913), 96.

20. Schultze, 106.

21. Theodor Bäuerle, *Technik und Volkserziehung* (Berlin: Ernst Siegfried Mittler und Sohn, 1917), 10–11.

22. Walter Benjamin, "Das Kunstwerk im Zeitalter seiner technischen Reproduzierbarkeit," in *Das Kunstwerk im Zeitalter seiner technischen Reproduzierbarkeit* (Frankfurt am Main: Suhrkamp, 2003), 7–44.

23. In the late eighteenth and early nineteenth centuries, there was a concerted effort to engineer and design more rapid forms of textual reproduction, most notably beginning in 1804 with Friedrich Koenig's "printing machine," which was rebuilt out of iron and powered by a steam engine by 1810. The first rotating press similar to contemporary presses was introduced in the United States in 1860 by William Bullock, followed by the *London Times*' double-sided printer, the "Walter Press," and the first German-produced rotary press produced in Augsburg in 1872. After 1872 the pace of innovation became ever-more accelerated. Eva Hanebutt-Benz, "Technik des Buches," in *Medienwissenschaft: Ein Handbuch zur Entwicklung der Medien und Kommunikationsform,* vol. 1, ed. Joachim-Felix Leonhard (Berlin: de Gruyter, 1999), 390–420. Katrin Völkner writes about the commercialization and capitalistic transformation of nineteenth-century ideals of Bildung with the introduction of Karl Robert Langewiesche's standard "Blaue Bücher" around 1900. Katrin Völkner, "*Bildung* for Sale: Karl Robert Langewiesche's Blaue Bücher and the Business of

'Reading-Up,'" in *Publishing Culture and the "Reading Nation": German Book History in the Long Nineteenth Century,* ed. Lynne Tatlock (Rochester, N.Y.: Camden House, 2010), 251–70.

24. Schultze, *Kulturfragen der Gegenwart,* 96.

25. Schultze, 102.

26. Bernhard Siegert, *Relais: Geschicke der Literatur als Epoche der Post* (Berlin: Brinkmann & Bose, 1993), 246.

27. Wilhelm von Humboldt, "Theorie der Bildung des Menschen," in *Werke,* vol. 1 (Berlin: B. Behr, 1903), 283. There was, of course, a universe of competing understandings of Bildung. See Johann Friedrich Herbart, "Zwei Vorlesungen über Pädagogik" (1802), in *Sämtliche Werke: In Chronologischer Reihenfolge,* vol. 1, ed. Karl Kehrbach (Langensalza: Hermann Beyer & Söhne, 1887), 279–90. Morgenstern also uses the term *Bildsamkeit* to describe a personal disposition benefiting from the insights of a work ("the nourishment of the spirit arising from such representations"). Karl Morgenstern, "Ueber das Wesen des Bildungsromans" (1820), reprinted in *Zur Geschichte des deutschen Bildungsroman,* ed. Rolf Selbmann (Darmstadt: Wissenschaftliche Buchgesellschaft, 1988), 66.

28. Herbart, "Zwei Vorlesungen über Pädagogik."

29. H., "Der Kampf gegen die Schundliteratur," *Geisteskultur* 4, no. 18 (1909): 101. This publication also features articles from Schultze. The cited material is essentially an account of the state of anti-Schund literature and major publications to that point. See Wilhelm Fronemann, "Die Schundliteratur nach dem Krieg," *Bücherei und Bildungspflege: Blätter für Volksbibliotheken* 1 (1921): 2–15. The tone of Fronemann's claim can be taken as highly satirical, referring to Brunners as "the dictator" and the publications he worked to shut down as "victims" (*Opfer*). However, Fronemann also tallies the results of Brunner's efforts, including the 152 series he worked to eliminate, and seems to earnestly protest the suggestive effects of pulp literature.

30. Oskar Planck, *Gegen das Kinowesen! Materialsammlung zur Kinoreform* (Wüttemberg: Evangelischer Volksverband für Wüttemberg, 1919), 9.

31. Planck, 9.

32. Planck, 9.

33. Walter Ong, *Orality and Literacy* (New York: Routledge, 2002), 68.

34. Franz Pfemfert, "Kino als Erzieher," *Die Aktion* 1, no. 18 (June 19, 1911): 562.

35. Pfemfert, 562. As has perhaps been well established by now, "Phantasie" was a defining element of literary education.

36. Oliver Gaycken, "The Cinema of the Future: Visions of the Medium as Modern Educator, 1895–1910," in *Learning with the Lights Off: Educational Film in the United States* (Oxford: Oxford University Press, 2012), 70. In this chapter, Gaycken writes about speculative assessments and projections about the value or detriment of early film for education in the United States and especially about Edison, his

assistant W. K. L. Dickson, and the industrial films commissioned by Westinghouse Electric & Manufacturing Company. Gaycken cites Johann Heinrich Pestalozzi and Jean-Jacques Rousseau, whose ideas of education "found an audience" in United States, as a way of situating distinctions being made in the United States in the late nineteenth century as a part of a theoretical migration from Europe.

37. Wilhelm Dilthey, "Goethe und die dichterische Phantasie," in *Das Erlebnis und die Dichtung: Lessing, Goethe, Novalis, Hölderlin* (Leipzig: B. G. Teubner, 1906), 146.

38. Dilthey, 149.

39. Dilthey, 149.

40. Friedrich Schiller, *Schillers Briefwechsel mit Körner, von 1784 bis zum Tode Schillers*, vol. 1, *1784–1792* (Berlin: Verlag von Veit und Comp., 1847), 396. Heinz Gockel details the conditions of Schiller's dispute with the editor and jurist Körner. Heinz Gockel, *Mythos und Poesie: Zum Mythosbegriff in Aufklärung und Frühromantik* (Frankfurt am Main: Vittorio Klostermann, 1981), 196.

41. Friedrich Schiller, "Über naïve und sentimentalische Dichtung," in *Werke und Briefe, Theoretische Schriften*, vol. 8 (Frankfurt am Main: Deutscher Klassiker, 1992), 734.

42. Schiller, 734.

43. Friedrich Schiller, "Über die ästhetische Erziehung des Menschen in einer Reihe von Briefen," in *Werke und Briefe, Theoretische Schriften*, vol. 8 (Frankfurt am Main: Deutscher Klassiker, 1992), 575.

44. Schiller, 575.

45. Schiller, 575.

46. Schiller, 575.

47. Wolfgang Iser, *The Fictive and the Imaginary: Charting Literary Anthropology* (Baltimore: Johns Hopkins University Press, 1993), 176–77.

48. Friedrich Kittler, *Gramophone, Film, Typewriter*, trans. Geoffrey Winthrop-Young and Michael Wutz (Stanford: Stanford University Press, 1999), 122.

49. Gilles Deleuze, *Cinema 2: The Time-Image*, trans. Hugh Tomlinson and Robert Galeta (Minneapolis: University of Minnesota Press, 1989), 127.

50. Schultze, *Kulturfragen der Gegenwart*, 111–12. Schultze's work and place in conversation with larger figures like Friedrich Wilhelm Foerster and Friedrich Paulsen are provided in Andrew Lees, *Cities, Sin, and Social Reform in Imperial Germany* (Ann Arbor: University of Michigan Press, 2002).

51. Schultze, *Kulturfragen der Gegenwart*, 80; Tom Gunning, "Cinema of Attraction: Early Film, Its Spectator and the Avant-Garde," *Wide Angle* 8, nos. 3–4 (1986): 63–70.

52. Schultze, *Kulturfragen der Gegenwart*, 80.

53. Schultze, 63–64.

54. Johann Wolfgang von Goethe, *Wilhelm Meisters Lehrjahre, Werke,* vol. 4, ed. Wilhelm Voßkamp and Waltraud Wiethölter (Frankfurt am Mian: Insel Verlag, 1998), 174, quoted in Schultze, *Kulturfragen der Gegenwart,* 82.

55. Nachdenken is a perpetual part of the Bildungs discourse since Goethe. This is discussed in greater detail in chapter 3.

56. O. Götze, "Jugendpsyche und Kinematograph," *Zeitschrift für Kinderforschung mit besonderer Berücksichtigung der pädagogischen Pathologie* 16 (1911): 417–18.

57. Götze, 418.

58. Götze, 418

59. Adolf Sellmann, *Kino und Schule* (Gladbach: Volkvereins, 1914), 7, 5.

60. Sellmann, 8.

61. Jay David Bolter and Richard Grusin, *Remediation: Understanding New Media* (Cambridge, Mass.: MIT Press, 2000). Outside of the strictly philosophical debates about transparency, which Bolter and Grusin do not address, there is also an important distinction in the field of media studies between "looking *at*" and "looking *through.*" See Richard A. Lanham, *The Electronic Word: Democracy, Technology, and the Arts* (Chicago: University of Chicago Press, 1993).

62. André Bazin, "The Myth of Total Cinema" (1946), in *What Is Cinema?,* vol. 1, trans. Hugh Gray (Berkeley: University of California Press, 2005), 21.

63. Bazin, 21.

64. Bolter and Grusin, *Remediation,* 70–71.

65. Friedrich Paulsen, *Moderne Erziehung und geschlechtliche Sittlichkeit: Einige pädagogische und moralische Betrachtungen für das Jahrhundert des Kindes* (Berlin: Reuther & Reichard, 1908), 44.

66. John William Adamson, *The Practice of Instruction: A Manual of Method General and Special* (London: National Society's Depository, 1907), 115.

67. W. A. Lay, *Experimentelle Didaktik: Ihre Grundlegung mit besonderer Rücksicht auf Wille und Tat* (Leipzig: Quelle & Meyer, 1910), 442.

68. Lay, 447.

69. Lay, 447. Such a mode of fantasizing had also been dissected in great detail by Ernst Mach, who, in keeping with the idea of scientized imaginary, was the first to introduce the term *thought experiments.* Ernst Mach, "Über Gedankenexperimente," in *Erkenntnis und Irrtum: Skizze zur Psychologie der Forschung* (Leipzig: Johann Ambrosius Barth, 1906), 183–99.

70. Lay, *Experimentelle Didaktik,* 444. The "combination method" is advanced in Herman Ebbinghaus, "Ueber eine neue Methode zur Prüfung geistiger Fähigkeiten und ihre Anwendung bei Schulkindern," *Zeitschrift für Psychologie und Physiologie der Sinnesorgane* 13 (1897): 401–58. See also Guy Montrose Whipple, *Manual of Mental and Physical Tests: A Book of Directions Compiled with Reference to the Experimental Study of School Children in the Laboratory or Classroom* (Baltimore:

Warwick & York, 1910), 446. The section of Whipple's book that addresses these experiments is appropriately titled "Imagination and Invention."

71. Whipple, *Manual of Mental and Physical Tests,* 446; Emil Kraepelin, "Ueber Ermüdungsmessungen," *Archiv für die gesamte Psychologie* 1 (1903): 9–30.

72. Lay, *Experimentelle Didaktik,* 452.

73. Lay, 452.

74. Lay, 27, 33.

75. One sees this most expressly undertaken in Heide Schlüpmann, *Abendröthe der Subjektphilosophie: Eine Ästhetik des Kinos* (Frankfurt am Main: Stroemfeld, 1998), 19.

76. Schlüpmann, 179.

77. Emilie Altenloh, *Zur Soziologie des Kino: Die Kino-Unternehmung und die sozialen Schichten ihrer Besucher* (Jena: Eugen Diederichs, 1914).

78. Altenloh, 98.

79. Niklas Luhmann, *Das Erziehungssystem der Gesellschaft* (Frankfurt am Main: Suhrkamp, 2002), 95–96.

80. Reinhart Koselleck, "Zur anthropologischen und semantischen Struktur der Bildung," in *Begriffsgeschichte: Studien zur Semantik und Pragmatik der politischen und sozialen Sprache* (Frankfurt am Main: Suhrkamp, 2006), 119.

81. Hugo Münsterberg, *The Photoplay: A Psychological Study* (New York: D. Appleton, 1916), 96–97.

82. Münsterberg, 88, 104.

83. Pasi Väliaho, *Mapping the Moving Image: Gesture, Thought and Cinema circa 1900* (Amsterdam: Amsterdam University Press, 2010), 10.

84. Kittler, *Gramophone, Film, Typewriter,* 246.

85. Friedrich Kittler, "Romantik—Psychoanalyse—Film: Eine Doppelgängergeschichte," in *Draculas Vermächtnis* (Leipzig: Reclam, 1993), 102–3.

86. Wolfgang Köhler, *Gestalt Psychology: An Introduction to New Concepts in Modern Psychology* (New York: Norton, 1992), 61–62. Of this development from psychophysics to gestalt, see Mitchell G. Ash, *Gestalt Psychology in German Culture, 1890–1967: Holism and the Quest for Objectivity* (Cambridge: Cambridge University Press, 1998), 260, 262: "Köhler himself recognized the considerable problems that remained to be solved before he could apply his heuristic postulate of psychophysical isomorphism to the whole of psychology." This problem was related more generally to larger scientific disputes about the possibility for disparate but related logics in "macro- to microlevel events," as found, for instance, in quantum mechanics. For Köhler, it was his "dual commitment to continuous-field physics and the unity of nature that made it seem natural to him to conceive the person-environment relationship and even the social realm as fields of forces paralleled by hypothetical field activity in the brain—*this in spite of the fact that he and his*

co-workers were discovering constantly how different the psychical order is from the physical" (emphasis mine).

87. Münsterberg, *The Photoplay,* 21.

88. Noël Burch, *Life to Those Shadows,* trans. Ben Brewster (Berkeley: University of California Press, 1990), 33.

89. Karel Reisz and Gavin Millar, *The Technique of Film Editing* (Oxford: Focal, 2010), 4.

90. Sabine Hake, "Weimar Film Theory," in *Weimar Thought: A Contested Legacy,* ed. Peter E. Gordon and John P. McCormick (Princeton, N.J.: Princeton University Press, 2013), 275. Kurt Pinthus's review "Quo vadis-Kino? Zur Eröffnung des Königspavillion-Theaters" (1913) is included in Anton Kaes, *Kino-Debatte: Texte zum Verhältnis von Literatur und Film, 1909–1929* (Tübingen: Niemeyer, 1978), 72–75. *Quo Vadis* is very often cited as an early example of diegetic maturity and "complex narrative structure," as for instance in Ivo Blom, *Jean Desmet and the Early Dutch Film Trade* (Amsterdam: Amsterdam University Press, 2003), 223.

91. Jacques Lacan, "The Mirror Stage as Formative of the *I* Function as Revealed in Psychoanalytic Experience," in *Écrits,* trans. Bruce Fink (New York: Norton, 2006), 75–81.

92. Schiller, "Über die ästhetische Erziehung des Menschen," 634.

93. Schiller, 634.

94. Christian Gottfried Körner, "Über Wilhelm Meisters Lehrjahre (aus einem Brief)," *Die Horen* 8, no. 12 (1796): 108.

95. Heinz-B. Heller, *Literarische Intelligenz und Film: Zu Veränderungen der ästhetischen Theorie und Praxis unter dem Eindruck des Film, 1910–1930 in Deutschland* (Tübingen: Max Niemeyer, 1985), 103.

96. Arguments for and against cinema's status as an art form and the precondition for evaluating its aesthetic, or lack of aesthetic, properties were a mainstay of debates about film through the middle of the twentieth century. For an analysis of the broad arcs of these debates, as well as a truly comprehensive view of the major figures in these aesthetic disputes, see Helmut H. Diederichs, "Frühgeschichte deutscher Filmtheorie: Ihre Entstehung und Entwicklung bis zum Ersten Weltkrieg" (PhD diss., J. W. Goethe-Universität, 1996).

97. Münsterberg, *The Photoplay,* 119.

98. Münsterberg, 119.

99. Marc Redfield, *Phantom Formations: Aesthetic Ideology and the Bildungsroman* (Ithaca, N.Y.: Cornell University Press, 1996), 55.

100. Frederick Winslow Taylor, *The Principles of Scientific Management* (New York: Harper and Brothers, 1911); Hugo Münsterberg, *Psychology and Industrial Efficiency* (New York: Houghton Mifflin, 1913). Münsterberg notes in the preface that his book is based on, but not a translation of, a work published in German less than a year after Taylor's book. See Hugo Münsterberg, *Psychologie und*

Wirtschaftsleben: Ein Beitrag zur angewandten Experimental-Psychologie (Leipzig: J. A. Barth, 1912).

101. Taylor, *The Principles of Scientific Management,* 114.

102. Quoted in Lise Sanders, *Consuming Fantasies: Labor, Leisure, and the London Shop Girl, 1880–1920* (Columbus: Ohio State University Press, 2006), 223n50.

103. Edward Cadbury, "Some Principles of Industrial Organisation: The Case for and against Scientific Management," *Sociological Review* 3, no. 2 (April 1914): 104.

104. Cadbury, 104.

105. The excerpt from the hearing is quoted in Daniel Nelson, *A Mental Revolution: Scientific Management since Taylor* (Columbus: Ohio State University Press, 1992), 5, emphasis mine. The original record of the hearings is available in U.S. House of Representatives, *Hearing before the Special Committee of the House of Representatives to Investigate the Taylor and Other Systems of Shop Management under the Authority of H. Res. 90,* vol. 11 (Washington, D.C., 1912), 1377–1508.

106. Cadbury, "Some Principles of Industrial Organisation," 100.

107. Münsterberg, *Psychology and Industrial Efficiency,* 49, 50.

108. Münsterberg, 57.

109. Münsterberg, 59.

110. Münsterberg, 59.

111. Münsterberg, 60.

112. Münsterberg, 60.

113. John C. Burnham discusses Münsterberg's work as part of a history of industrial psychological testing for the purpose of identifying employees predisposed to accidents and its influence of hiring practices for Dallas streetcar operators. John C. Burnham, *Accident Prone: A History of Technology, Psychology, and Misfits of the Machine Age* (Chicago: University of Chicago Press, 2009).

114. Robert H. Wozniak notes that scientific worker selection procedures were already in place by the time of Münsterberg's arrival on the scene, though he "took the general problem of selection a step further by developing a series of experimental tests specifically designed to assess particular characteristics needed for specialized occupations." Robert H. Wozniak, *Classics in Psychology, 1855–1914: Historical Essays* (Bristol, UK: Thoemmes, 1999).

115. Hugo Münsterberg, *Grundzüge der Psychotechnik* (Leipzig: Verlag von Johann Ambrosius Brath, 1914), 414.

116. Münsterberg, 415, emphasis mine.

117. Brian Price notes that Gilbreth had developed scientific managerial techniques, integrated industrial and office systems, and speed techniques prior to meeting Taylor in 1907. Taylor even integrated Gilbreth's 1908 motion studies on bricklaying in his 1911 opus *The Principles of Scientific Management.* Brian Price, "Frank and Lillian Gilbreth and the Motion Study Controversy, 1907–1930," in *A*

Mental Revolution: Scientific Management since Taylor, ed. Daniel Nelson (Columbus: Ohio State University Press, 1992), 58–76. Much of the work published under Frank's name was the result of a joint effort with his wife, Lillian Gilbreth, who had, not surprisingly, a PhD in psychology. A great deal has been written about the Gilbreths' contributions to scientific management, Lillian Gilbreth's work in psychology, their motion studies, and the wide application of their methods across fields from medicine to agriculture. See the collected two-part volume *Frank and Lillian Gilbreth: Critical Evaluations in Business and Management,* ed. Michael C. Wood and John C. Wood (New York: Routledge, 2003).

118. Frank B. Gilbreth, *Bricklaying System* (New York: Myron C. Clark, 1909).

119. Brian Price, "Frank and Lillian Gilbreth and the Manufacture and Marketing of Motion Study, 1908–1924," *Business and Economic History* 18 (1989): 3.

120. Lillian Evelyn Moller Gilbreth, *The Psychology of Management: The Function of the Mind in Determining, Teaching and Installing Methods of Least Waste* (New York: Sturgis & Walton, 1914), 36.

121. Karl Bücher, *Arbeit und Rhythmus* (Leipzig: B. G. Teubner, 1899), 419.

122. Charles Musser, *Before the Nickelodeon: Edwin S. Porter and the Edison Manufacturing Company* (Berkeley: University of California Press, 1991), 194.

123. Max Horkheimer and Theodor W. Adorno, *Dialectic of Enlightenment: Philosophical Fragments,* trans. Edmund Jephcott (Stanford: Stanford University Press, 2002), 99.

124. Ramon Reichert, *Im Kino der Humanwissenschaft: Studien zur Medialisierung wissenschaftlichen Wissens* (Bielefeld: Transcript, 2007), 125.

125. Geoff Alexander, *Academic Films for the Classroom: A History* (Jefferson, N.C.: McFarland, 2010), 15; Ian Aitken, ed., *Encyclopedia of Documentary Film* (New York: Routledge, 2006), 331–32.

126. Edward Wirth, *Thomas Edison in West Orange* (Charleston, S.C.: Arcadia, 2008), 89. The fire was widely reported in East Coast newspapers on December 10, including the *New Haven Register, Newark News, New York Post,* and *Boston Globe.*

127. Anthony Slide, *Early American Cinema* (Metuchen, N.J.: Scarecrow, 1994), 7.

128. Frederick James Smith, "The Evolution of the Motion Picture," *New York Dramatic Mirror,* July 9, 1913, 24, quoted in Anthony Slide, *Before Video: A History of the Non-Theatrical Film* (New York: Greenwood, 1992), 2.

129. "Edison Talks of the Future," *Motion Picture News* 14, no. 26 (December 1916): 4177, quoted in Slide, *Early American Cinema,* 7.

130. "Edison Company in Detroit," *Edison Kinetogram* 12, no. 3 (November 1, 1915): 5.

131. Walter Benjamin, "Über einige Motive bei Baudelaire," in *Gesammelte Schriften,* vol. 1 (Frankfurt am Main: Suhrkamp, 1991), 630–31.

132. The Gaumont film is discussed in great detail in Alain P. Michel, "Corporate Films of Industrial Work: Renault (1916–1939)," in *Films That Work: Industrial Films and the Productivity of Media,* ed. Vinzenz Hediger and Patrick Vonderau (Amsterdam: Amsterdam University Press, 2009), 167–85. The film of the Opel factory is discussed at length in Martin Loiperdinger, "Early Industrial Moving Pictures in Germany," in *Films That Work: Industrial Films and the Productivity of Media,* ed. Vinzenz Hediger and Patrick Vonderau (Amsterdam: Amsterdam University Press, 2009), 65–73.

133. Loiperdinger, "Early Industrial Moving Pictures in Germany," 71, 72.

134. Loiperdinger, 69.

5. The Cinema of Afflictions

1. Robert Musil, *The Man without Qualities,* trans. Sophie Wilkins and Burton Pike (London: Picador, 2017), 4.

2. Musil, 4.

3. Musil, 5.

4. See Edward Eigen's wonderful book, *On Accident: Episodes in Architecture and Landscape* (Cambridge, Mass.: MIT Press, 2018).

5. See Catherine Wilson, "Mach, Musil, and Modernism," *The Monist* 97, no. 1 (January 2014): 138–55.

6. Jacques Lacan, *The Seminar of Jacques Lacan, Book III: The Psychoses, 1955–1956,* trans. Russell Grigg (New York: Norton, 1997), 9.

7. As Orit Halpern notes, this was a question that was also raised in the context of cybernetics where, at a conference in 1948, Warren McCulloch asked about whether "finite state automata, those models of calculative and computational reason, the templates for programming, the very seats of repetition, reliability, mechanical, logical, and anticipatable behavior, might be 'psychotic' just as brains can sometimes be." Orit Halpern, "Cybernetic Rationality," *Distinktion: Scandinavian Journal of Social Theory* 15, no. 2 (2014): 1.

8. German E. Berrios, *The History of Mental Symptoms: Descriptive Pathology since the Nineteenth Century* (Cambridge: Cambridge University Press, 2002), 26.

9. Wilhelm Griesinger, *Mental Pathology and Therapeutics,* trans. C. Lockhart Robertson and James Rutherford (London: New Sydenham Society, 1867), 62. This passage is also referenced in David Trotter, *Paranoid Modernism: Literary Experiment, Psychosis, and the Professionalization of English Society* (Oxford: Oxford University Press, 2001), as well as in Berrios, *The History of Mental Symptoms.*

10. Trotter, *Paranoid Modernism,* 36.

11. Georges Canguilhem, *The Normal and the Pathological,* trans. Carolyn R. Fawcett (Cambridge, Mass.: MIT Press, 1991), 78.

12. Oswald Külpe, "Ueber die Objectivirung und Subjectivirung von Sinneseindrücken," *Philosophische Studien* 19 (1902): 551.

13. Dziga Vertov, "We: Variant on a Manifesto," in *Kino-Eye: The Writings of Dziga Vertov,* trans. Kevin O'Brien (Berkeley: University of California Press, 1984), 8, 7.

14. Vertov, 8.

15. Vertov, 9.

16. Yuri Tsivian has extended this observation to Vertov's frequent attacks on literature, remarking that the "goal of divorcing films from literature which Vertov relentlessly pursued was complemented by no less manifest intentions to wed them to science . . . which in Vertov's frame of reference was the same as saying that cinema must become Marxist." Yuri Tsivian, introduction to *Lines of Resistance: Dziga Vertov and the Twenties,* ed. Yuri Tsivian (Pordenone: Le Giornate del Cinema Muto, 2004), 9.

17. Malcom Turvey, "Introduction: A Return to Classical Film Theory," *October,* no. 148 (Spring 2014): 3. D. N. Rodowick notes that it was not until 1975 that contemporary film theory had its "psychoanalytic moment," which he credits to Julia Kristeva's integration of Lacan into the conception of "*significance* and signifying practice." D. N. Rodowick, *Elegy for Theory* (Cambridge, Mass.: Harvard University Press, 2014), 219.

18. Jean-Louis Baudry and Alan Williams, "Ideological Effects of the Basic Cinematographic Apparatus," *Film Quarterly* 28, no. 2 (Winter 1974–75): 46.

19. Jacques Lacan, *The Seminar of Jacques Lacan, Book II: The Ego in Freud's Theory and in the Technique of Psychoanalysis, 1954–1955,* trans. Jacques-Alain Miller (New York: Norton, 1991).

20. Lacan, 52.

21. Sigmund Freud, *The Interpretation of Dreams,* trans. James Strachey (New York: Basic Books, 2010).

22. Lacan, *The Seminar of Jacques Lacan, Book II,* 50.

23. The concept of "narrative space" became an important tool for understanding the reliance of montage on spatiotemporal discontinuities following the publication of Stephen Heath's essay "Narrative Space," *Screen* 17, no. 3 (Autumn 1976): 68–112.

24. Friedrich A. Kittler, "Romanticism, Psychoanalysis, Film: A Story of Doubles," in *The Truth of the Technological World,* trans. Erik Butler (Stanford: Stanford University Press, 2013), 77.

25. Kittler, 79.

26. Jean-Pierre Oudart, "Cinema and Suture" (1969), in *Cahiers du Cinéma,* vol. 3, *1969–1972: The Politics of Representation,* ed. Nick Browne (London: Routledge, 1990), 45.

27. Oudart, 45.

28. Oudart, 45.

29. Christian Metz, *The Imaginary Signifier: Psychoanalysis and the Cinema,* trans. Celia Britton, Annwyl Williams, Ben Brewster, and Alfred Guzzetti (Bloomington: University of Indiana Press, 1982), 35.

30. Viktor Tausk, "Über die Entstehung des 'Beeinflussungsapparates' in der Schizophrenie," *Internationale Zeitschrift für Ärtzliche Psychoanalyse* 5 (1919): 1–33.

31. By 1914, when Otto Rank countenanced the possibility that films like *Der Student von Prag* (1913) could "express certain psychological facts and relationships" that a "writer is often unable to describe with verbal clarity," film was already a contentious object of psychoanalytic interest. Otto Rank, *The Double: A Psychological Study,* trans. Harry Tucker Jr. (Chapel Hill: University of North Carolina Press, 1971), 4. Freud himself refused to even meet with Samuel Goldwyn, who purportedly offered him $100,000 to act as an advisor for a film about Antony and Cleopatra and famously "disliked" the "business of making a film" that demonstrated the mechanisms of psychoanalysis. That film, *Geheimnisse einer Seele,* was nevertheless made in 1926 by G. W. Pabst with the help of members of Freud's psychoanalytic circle, Hanns Sachs and Karl Abraham, much to Freud's irritation. Ernest Jones, *The Life and Work of Sigmund Freud,* vol. 3, *The Last Phase, 1919–1939* (New York: Basic Books, 1957), 114; Sigmund Freud, *The Complete Correspondence of Sigmund Freud and Ernest Jones, 1908–1939,* ed. R. Andrew Paskauskas (Cambridge, Mass.: Belknap Press of Harvard University Press, 1993), 586.

32. See Sigmund Freud, *Entwurf einer Psychologie* (1895), in *Nachtragsband: Texte aus den Jahren 1885 bis 1938* (Frankfurt am Main: S. Fischer, 1964), 387–477.

33. John Haslam, *Illustrations of Madness* (New York: Routledge, 1988). Matthews was also a talented draughtsman and made beautiful and involved diagrams of the machines as well as architectural blueprints for the redesign of the Bethlem hospital.

34. Daniel Paul Schreber, *Denkwürdigkeiten eines Nervenkranken* (Leipzig: Oswald Wuße, 1903), 159. Freud's analysis of the case is published as Sigmund Freud, "Psychoanalytische Bemerkungen über einen autobiographisch beschriebenen Fall von Paranoia (Dementia Paranoides)" (1911), in *Gesammelte Werke,* vol. 8 (Frankfurt am Main: S. Fischer, 1967), 240–316.

35. Friedrich Kittler, *Discourse Networks 1800/1900,* trans. Michael Metteer and Chris Cullens (Stanford: Stanford University Press, 1990), 298–99.

36. Tausk, "Über die Entstehung des 'Beeinflussungsapparates' in der Schizophrenie," 2.

37. Tausk, 2.

38. Tausk, 2.

39. Tausk, 2.

40. Tausk, 2, 8.

41. Tausk, 3, 5, 11.

42. Tausk, 22; Sigmund Freud, “Zur Einführung des Narzißmus” (1914), in *Gesammelte Werke*, vol. 10 (Frankfurt am Main: S. Fischer, 1967), 138–70. Though Tausk is referencing Freud’s earlier work on narcissism, the distinctions he makes between the two periods of narcissism are different from Freud’s.

43. Tausk, “Über die Entstehung des ‘Beeinflussungsapparates’ in der Schizophrenie,” 17.

44. Tausk, 14.

45. Tausk, 18.

46. Freud, “Psychoanalytische Bemerkungen über einen autobiographisch beschriebenen Fall von Paranoia.”

47. Freud, 303.

48. Freud, 303.

49. Metz, *The Imaginary Signifier*, 48.

50. Metz, 49.

51. Kittler, “Romanticism, Psychoanalysis, Film,” 76.

52. Kittler, 79.

53. Baudry and Williams, “Ideological Effects of the Basic Cinematographic Apparatus,” 42.

54. Tausk, “Über die Entstehung des ‘Beeinflussungsapparates’ in der Schizophrenie,” 9.

55. Tausk, 13.

56. Tausk, 3.

57. Tausk, 24. Here he is referring to an early draft of Freud’s “Metapsychologische Ergänzung zur Traumlehre” (1915), in *Gesammelte Werke*, vol. 10 (Frankfurt am Main: S. Fischer, 1967), 412–26.

58. Lou Andreas-Salomé, *In der Schule bei Freud: Tagebuch eines Jahres, 1912–1913* (Zurich: Max Niehans, 1958), 102.

59. Max Wertheimer, “Experimentelle Studien über das Sehen von Bewegung,” *Zeitschrift für Psychologie* 61 (1912): 161–265; Hugo Münsterberg, *The Photoplay: A Psychological Study* (New York: D. Appleton, 1916).

60. Andreas-Salomé, *In der Schule bei Freud*, 191. Tausk was acknowledged as one of the most promising members of the early circle, with an aptitude for metapsychology. However, after being fully marginalized and having his analysis terminated by Helene Deutsch on Freud’s suggestion, Tausk committed suicide on July 3, 1919, leaving a rich trove of psychoanalytical writings. Freud is also reported to have called Tausk “a threat to the future.” See Paul Roazen, *Brother Animal: The Story of Freud and Tausk* (New York: Alfred A. Knopf, 1969), 140. In *The Historiography of Psychoanalysis* (New Brunswick, N.J.: Transaction, 2001), Roazen claims that resistance to Tausk from the Freudian psychoanalytic institution was so fierce that it prevented the publication of his work until many years after his death.

61. Leo Strauss, *Persecution and the Art of Writing* (Chicago: University of Chicago Press, 1988), 24.

62. Friedrich A. Kittler, *Gramophone, Film, Typewriter,* trans. Geoffrey Winthrop Young (Stanford: Stanford University Press, 1999), 89. In this passage, Kittler is claiming that the phonograph, not film, represented the primary "enemy" of psychoanalysis.

63. Stephen Heath argues that "film for Freud is the intruder with whom psychoanalysis cannot negotiate." Stephen Heath, "Cinema and Psychoanalysis: Parallel Histories," in *Endless Night: Cinema and Psychoanalysis, Parallel Histories,* ed. Janet Bergstrom (Berkeley: University of California Press, 1999), 29.

64. Heath, "Narrative Space," 86–87. Later in the essay, he writes: "Classical continuity is built on fragmentation rather than the long take—on a segmentation for recomposition that can bind the spectator in the strong articulations of the unity it seeks to create" (90).

65. Tausk, "Über die Entstehung des 'Beeinflussungsapparates' in der Schizophrenie," 8.

66. Tausk, 8, emphasis mine.

67. Tausk, 8, emphasis mine.

68. Sigmund Freud, "Das Unbewusste" (1915), in *Gesammelte Werke,* vol. 10 (Frankfurt am Main: S. Fischer, 1967), 286.

69. Tausk, "Über die Entstehung des 'Beeinflussungsapparates' in der Schizophrenie," 25.

70. Lacan, *The Seminar of Jacques Lacan, Book II,* 52.

71. Werner Michael Schwarz, *Kino und Kinos in Wien: Eine Entwicklungsgeschichte bis 1934* (Vienna: Turia & Kant, 1992), 22, 295.

72. Noël Burch, *Life to Those Shadows,* trans. Ben Brewster (Berkeley: University of California Press, 1990).

73. Burch, 189.

74. Burch, 186, 188.

75. Andreas Killen, "The Scene of the Crime: Psychiatric Discourses on the Film Audience in Early Twentieth Century Germany," in *Film 1900: Technology, Perception, Culture,* ed. Annemone Ligensa and Klaus Kreimeier (New Burnet, UK: Barnet Libbey, 2009), 99–111.

76. Laurent Mannoni, *The Great Art of Light and Shadow: Archaeology of the Cinema,* ed. and trans. Richard Crangle (Exeter: University of Exeter Press, 2000), 294.

77. In his consideration of Lapierre, one of the most artful and "cinematic" practitioners of the magic-lantern show, Mannoni writes that the advanced narrative quality of his performances is evident in the remaining slides from his "second period." He argues that the slides "display some narrative features which suggest the language of the cinema. The Lapierre studio used 'close-ups,' 'medium-shots,'

'establishing shots,' and 'long-pans.' Framed texts were interspersed between the images, suggesting the explanatory 'intertitles' of the silent cinema. A desire for cutting and mise-en-scène seems evident in the way that the stories were presented for the screen" (292). However, it is clear from his descriptions that even the "best" magic-lantern performances relied heavily on verbal narrative structuring from the projectionist or narrator.

78. Even with the Lumières' much-improved cinematograph, the conditions for the illusion of movement were painfully evident. Mannoni comments that the Lumière machine "did have the tendency to shake the image," and "for many years, film projectors continued to make spectators weep; there was even talk, later, of 'cinematophthalmia' or 'cinema blindness'" (465).

79. Robert Gaupp, *Zur Psychologie des Massenmords: Hauptlehrer Wagner von Degerloch; eine kriminalpsychologische und psychiatrische Studie,* Verbrechertypen 1, no. 3, ed. Hans W. Gruhle and Albrecht Wetzel (Berlin: Julius Springer, 1914). As David Trotter has rightly noted, "Wagner, unlike Daniel Paul Schreber . . . has not yet attracted any attention from cultural historians." Trotter, *Paranoid Modernism,* 19. The case has remained a mere curiosity that has been the subject of almost no scholarship, though it has been referenced infrequently in contemporary journalism as an early example of the *Amokläufer* that have become fixtures of the late twentieth- and early twenty-first-century media landscape. During its time, however, the case was a cultural and literary wellspring. It was also the premise for Hermann Hesse's novella *Klein und Wagner,* which is quoted in the epigraph to this chapter.

80. The unfolding of events was, in fact, rather complicated, involving multiple stops; a failed attempt to cut the telephone and telegraph wires, which had been a part of his design for the rampage; and a visit to the house of his brother, who was not home at the time. Gaupp's study is very thorough, detailing every stage of the events and commenting at length on Wagner's verbal and written accounts as well as collections of letters, diaries, and several plays he wrote ("Nero" and "Saul und David") as a part of his formal psychological evaluation, which spans roughly two hundred pages.

81. The same volume also includes the official recommendation (*Gutachten*) from Professor Dr. Wollenberg. In it, he adumbrates Gaupp's observations and recommendations. He concludes that Wagner committed the acts of violence "in a condition of pathological disturbance of mental activity" in which his "determinations of will was excluded" (Gaupp, 216). This repeats Gaupp's own assessment, which found that Wagner was "exempt from prosecution" (188).

82. Gaupp, 45, 37.

83. A professional biography of Gaupp and his relationship with Karl Bonhoeffer, Kraepelin, and Wernicke is available in *The University Department of Psychiatry in Munich: From Kraepelin and His Predecessors to Molecular Psychiatry,* ed.

Hanns Hippius, Hans-Jürgen Möller, Norbert Müller, and Gabriele Neundörfer-Kohl (Heidelberg: Springer Medezin, 2008).

84. This was a part of what has been called "Kraepelin's Dichotomy," which asserts a total distinction between manic depression and dementia praecox, or what would soon be redescribed as "schizophrenia." Karl Leonhard notes that there was more nuance to Kraepelin's distinctions but that his "successors did not pay attention to this, they saw only the gross division of endogenous psychosis into dementia praecox or schizophrenia and manic-depressive illness." Karl Leonhard, *Classification of Endogenous Psychoses and Their Differentiated Etiology* (Vienna: Springer, 1999), 1. Leonhard also observes that this distinction would not likely have been allowed to persist as far into the twentieth century as it did had Wernicke, Kraepelin's rival, lived longer.

85. Gaupp, *Zur Psychologie des Massenmords,* 186; Emil Kraepelin, *Psychiatrie: Ein Lehrbuch für Studierende und Aerzte,* vol. 2, 6th ed. (Leipzig: Johann Ambrosius Barth, 1899), 430.

86. See the short entry on Gaupp's "reactive paranoia (abortive paranoia)" in Edward Shorter, *A Historical Dictionary of Psychiatry* (Oxford: Oxford University Press, 2005), 210. This divergence from Kraepelin also had implications for Gaupp's understanding of criminality. Richard F. Wetzell notes that Gaupp "acknowledged that environmental factors played a role in criminal behavior but that this was not an argument against the sterilization of criminals" because those same conditions along with certain predispositions and a general milieu were likely to produce criminality in their children. Richard F. Wetzell, *Inventing the Criminal: A History of German Criminology, 1880–1945* (Chapel Hill: University of North Carolina Press, 2000), 243. Gaupp, unlike some of his radical contemporaries who emphasized the genetic underpinnings of criminality, was more interested in environmental and media-technical factors associated with modern living and the propensity for criminal behavior. In the extensive records Gaupp made of his interactions with Wagner at the clinic and his observations on Wagner's literary and biographical writing, Gaupp is tremendously empathetic, which is striking given his more hard-line treatises on film. Gaupp frequently makes note of Wagner's reference to philosophical theories opposing the notion of free will and seems to see a certain cultural and media-technological inevitability to Wagner's case.

87. Ernst Kretschmer, *Der sensitive Beziehungswahn: Ein Beitrag zur Paranoiafrage und zur psychiatrischen Charakterlehre* (1918; repr., Berlin: Springer, 1927). This was a term that was also frequently used by Eugen Bleuler.

88. These historical debates through which diagnostic categories were elaborated at the end of the nineteenth century and the beginning of the twentieth century, especially with respect to manic depression, paranoia, schizophrenia, and dementia praecox, underwent various convergences and divergences in their classification and treatment. For an overview, see Berrios, *The History of Mental Symptoms.*

In short, there was a prevailing dispute about whether paranoia could be subsumed under the category of schizophrenia, whether schizophrenia and related disorders represented the far end of a continuum between healthy and unhealthy or whether there were fundamental differences in the psychological and neurophysiological configuration of the patients in question, and whether these extreme instances of psychopathology were exogenous or endogenous.

89. Trotter, *Paranoid Modernism,* 44.

90. Trotter, 44.

91. Louis A. Sass, *Madness and Modernism: Insanity in the Light of Modern Art, Literature, and Thought* (Cambridge, Mass.: Harvard University Press, 1992), 178. This is the same reason, as noted earlier, that Freud found schizophrenics "incurable" through psychoanalysis.

92. This distinction between paranoia and schizophrenia also perhaps underlies the frequent invocation of schizophrenia in modernism. Sass writes in *Madness and Modernity* that "schizophrenics will often attend to material qualities of the signifier, to the sounds of words or their graphic appearance on the page, or they will become aware of a large number of the potential, but normally irrelevant, meanings of words" (178).

93. Gaupp, *Zur Psychologie des Massenmords,* 123. As it turns out, Wagner did achieve canonical literary recognition, though not in the way he would have wanted. In 1919 Hermann Hesse published the novella *Klein und Wagner,* about the psychological unraveling of a bourgeois man who embezzles money from his employer and leaves his family to travel south with a false passport to Italy, where he becomes infatuated with a young woman. Throughout the story, the character is confronted with the specter of a mass murderer named Wagner, who is not explicitly identified as Ernst Wagner but whom we can infer to be him, as he is described as a media sensation discussed by coworkers, a schoolteacher, and an otherwise normal man who killed his family. It has also been suggested that the indeterminacy of the name Wagner uses the coincidence between the last names of Ernst Wagner and Richard Wagner to critique the latter. The parallels between the story and Gaupp's account are discussed in Stefan Höppner, "Klein und Wagner," in *A Companion to the Works of Hermann Hesse,* ed. Ingo Cornils (New York: Camden House, 2009), 117–38.

94. Gaupp, *Zur Psychologie des Massenmords,* 45. This corresponds word-for-word with Kraepelin's terminology in the definition of paranoia. Emil Kraepelin, *Psychiatrie: Ein Lehrbuch für Studierende und Aerzte,* vol. 4, 8th ed. (Leipzig: Johann Ambrosius Barth, 1915), 1761. The description of typical cases of paranoia is repeated in Kraepelin's lecture on the subject and parallels Gaupp's observations exactly. Emil Kraepelin, *Einführung in die Psychiatrische Klinik: Zweiunddreißig Vorlesungen* (Leipzig: Johann Ambrosius Barth, 1905), 153.

95. Gaupp, *Zur Psychologie des Massenmords,* 25.

96. Gaupp, 28.

97. Gaupp, 28, 31.

98. Gaupp, 59.

99. Gaupp, 184.

100. Drawing from Kraepelin's diagnostic categories, Bleuler writes that while "hallucinatory excitement" could be found "in the histories on many schizophrenics with delusional ideas in general," in cases of "non-paranoia they play a very minor role," although "there are also paranoids without hallucinations." Eugen Bleuler, *Dementia Praecox oder Gruppe der Schizophrenien* (1911; repr., Tübingen: Diskord, 1988), 189. For a good overview of the development of paranoia as a distinct diagnostic category, see Aubrey Lewis, "Paranoia and Paranoid: A Historical Perspective," *Psychological Medicine* 1 (1970): 2–12.

101. Gaupp, *Zur Psychologie des Massenmords,* 6.

102. Gaupp, 24.

103. Gaupp, 40.

104. Gaupp, 28.

105. Gaupp, 61.

106. Gaupp, 61.

107. Gaupp, 142.

108. Gaupp, 144.

109. Gaupp, 186.

110. Gaupp, 153.

111. Gaupp, 144.

112. Gaupp, 52.

113. Kittler, *Discourse Networks,* 292.

114. Kittler, 355, quoting Gottfried Benn, "Der Aufbau der Persönlichkeit" (1930), in *Sämtliche Werke, Stuttgarter Ausgabe,* vol. 3., ed. Gerhard Schuster (Stuttgart: Klett-Cotta, 1987), 263–76.

115. Gaupp, *Zur Psychologie des Massenmords,* 132.

116. Gaupp, 132–33.

117. Gaupp, 133.

118. Kittler, *Discourse Networks,* 301.

119. Kittler, 240.

120. Georg Lukács, "Thoughts on and Aesthetics of Cinema," in *German Essays on Film,* trans. Lance W. Garmer, ed. Richard W. McCormick and Alison Guenther-Pal (New York: Continuum, 2004), 13.

121. Kittler, *Discourse Networks,* 214.

Coda

1. Jocelyn Szczepaniak-Gillece, introduction to *Ends of Cinema,* ed. Richard Grusin and Jocelyn Szczepaniak-Gillece (Minneapolis: University of Minnesota Press, 2020), vii.

2. James Vincent, "Hollywood Is Quietly Using AI to Help Decide Which Movies to Make," *The Verge*, May 28, 2019, https://www.theverge.com.

3. Ronald R. Kline, *The Cybernetics Moment: Or Why We Call Our Age the Information Age* (Baltimore: Johns Hopkins University Press, 2015), 46.

4. Ralph W. Gerard, "Some of the Problems Concerning Digital Notions in the Central Nervous System," in *Cybernetics: The Macy Conferences, 1946–1953, The Complete Transactions*, ed. Claus Pias (Berlin: Diaphanes, 2016), 181–82.

5. For more about the history of his visit, see George Dyson's excellent book *Turing's Cathedral: The Origins of the Digital Universe* (New York: Pantheon, 2012).

6. Gerard, "Some of the Problems Concerning Digital Notions in the Central Nervous System," 176.

7. Gerard, 177.

8. Gerard, 171.

9. Ernst Kapp, *Elements of a Philosophy of Technology: On the Evolutionary History of Culture*, ed. Jeffrey West Kirkwood and Leif Weatherby, trans. Lauren K. Wolfe (Minneapolis: University of Minnesota Press, 2018), 103.

10. John D. Kelleher, *Deep Learning* (Cambridge, Mass.: MIT Press, 2019), 39.

11. Frank Pasquale details the many dangerous social consequences of forfeiting essential human judgment to artificial intelligence. Frank Pasquale, *New Laws of Robotics: Defending Human Expertise in the Age of AI* (Cambridge, Mass.: Belknap Press of Harvard University Press, 2020).

12. Kate Crawford, *Atlas of AI: Power, Politics, and the Planetary Costs of Artificial Intelligence* (New Haven, Conn.: Yale University Press, 2021), 117–18.

13. Arthur P. Shimamura, "Psychocinematics: Issues and Directions I," in *Psychocinematics: Exploring Cognition at the Movies*, ed. Arthur P. Shimamura (Oxford: Oxford University Press, 2013), 15, 18.

14. Alan Turing, "Systems of Logic Based on Ordinals" (PhD diss., Princeton University, 1938), 13. Turing also claims that such a machine "cannot be a machine." Dyson describes the function of this abstract hypothetical postulate in a way that makes clear the informational relationship between continuity and discontinuity in questions of intelligence when he writes: "The Universal Turing Machine of 1936 gets all the attention, but Turing's O-machines of 1939 may be closer to the way intelligence (real and artificial) works: logical sequences are followed for a certain number of steps, with intuition bridging the intervening gaps." Dyson, *Turing's Cathedral*, 252.

15. Friedrich Kittler, "There Is No Software," in *Literature, Media, Information Systems*, ed. John Johnston (Amsterdam: G+B Arts, 1997), 151.

16. Jean-Louis Comolli, "Machines of the Visible," in *The Cinematic Apparatus*, ed. Teresa de Lauretis and Stephen Heath (New York: St. Martin's, 1980), 125, 126.

17. Gregory Bateson, *Mind and Nature: A Necessary Unity* (New York: E. P. Dutton, 1979), 228.

18. For more about the central concepts and organization of quantum computers, see Chris Bernhardt, *Quantum Computing for Everyone* (Cambridge, Mass.: MIT Press, 2019); and Martin Giles, "Explainer: What Is a Quantum Computer," *MIT Technology Review*, January 29, 2019, https://www.technologyreview.com.

Index

JEFFREY WEST KIRKWOOD is associate professor of art history at Binghamton University. He is coeditor of Ernst Kapp's *Elements of a Philosophy of Technology: On the Evolutionary History of Culture* (Minnesota, 2018).